INTERPRETATION AND GAP FILLING IN INTERNATIONAL COMMERCIAL CONTRACTS

INTERPRETATION AND GAP FILLING IN INTERNATIONAL COMMERCIAL CONTRACTS

Ayşe Nihan Karadayi Yalim

intersentia
Cambridge – Antwerp – Chicago

Intersentia Ltd
8 Wellington Mews
Wellington Street | Cambridge
CB1 1HW | United Kingdom
Tel.: +44 1223 736 170
Email: mail@intersentia.co.uk
www.intersentia.com | www.intersentia.co.uk

Distribution for the UK and Ireland:
NBN International
Airport Business Centre, 10 Thornbury Road
Plymouth, PL6 7PP
United Kingdom
Tel.: +44 1752 202 301 | Fax: +44 1752 202 331
Email: orders@nbninternational.com

Distribution for Europe and all other countries:
Intersentia Publishing nv
Groenstraat 31
2640 Mortsel
Belgium
Tel.: +32 3 680 15 50 | Fax: +32 3 658 71 21
Email: mail@intersentia.be

Distribution for the USA and Canada:
Independent Publishers Group
Order Department
814 North Franklin Street
Chicago, IL 60610
USA
Tel.: +1 800 888 4741 (toll free) | Fax: +1 312 337 5985
Email: orders@ipgbook.com

Interpretation and Gap Filling in International Commercial Contracts

ISBN 978-1-78068-808-4
D/2019/7849/122
NUR 822

British Library Cataloguing in Publication Data. A catalogue record for this book is available from the British Library.

To my parents Erhun and Handan Karadayı

ACKNOWLEDGMENTS

I would like to thank Prof. Dr. Matthias Storme for his valuable guidance that shed a light on this research. I would also like to thank Prof. Dr. Marta Pertegas, Prof. Dr. Alois Van Oevelen, Prof. Dr. Filip De Ly, Prof. Dr. Christoph Van der Elst and Prof. Dr. Denis Philippe for providing their valuable comments and suggestions that improved the quality of my research.

I would like to thank Ms. Ingeborg Jongbloet for her administrative support.

Last but not the least, I would like to thank my parents, Erhun and Handan Karadayı, my husband Sarp Yalım, my daughter Jülide Lâl Yalım and the members of my family Rahşan, Ferit, Erkut and Rukset Attar, Perihan and Behiç Ayral, Nalan, Cengiz and Dicle Mutel for their constant support, encouragement and endless love throughout my life and my research career.

CONTENTS

LIST OF CASES

SUPRANATIONAL

NATIONAL

EUROPE (EXCLUDING THE UNITED KINGDOM)

UNITED KINGDOM

UNITED STATES

OTHER JURISDICTIONS

INTRODUCTION

The main objective of this book is to examine the mechanisms of two main tools serving to determine the content of international commercial contracts, namely interpretation and gap filling. It essentially focuses on a comparative analysis of the rules provided by four main – uniform and harmonized – sets of rules conceived according to the needs of international trade. While doing so, it discusses various important theoretical aspects of contract interpretation in general and refers to different interpretation approaches which are traditionally used in different law systems by also taking into account the specific context of international commercial contracts. Accordingly, it treats not only the practical solutions to be extracted from harmonized instruments but also theoretical perspectives which could help clarify the content of the rules provided by these instruments.

To start with, contract interpretation can be briefly described as the understanding of the language (or the meaning) of a contract and of rights and obligations that are created by it. It is a topic which has long been treated by lawyers and scholars coming from all different legal systems. Yet it seems that the thousands of pages which have been written so far fall short to settle questions and controversies related to it.

This seems to be mainly because "language" which serves as the most important tool both to conclude and to interpret the contract is far from being a static and easy-to-deal-with tool, as it changes from one context to another. That explains why approaches which consider language as a common tool to be used in the same manner by its all competent users cannot answer the question why there are so many differences of opinion when it comes to ascertaining the meaning of an actual text. This is, indeed, a phenomenon that we all can observe in our lives and that is also confirmed by research.

With a more focused analysis, it can be seen that contractual interpretation cannot be fully explained without reference to different types of context and is not just a topic to be addressed with dictionaries. From that point of view, first there are facts inherent to contractual parties such as their abilities (including linguistic) and the "context" in which each of them is situated by the time of contracting. Second there are elements inherent to the contract itself and the "context" in which the contract itself is concluded. And finally there is the "interpreter" or the "reader" who, after the occurrence of a disagreement between the parties on the meaning of contractual terms, aims to interpret the contract by using the tool called "language". He/she will decide on the "contractual meaning" and on which elements should be taken into account and to what extent in order to extract that meaning.

It should not be forgotten that the interpreter is also situated in a "context" which is mainly constituted of his/her linguistic, cultural and legal background. Accordingly, as a user of the language he/she has a view concerning the meanings of words used by contracting parties (that he/she can "extract" with more or less reference to the contextual matrix of the contract) as well as the purpose and the function of contract interpretation. He/she has a view on fairness and on to what extent it should be taken into account when interpreting a particular contract and so forth.

When we consider all these elements we can understand why thousands of pages of literature cannot resolve existing controversies in this field.

The object of this book is also situated in a particular context, as it is focused only on "international commercial" contracts. The setting of international commercial contracts is a particularly difficult setting, especially when it comes to interpretative issues, as two "*competing*" contexts, namely the "international context" and "commercial context" come together in order to form one factual matrix in which a particular contract is placed.

While, the international character of the contract is susceptible to rendering "contractual language" an "even less reliable tool" because of the risk of divergences (of meanings attributed by the parties and/or the interpreter to the same wording) that reaches its highest level as their legal, cultural and linguistic backgrounds are generally different; the commercial character, itself, causes concerns of function such as efficiency, predictability and certainty in commercial relations.

The book also examines the gap-filling mechanisms provided by these instruments. As it is not possible in real life for the parties to a contract to predict all contingencies at the time of contracting and provide for them, together with "interpretation", the process of "*gap filling*" determines the content of a contract in case of such contingency. In this context, the notions of *force majeure* and hardship are also addressed as they also constitute consequences of a lack of foresight at the time of contracting.

Legal instruments that are used (the 1980 United Nations Convention on Contracts for the International Sale of Goods (CISG), the UNIDROIT Principles of International Commercial Contracts (PICC),[1] the Principles of the European Contract Law (PECL) and the Draft Common Frame of Reference (DCFR)) represent efforts to reach legal uniformity or harmonization. Because of the above-mentioned difficulties existing in the field of contractual interpretation and more specifically in the field of interpretation of international commercial contracts, such efforts become particularly important.

The aim of this book is to make an autonomous and horizontal analysis of the interpretation and gap-filling rules contained in these uniform and harmonized instruments to extract practical solutions to current problems. In order to do so, it does not only seek to understand "what" the contents of the sets of rules provided by these instruments are but also "why" certain "interpretative" approaches are preferred over others by their authors, which also requires some theoretical perspectives. In order to better understand the contents of these rules, examples of related case law will also be shown.

In Chapter 1 of this book, general rules of interpretation contained in the CISG, PICC, PECL and DCFR will be examined. In order to do so, first the notions of "meaning" and "intent" will be explained and two main approaches of contract interpretation, namely "subjective" and "objective" theories of contract interpretation which form the "inter-subjective" interpretation method[2] adopted by the CISG, PICC, PECL and DCFR, will be dealt with. For this purpose, the "*relevant circumstances*" to be used in order to interpret contracts governed by the CISG, PICC, PECL and DCFR will also be discussed and the choice of these instruments on this matter will be analyzed.

In Chapter 2 specific rules of interpretation, such as *contra proferentem*, all terms to be given effect, linguistic discrepancies, etc. will be addressed. In Chapter 3, the principle of good faith and fair dealing and its scope

---

1 The Principles of International Commercial Contracts (PICC) of 2016 is a document drawn up by UNIDROIT, intended to help harmonize international commercial contracts law. Its first edition was published in 1994, its second, enlarged edition was published in 2004 and a third edition was published in 2010. In this book, unless otherwise specified, the 2016 version is referred to.

2 For this term see DiMATTEO, L., OSTAS, D.L., "*Comparative Efficiency in International Sales Law*", 26 Am. U. Int'l L. Rev. p. 410.

of application in the context of interpretation and gap filling in terms of the CISG, PICC, PECL and DCFR will be examined. It will also be seen that the main topic of this book cannot be fully explained without reference to the principle of good faith and fair dealing because of the broadness of its scope of application in the fields of contract interpretation and gap filling in terms of these instruments. Chapter 4 of this book is on gap filling in the CISG, PICC, PECL and DCFR. In this context, not only the gap-filling rules, but also some examples of default gap fillers that these instruments provide will be treated. Finally, the notions of *force majeure* and *hardship* in terms of these instruments will be analyzed. The final chapter of the book is where conclusive remarks will be presented.

CHAPTER 1

GENERAL AND SPECIFIC RULES ON INTERPRETATION

1. GENERAL RULES ON INTERPRETATION

1.1. MEANING AND INTENT

In legal dictionaries, the word "interpretation"[1] is defined as the act of explaining or telling "the meaning" (of a document – and in our case of a contract), especially in order to determine "intent".[2] The term "meaning" is a highly ambiguous concept which itself has 16 different meanings when used by philosophers, according to the classification made by Ogden and Richards.[3] We will not examine here the notion of meaning as a linguistic and philosophical concept. Instead we will focus on "the meaning" in contract law, which can be distinguished by an aspect of paramount importance, namely the notion of "understanding of contracting parties". We will, thus, examine the "meaning attached to contractual clauses by contracting parties", and try to understand its relevance and to what extent and how it can be taken into account in the interpretation process.

---

1 It should first be emphasized that in terms of this book we understand the term "contract interpretation" in a broader sense, meaning to cover all "understanding of contractual language" and not as a tool to ascertain the "meaning" if "reading" does not yield to a solution. Thus, a distinction between "the reading of the language" and "interpretation of the language" is not made here. On this matter, see n 10 below.

2 See, Merriam-Webster's Dictionary of Law, 1996.

3 See OGDEN, C.K., RICHARDS, I.A., *The Meaning of Meaning*, Routledge & Kegan Paul Ltd., London 1969, pp. 186–187.

From this point of view, three competing definitions of "meaning", the roots and evolutions of which are shown by Farnsworth, can be seen.[4] Accordingly, the meaning can be understood as:

1. That to which either party ought to be referring according to the "common" or "ordinary" usage of the words.
2. That to which either party has reason to believe the other to be referring.
3. That to which either party refers.[5]

While the first definition does not take into account "intent" of the contracting parties in the ascertainment of contractual meaning and takes the position of an ordinary objective user of the language, the second and the third, both construe contracting language from the perspective of a different party, namely the promisee and the promisor. It can be said that, in this sense, these three definitions give three solutions grading from the most "objective" test to the most "subjective" one.

Accordingly, the first definition reflects the textualist approach, suggesting that the plain meaning of contractual terms is preferred to any other specific meaning which may be intended by contracting parties, to the extent that it yields to a solution.[6]

The second definition takes the perspective of the promisee as the point of inquiry and "objectifies" the intent of the promisor in order to protect reliance by construing a sort of a "presumed" or "apparent" intent.[7] The reference to intent should not erroneously be understood such that

---

4 See FARNSWORTH, E.A., "'*Meaning' in the Law of Contract*", 76, Yale L.J. 939 (1967) p. 946.

5 To the extent that it corresponds to "that to which the other party refers or believes or has reason to believe the first party to be referring": See FARNSWORTH, E.A., ibid.

6 For an analysis of the notion of plain meaning, see for instance, PERELL, P.M., "*Plain Meaning for Judges, Scholars and Practitioners*", 20 Advoc. Q. 24–84 (1998). For critics of the plain meaning see for instance Lord HOFFMANN, "*The Intolerable Wrestle with Words and Meanings*", 114 S. African L.J. 656 (1997), GOLDSTEIN, B.H., "*The Plain Language Law: Some Reflections on its Basic Assumptions*", 1 Comm. & L. 69 (1979), p. 72, DEWEY, J., *Logic – The Theory of Inquiry*, Henry Holt and Company, New York 1938, p. 135, CHERRY, C., *On Human Communication – A Review, a Survey and a Criticism*, 3rd ed., MIT Press, Cambridge MA August 1980, p. 10.

7 See Lord Diplock in *Pioneer Shipping Ltd v BTP Tioxide Limited* [1982] A.C. 724: "The object sought to be achieved by construing any contract is to ascertain what the mutual intentions of the parties were as to the legal obligations each assumed by the contractual words in which they sought to express them". This reflects the traditional approach of the English Law to contract interpretation. See LEWISON, K., *The Interpretation of Contracts*, Sweet & Maxwell, London 2007, p. 6.

the task of the courts is to ascertain the *actual* intention of the parties under this definition.[8] Thus, this second approach may be considered as concerned with "party intent", not as the subjective intention of the parties themselves but as the "intention of reasonable persons in similar context".[9]

Let us note that this second definition may be adopted from the beginning of the inquiry into meaning, or follow the application of the first definition in accordance with the argument suggesting that "interpretation begins only when 'reading' does not yield to a solution because of a linguistic defect".[10]

Finally, the third definition places the promisor in the center of the inquiry and aims to reveal his or her "actual" or "subjective" intent.

1.2. INTENT: A RATHER CONTROVERSIAL TERM

Before examining different methods used in ascertaining contractual intent, whether actual or presumed, let us first focus on the textualist approach to meaning, rejecting a "party-based" inquiry, and also on some

8 See LEWISON, K., *The Interpretation of Contracts*, Sweet & Maxwell, London 2007, p. 21.

9 See Mr. Justice Warren in *Cofacredit S.A. v. Clive Morris & More UK Ltd. (in liquidation)* [2006] EWHC 353 (Ch. D.) at [37]; Cf. DiMATTEO, L.A., "*The Counterpoise of Contracts: The Reasonable Person Standard and the Subjectivity of Judgement*", 48 South Carolina L. Rev. 293–355 (Winter 1997), p. 297: submitting that the descriptive reasonable person of the objective theory is simply placed in the shoes of the parties to determine their intended meaning.; Compare also "intent" with the modern notion of purposive interpretation in objective theory expressed in *Antaios Compania SA v. Salen AB* [1985] AC 191, 201.

10 From one point of view, every understanding of the contract necessitates an "interpretation". See for instance, CANARIS, C.W., GRIGOLEIT, H.C., "*Interpretation of Contracts": Towards a European Civil Code*, 4th ed., Kluwer Law International, 2011, p. 618: interpretation is an "omnipresent phenomenon" in contract law because "every understanding of a contract presupposes and is – albeit often unsaid – based on interpretation"; see also HERBOTS, J.H., "*What Precisely is Interpretation?*" in *Elgar Encyclopedia of Comparative Law*, 2nd ed., Jan M. Smits (ed.), Edward Elgar, Cheltenham 2012, p. 438. From another point of view, however, the term has a narrower scope as it is put forward that if every reading is considered as an act of interpretation there is no starting point to inquiry. Thus, there must be cases where the meaning is clear and there is no room for interpretation. In favour of this approach, See for instance, SIMMONDS, N.E., "*Imperial Visions and Mundane Practices*", 46 C.L.J. 465–488 (1987), pp. 465–472; PATTERSON, D., "*Interpretation in Law*", 42 San Diego L.R., 685 (2005), p. 690. For a general discussion on this matter see MITCHELL, C., *Interpretation of Contracts, Current Controversies in Law*, Routledge-Cavendish, London 2007, p. 11.

discussions over the existence of "intent" in relation with future events that occur in the life of a contract.

Accordingly, we will examine both the textualist definition of "meaning" presented above and the argument put forward by Curtis stating that any party intent in relation to future events is generally non-existent when formulating contractual clauses because of the lack of information about the future that we all share.[11]

The first question to be taken into account is that of deciding on what constitutes the object of our inquiry while ascertaining the meaning of an utterance. Is it what the contractual language used by the parties "ought to" mean according to an objective third party user of the language, or what is actually or presumably intended according to some sort of party-based inquiry?

We should note that we do not discuss here the possible adoption by courts of the meaning that each party "ought to be referring to" by applying overriding legal rules such as the principle of good faith and fair dealing, which may alter contractual meaning subsequent to any "interpretative" effort. This latter aspect of contractual interpretation will be examined further in this book. Here, we only deal with "meaning" in relation to determination of party intent.[12]

Therefore, it should first be noted that from an intentionalist point of view, there is no meaning and no language apart from "intention". In this direction, Fish points out that text alone, no matter how long and dense, can never yield meaning without intention, whether assumed, discovered, or revealed. He suggests that if no intention were in place, not only would there not be a meaning, but also there would be no reason to seek one.[13]

It must be noted here that all understanding of language is necessarily construed against contextual background knowledge, even if this fact might sometimes go unnoticed by the users of the language.[14] When, for instance, the author of an utterance uses the sentence "blue bicycle", he/she necessarily refers to background information on the color called

---

[11] See CURTIS, C.P., "*A Better Theory of Legal Interpretation*", 3 Vand. L. Rev. 407 (1949–1950).

[12] For a linguistic analysis of the "speaker meaning" as compared to a "sentence meaning" see also PERCONTI, P., "*An Epistemic Commitment in the Very Idea of 'Speaker's Intention'*" in *Pragmemes and Theories of Language Use*, Allan K., Capone A., Kecskes I. (eds.), Springer, 2016, pp. 791–798.

[13] FISH, S., "*There is no Textualist Position*", 42 San Diego L. Rev. 629 (2005), p. 632.

[14] See Lord HOFFMANN, "*The Intolerable Wrestle with Words and Meanings*", 114 S. African L.J. 656 (1997).

"blue" and the object called "bicycle." Accordingly, in order to "understand" this sentence, the listener would need to have the knowledge of that background information.

As language operates across all kinds of human activity, it is, however, hard to conclude that language in general has meaning only when the author's (whether subjective or objective) intention is at stake. Indeed, if we take the example provided by Farnsworth, when the author communicates scientific data such as "Water will boil at 100°C", his or her actual or presumed intention does not play an important role for the reader or listener in understanding this descriptive language as the main concern is with its truth.[15]

In interpreting the prescriptive language of the contract, however, if one is even slightly concerned with preserving the essence of "party autonomy", meaning should inevitably be considered with reference to the intention of the contracting parties, whether actual (subjective) or presumed (objective). This is, in this author's opinion, to treat the contract as an agreement and not merely as a written document.

Against this position stands a strict textualist position, as put forward by Judge Learned Hand, while suggesting that a contract has nothing to do with the personal, or individual, intent of the parties and that parties should be held to the "usual meaning which the law imposes upon their words" unless there is some mutual mistake or something else of the sort.[16] From a textualist point of view, such an approach is not seen in contradiction to the notion of party autonomy; on the contrary, it is considered as reflecting party autonomy better.

On this matter, Justice Scalia puts forward the view in relation to interpretation of legislative texts that "The practical threat (of taking intention as the object of interpretation) is that, under the guise or even the self-delusion of pursuing unexpressed legislative intents … judges will in fact pursue their own objectives and desires". According to Justice Scalia, the search for meaning in legislative texts will surely bring the interpreter to the conclusion that "the law means what you think it ought to mean".[17]

---

15 See FARNSWORTH, E.A., "*'Meaning' in the Law of Contract*", 76, Yale L.J. 939 (1967), p. 942.

16 See, *Hotchkiss v. National City Bank*, 200 F. 287, 293 (S.D.N.Y. 1911).

17 SCALIA, A., "*Common Law Courts in a Civil Law System: The Role of the United States Federal Courts in Interpreting the Constitution*" in A. Scalia, *A Matter of Interpretation: Federal Courts and the Law*, Amy Gutmann (ed.), Princeton University Press, Princeton N.J., 1997, pp. 3, 17.

It should be noted that there might be significant differences between *statutory* interpretation and interpretation of *contracts* when it comes to the search for "intent", as the connection between the text and its author is not the same for these two types of texts.[18] It should be noted that despite the differences between the two types of text, the textualist argument on minimization of judicial interference, is generally put forward against intentionalism for both contractual and statutory interpretation.[19] Accordingly, textualism would prevent judges from making the contract for contracting parties according to their own beliefs.

A very interesting study conducted by Solan, Rosenblatt and Osherson[20] shows, however, that this suggestion of the textualist approach might not be accurate, as in borderline cases where an object is not a central case example of a particular category, people (even judges) not only disagree but also have a "false consensus bias" that their own interpretation is shared by other people as the predominant view. Accordingly, it seems not always easy to decide whether "a lamp is furniture"[21] or "a burrito is a sandwich".[22]

---

18 For differences between these two kinds of texts see for instance, GREENAWALT, K., "A Pluralist Approach to Interpretation: Wills and Contracts", 42 San Diego L. Rev. 533 (2005), p. 539. See also HERBOTS, J.H., "*What Precisely is Interpretation*" in *Elgar Encyclopedia of Comparative Law*, 2nd ed., Jan M. Smits (ed.), Edward Elgar, Cheltenham 2012, p. 422, For a comparison between interpretation of these two kinds of texts see also MITCHELL, C., *Interpretation of Contracts, Current Controversies in Law*, Routledge-Cavendish, London 2007, pp. 18–19, where the author suggests that contracts raise similar issues about the balance of power and authority between the interpreter (the judge) and the creators (the parties) although underlying concerns over political legitimacy and the judicial function are much more significant in statutory interpretation where stakes are higher. For a criticism of intentionalism in statutory interpretation, see McGOWAN, M.O., "*Against Interpretation*", 42 San Diego L. Rev. 711 (2005).

19 See MITCHELL, C., *Interpretation of Contracts, Current Controversies in Law*, Routledge-Cavendish, London 2007, pp. 18–19.

20 See SOLAN, L., ROSENBLATT, T., OSHERSON, D., "*False Consensus Bias in Contract Interpretation*", 108 Columbia L. Rev. 1268 et seq.

21 Example given by SOLAN, L., ROSENBLATT, T., OSHERSON, D., "*False Consensus Bias in Contract Interpretation*", 108 Columbia L. Rev. 1268 et seq.

22 For the latter example see the famous case of *White City Shopping Center v PR Restaurants* LLC, No. 2006196313, 2006, WL 3292641, Mass. Super. Ct. October 31, 2006. For critics of this case see, for instance, FLORESTAL, M., "*Is a Burrito a Sandwich? Exploring Race, Class, and Culture in Contracts*", 14(1) Michigan Journal of Race and Law 1–60 (2008) exploring the notion of cultural bias in contract interpretation; see also DiMATTEO, L.A., MORANT, B.D., "*Contract in Context and Contract as Context*", 45 Wake Forest L. Rev. 549 (2010). For another borderline

In the present author's opinion, although it is true that there is always a risk for the judges to interfere in the content of parties' agreement, a plain meaning approach seems to be far from protecting the contract from such interference.

Second, there is the argument put forward by Curtis, who expressed his skepticism on the existence of a party intent leading to one specific meaning, discernable *ex post*. As it is impossible to predict the future, it is impossible for contracting parties to write down contractual clauses that will show one particular "intent" in relation to a particular future event. Accordingly, Curtis suggests that any rule, designed in order to either reveal the inner intent of the promisor or protect reliance of the promisee – seeking one specific "meaning" in contracts – is misleading, because contractual clauses will always have a number of possible meanings when applied to future events due to the lack of foresight which affects all of us.

He, thus, points out that the author should be skillful and should do his or her best to limit properly the space of freedom of those people who will be concerned with these contractual clauses in the future – first the other party and then the court – and try to control their behavior by drafting clauses which are neither too specific nor too vague. The other party then will be invited to act within the limits of the clause and the court will decide whether his or her behavior might be considered reasonable given the wording of the contract. Thus, the court will only be concerned with the reasonableness of the specific behavior of the other party and will not inquire in general what a reasonable person would do if he or she were in the other party's place.[23]

In the opinion of the present author, although it may be difficult to predict the future in general, there might always be a particular intent, either expressed by one party or reasonably understood by the other party, in the contract with regard to a particular future event which may occur and thus, one "meaning" which can be extracted from the text in the light of particular given circumstances. The aim of the interpreter should be to look, before everything else, for this one "meaning" that the language of the contract could bear in the circumstances of the case.

---

case, see *Polpen Shipping Co. v. Commercial Union Assurance Co.*, [1943] 1 K.B. 161, where the insurance contract covered collision with any "other ship or vessel". Can an "anchored flying boat" be considered covered?

23 See CURTIS, C.P., "*A Better Theory of Legal Interpretation*", 3 Vand. L. Rev. 407 (1949–1950).

1.3. SUBJECTIVE AND OBJECTIVE THEORIES OF INTERPRETATION

If we put aside the plain meaning approach, which is more related to the "understanding of the language" than "interpretation", we observe that there are two competing "interpretative" approaches to contractual meaning, each corresponding to one of the second and third definitions given above, namely objective and subjective theories of contract interpretation.

In a subjective approach, the aim of the interpretation is to ascertain the parties' "actual intention". Accordingly, interpretation is the establishment of the meaning that the parties actually attributed to the expressions contained in the contract, and thus the determination of the existence of the "parties' common intention" at the time of contracting.[24] The following definitions of the interpretation process given by French scholars reflect this point of view:

> Interpreting an imperfect contract consists of searching for its exact signification, of fixing the meaning and the scope of its deficient clauses through diverse techniques allowing one to respect as faithfully as possible the badly expressed thoughts of the contracting parties.[25]

Interpretation is considered to be the art of discovering the thoughts expressed by words and writings.[26] "The first duty of the judge consists of a sincere search of the inner wills, as the judge is the natural guardian of contractual faith".[27]

A subjective approach stems from the basis of the contractual relationship which is to be found in the parties' freedom of contract, and, if freedom of contract and party autonomy are to be taken seriously, it is viewed as necessary to give effect to the parties' actual intention that underlies the contract they have concluded.[28]

---

[24] See KORNET, N., *Contract Interpretation and Gap-Filling: Comparative and Theoretical Perspectives*, Intersentia, Antwerpen-Oxford 2006, p. 235.

[25] JOSSERAND, L., *Cours de droit civil positif français*, 2nd ed., Sirey, Paris 1932, p. 125, para. 238. Author's translation.

[26] TOULLIER, C.B.M., *Le droit civil français suivant l'ordre du Code*, 5th ed., Paris 1842, vol. IV, para. 304. Author's translation.

[27] DUPICHOT, J., *"Pour un retour aux textes : Défense et illustration du petit guide-âne des articles 1156 à 1164 du Code Civil"*, in *Etudes offertes à Jacques Flour*, Defrenois, Paris 1979, p. 179. Author's translation.

[28] KORNET, N., *Contract Interpretation and Gap-Filling: Comparative and Theoretical Perspectives*, Intersentia, Antwerpen-Oxford 2006, p. 238.

Again, it should be noted that, like a contextual objective approach, a subjective approach can be adopted in a legal system either from the beginning of the interpretation process or subsequent to a plain meaning reading which does not yield a solution. The scope of the term "interpretation" adopted in a given legal system is decisive on this matter.

The approach of the subjective theory is said to be in accordance with the will theory of contract.[29]

In fact, different theories of contractual obligation have been developed by scholars in order to provide a basis which would justify the binding force of an agreement. The first category of theories is called "party-based" theories, and the interaction between these theories has an important influence on the interpretation process. Party-based theories are said to be one sided since they focus on protecting a particular party of the transaction; a will theory of contract focuses on the protection of the promisor, while a reliance theory takes the side of the promisee.

According to will theory, commitments are enforceable because the promisor has willed or chosen to be bound by his commitment and the will is something worthy of respect. The counterpart, with a slight difference, of the will theory in common law systems is the promise theory of contract. The concept of promise, however, is somewhat narrower than the will, and contracts are regarded, on this view, not just as the products of intentional acts, but as the products of acts expressing an intention to undertake an obligation.[30]

In any case, the main idea lying behind both will and promise theories is the self-imposed character of the contractual obligation. This constitutes an affirmation of the principle of freedom of contract. "After all, the theory can hardly be based on will if the obligation was not chosen by the individual but instead was imposed by law."[31]

As regards the principle of freedom of contract, the parties determine the content of their agreement, will theory suggests that contractual obligations are self-imposed and the result of parties' voluntary acts; in other words, they are created by the parties' will or intention.[32] This position leads to an inquiry of the parties' will or intention, and as to the

---

29 See for instance ZWEIGERT, K., KOTZ, H., *An Introduction to Comparative Law*, 3rd ed., T. Weir (trans.), 1998, para. 400-1.

30 SMITH, S.A., *Contract Theory*, Oxford University Press, Oxford 2004, p. 56.

31 BARNETT, R.E., "*A Consent Theory of Contract*", 86 Columbia L. Rev. 269 (1986), p. 272.

32 See KORNET, N., *Contract Interpretation and Gap-Filling: Comparative and Theoretical Perspectives*, Intersentia, Antwerpen-Oxford 2006, pp. 274–275.

promisor's actual state of mind at the time of agreement: the so-called "subjective viewpoint".[33]

In practice, however, it is difficult to establish the parties' actual intention. So, it is submitted that if the parties' subjective intent *cannot* be discerned, then it will be assumed that this intention corresponds to objectively manifested intentions. But whenever this intention *can* be shown, it should prevail even if it is contrary to objectively manifested behavior if the moral integrity and logic of a will theory are to be preserved.[34] This conception of the contractual obligation is consistent with an interpretation technique which is based on the establishment of the parties' actual intention thus with a subjective approach to interpretation.

Conversely, from an objectivist point of view, the meaning in contracts should be that to which each party has reason to believe the other to be referring. Thus, the contracts should not be interpreted by looking into the parties' actual intent but rather by looking into what parties have expressed and written down.

The following definition of interpretation given by Lord Hoffman in *Investors Compensation Scheme v. West Bromwich Building Society*[35] reflects the objective theory of contract interpretation. Accordingly,

> Interpretation is the ascertainment of the meaning which the document would convey to a reasonable person having all the background knowledge which would reasonably have been available to the parties in the situation in which they were at the time of the contract.[36]

---

33 BARNETT, R.E., "*A Consent Theory of Contract*", 86 Columbia L. Rev. 269 (1986), p. 272.

34 BARNETT, R.E., "*A Consent Theory of Contract*", 86 Columbia L. Rev. 269 (1986), p. 272.

35 [1998] 1 W.L.R. 896.

36 This definition is in fact presented as the first rule of the law about interpretation and is completed with four others. Accordingly, the factual matrix is taken into consideration with the exclusion of previous negotiations and parties' declarations of private intent. The decision states that although we accept that people generally do not make mistakes in a formal document, if, nevertheless, one would conclude from the background that something must have gone wrong with the language, a plain meaning interpretation is not followed; see LEWISON, K., *The Interpretation of Contracts*, Sweet & Maxwell, London 2004, p. 2; see also *Chartbrook Ltd. v. Persimmon Homes Ltd.*, which is in line with *Investors Compensation Scheme v. West Bromwich Building Society* as, although the owner's construction was in accordance with "conventional syntax", it made no commercial sense. In *Arnold v. Britton* the court retained the literal meaning of the words, suggesting that there was no reason to reject the natural language simply because it has worked out badly for one party. For these decisions, see also BURROWS, A., *A Casebook on Contract*, 5th ed., Hart Publishing, Oxford 2016, pp. 243–254.

McMeel acknowledges that in Lord Hoffmann's opinion, the objective approach to interpretation is inescapable, not because of any skepticism about the existence of subjective intention, but because all efforts at construction are conditioned by the listener's background. Consequently, in contractual interpretation, the author of an utterance is a fictional, impersonal construct of law.[37]

In order to support the objective theory, it is often said that it is impossible to read the parties' mind to ascertain their subjective intention. From that point of view, every inquiry of the parties' intention is necessarily objective because it is ascertained by following signs, intrinsic to the contract or not, that are always objective data.[38]

It is also submitted in legal literature that in commercial contracts "the intention of contracting parties", as put forward by the subjective approach, is synonymous with "discovering the commercial purpose of the agreement", or "adopting an interpretation that accords with business common sense" as applied by the modern objective approach, because in commercial contracts, parties "will intend (objectively and subjectively) that their agreement is *effective to achieve 'some' purpose*".[39] The progress from ancient formalism to modern purposive approaches is described as more commercial and commonsensical.[40]

The conception of the objective theory of interpretation is said to be in accordance with the reliance theory of contracts. A reliance theory focuses on the protection of the promisee's reliance induced by the declarations and conduct of the promisor.

Accordingly, from the perspective of the reliance theory,

> we ought to be liable in contract law for our assertive behavior when it creates "foreseeable" and "justifiable" (or reasonable) reliance in others, in much the same way that we are held liable in tort law for harmful consequences of other acts.[41]

---

37 McMEEL, G., "*Language and the Law Revisited: An Intellectual History of Contractual Interpretation*", 34 Comm. L. World Rev. 256 (2005), p. 284.

38 KASSIS, A., *Théorie générale des usages du commerce, Droit Comparé, Contracts et Arbitrage Internationaux, Lex Mercatoria*, L.G.D.J., Paris 1984, p. 152.

39 MITCHELL, C., *Interpretation of Contracts, Current Controversies in Law*, Routledge-Cavendish, London 2007, p. 48.

40 McMEEL, G., *The Construction of Contracts*, 3rd ed., Oxford University Press, Oxford 2017, p. 26.

41 BARNETT, R.E., "*A Consent Theory of Contract*", 86 Columbia L. Rev. 269 (1986), p. 274.

Thus, a person may be bound by the common meaning of his or her words regardless of his or her intention. This priority given to the understanding of the listener leads to a more objective inquiry of the "intent", where the "foreseeable character" and the "reasonableness" of the listener's understanding are questioned.

This conception is consistent with an objective approach to the contract interpretation where justifiable expectations of the promisee rather than the subjective will of the promisor are taken into account.[42] At first, will theorists viewed the reasonable person standard of the objective theory which will be examined below as merely providing evidence of the subjective understanding of the parties, but the test gradually became more objective.[43]

Accordingly, a major objection against the promissory theorists coming from the common law tradition is that the promissory theories are inconsistent with the objective interpretation of contracts generally accepted in common law systems.[44] From that point of view, if contracts are truly based on promises, judges should look at the parties' subjective or inner intent, and an objective approach is required if reliance is to be protected based on external appearances on which parties rely.[45]

Smith explains that this argument weakens once the difference between the determination of the *existence* of a contract and the determination of the *meaning* of a contract is acknowledged, the latter being an objective test which is not disputed by promissory theories.[46]

In conclusion, in order to show the difference between the two approaches, it can be said that the subjective approach looks for what the author meant whereas the objective approach looks for what he or she said. To determine the content of what the parties said, an "objective" point of view is needed. This point of view is called the "reasonable person".

The reasonable person's ancestral roots can be found in Roman contract law, which was structured upon objective formality rather than

---

42 See FARNSWORTH, E.A., "'Meaning' in the Law of Contract", 76 Yale L.J. 939 (1967), pp. 942–943.

43 See DiMATTEO, L.A., "*The Counterpoise of Contracts: The Reasonable Person Standard and the Subjectivity of Judgement*", 48 South Carolina L. Rev. 293–355 (Winter 1997), p. 297.

44 See ATIYAH, P.S., *Promises, Morals and Law*, Clarendon Press, Oxford 1981, p. 21.

45 See SMITH, S.A., *Contract Theory*, Oxford University Press, Oxford 2004, p. 173.

46 See SMITH, S.A., *Contract Theory*, Oxford University Press, Oxford 2004, p. 174.

subjective intent and where completion of the formalities rather than the consent was determinative.[47]

According to Durkheim,

> the undertaking is sacred as soon as the wills in question have been declared by words accompanied by words consecrated formulas. Even in this instance, the moral value of the undertaking does not come about through the consent of the wills but by the formula used. If the solemn ritual is lacking, there is no contract.[48]

DiMatteo writes that the notion of manifestation of intent can be seen as a modern substitute for these ancient rituals, and that implicit in the notion of manifestation of intent is the need to measure and judge that manifestation.[49]

It can be said that the main criterion which distinguishes subjective approaches from objective approaches is that the former take the understanding of contracting parties as their starting point whereas the latter often adopt the position of an objective third party.[50] It should be noted, however, that the "degree of objectivity" of the reasonable person and the extent of the person's "third party" character depend on its construction (as a normative *v.* descriptive reasonable person) and the degree of context to be taken into account (more like a third party listener *v.* more party-based reasonable person).

Accordingly, any construction of the reasonable person may be situated on a scale between "a neutral, third-party listener" who could also dictate moral judgements to contractual parties, and "a highly approached objectified substitute for the actual parties".

As to the context to be taken into account, it should be noted that while subjective approaches to contract interpretation are by definition always contextual, objective approaches may have important variations on this matter.

---

47 See DiMATTEO, L.A., "*The Counterpoise of Contracts: The Reasonable Person Standard and the Subjectivity of Judgement*", 48 South Carolina L. Rev. 293–355 (Winter 1997), p. 295.

48 DURKHEIM, E., quoted in *Durkheim and the Law*, Steven Lukes, Andrew Scull (eds.), Martin Robertson, Oxford 1983, p. 200.

49 See DiMATTEO, L.A., "*The Counterpoise of Contracts: The Reasonable Person Standard and the Subjectivity of Judgement*", 48 South Carolina L. Rev. 293–355 (Winter 1997), p. 296.

50 See KORNET, N., *Contract Interpretation and Gap-Filling: Comparative and Theoretical Perspectives*, Intersentia, Antwerpen-Oxford 2006, p. 235.

When the reasonable person is placed in the shoes of the contracting parties, the test of the reasonable person may become more party-based and in this sense more "subjective" if it is construed as an objective substitute for the actual parties.[51]

Conversely, it is also possible for this person to be construed merely as a properly informed ordinary speaker of the language, as suggested by Lord Steyn.[52] All depends on the weight given to the text and the degree of context taken into account in its construction. Indeed, even in a legal system which exclusively adopts an objective test on interpretation, the presence of context may reach a point where it could be "difficult to distinguish admissible context from declarations of subjective intent."[53]

It is thus impossible to construe the reasonable person in the abstract without referring to the "context" to which the interpreter is allowed to have access in a legal system in general and also to which he or she chooses as a relevant matter to have access in particular.

Conversely, the reasonable person may be not a descriptive but a more normative person, and fairness might be in consideration and the test may become more objective in this sense. The battle between descriptive and normative reasonable persons is said to be the battle between the competing notions of freedom of contract and fairness in exchange.[54]

We will examine this normative aspect of contractual interpretation further in this book but it would be useful to underline here that the normative reasonable person may serve well in a legal system such as English Law which does not recognize a general duty of good faith, in order to provide "piecemeal solutions in response to demonstrated problems of unfairness" in the issues of interpretation and gap-filling, and the results that it may lead to would generally be reached in other legal systems by the application of a general requirement of good faith.[55]

---

51 DiMatteo states that "the descriptive reasonable person is simply placed in the shoes of the parties to determine their intended meaning". See DiMATTEO, L.A., "*The Counterpoise of Contracts: The Reasonable Person Standard and the Subjectivity of Judgement*", 48 South Carolina L. Rev. 293–355 (Winter 1997), p. 297.

52 See Lord Steyn, "*Written Contracts: To What Extent may Evidence Control Language*", 41 C.L.P. 23 (1998).

53 See MITCHELL, C., *Interpretation of Contracts, Current Controversies in Law*, Routledge-Cavendish, London 2007, pp. 71–72.

54 For descriptive and normative reasonable man, see, DiMATTEO, L.A., "*The Counterpoise of Contracts: The Reasonable Person Standard and the Subjectivity of Judgment*", 48 South Carolina L. Rev. 293–355 (Winter 1997), p. 294.

55 See, WHITTAKER, S., ZIMMERMANN, R., "Good Faith in European Contract Law: Surveying the Legal Landscape" in *Good Faith in European Contract Law*, Zimmermann, R., Whittaker, S. (eds.), Cambridge University Press, Cambridge 2000, pp. 45–46.

In this direction, Lord Steyn submits that "There is not a world of a difference between the objective requirement of good faith and the reasonable expectations of the parties".[56] In German law, for instance such objectification of the interpretation process is realized with the application of the good faith principle in order to protect the recipient's reliance.[57]

This point is especially interesting for the CISG, which contains no express provision that imposes a duty of good faith on the parties, as opposed to the PICC, PECL and DCFR. As will be shown further, the question of the recognition of a duty of good faith by this instrument is a matter of controversy as, in literature, there are competing approaches to the question. Accordingly some scholars take the language of the Convention literally and reject any duty to act in good faith imposed by CISG, while other scholars recognize a duty of good faith based on different grounds.[58]

Finally, as the reliance and will theories are one-sided and protect only the interests of one particular party to the contract, they are generally combined in practice.[59] Accordingly, "the will theory is generally combined with elements of the reliance theory or the intention of the parties is

---

56 STEYN, J., "Contract Law: Fulfilling the Reasonable Expectations of Honest Men", 113 L.Q.R. 433 (1997), 446–450.

57 See in general, KORNET, N., *Contract Interpretation and Gap-Filling: Comparative and Theoretical Perspectives*, Intersentia, Antwerpen-Oxford 2006, pp. 96–97.

58 For discussions on this matter see for instance, FARNSWORTH, E.A., "*Duties of Good Faith and Fair Dealing under the Unidroit Principles, Relevant International Conventions, and National Laws*", 3 Tulane Journal of International and Comparative Law 47–64 (1995). HONNOLD, J.O., *Uniform Law for International Sales*, 3rd ed., Kluwer Law International, The Hague 1999, pp. 100–101. GOODE, R., KRONKE, H., MCKENDRICK, E., *Transnational Commercial Law, Text, Cases and Materials*, Oxford University Press, Oxford 2007, p. 281. BONELL, M.J., "Interpretation of Convention" in *Commentary on the International Sales Law*, C.M. Bianca, M.J. Bonell (eds.), Giuffrè, Milan 1987, pp. 84–94. EORSI, G., "*General Provisions*" in *The UN Convention on Contracts for the International Sale of Goods*, N.M. Galston, H. Smit (eds.), Matthew Bender, New York 1984, para. [2.03]. SCHROETER, U.G., "*Freedom of Contract: Comparison between Provisions of the CISG (Art. 6) and Counterpart Provisions of the Principles of European Contract Law*", July 2002, http://www.cisg.law.pace.edu/cisg/text/peclcomp6.html. SCHLECHTRIEM, P., "Uniform Sales Law", 1986, p. 39. WEISZBERG, G., "*Le raisonnable en Droit du Commerce International*", http://www.cisg.law.pace.edu/cisg/biblio/Reasonableness.html, §258. SIM, D., "*The Scope and Application of Good Faith in the Vienna Convention on Contracts for the International Sale of Goods*", http://www.cisg.law.pace.edu/cisg/biblio/sim1.html.

59 See ZWEIGERT, K., KOTZ, H., *An Introduction to Comparative Law*, 3rd ed., T. Weir (trans.), Oxford University Press, Oxford 1998, para. 400-1: "Construction may start from either two opposed premises neither of which is found in the pure form in practice today."

determined on an objective basis."[60] Thus, the rules on interpretation of contracts in most systems combine the subjective and objective theories and adopt tempered solutions.[61]

This point can be better understood if we consider that each system adopts a degree of "objectivity" and "subjectivity" in ascertaining the meaning of a contract, which is determined mainly with reference to different textual and contextual elements. Accordingly, while the use of "objective" data such as textual data (dictionary meaning, grammar etc.) or objective contextual circumstances (the nature of the contract, meaning commonly given to terms and expressions in the trade concerned, etc.) renders the interpretation more "objective", the use of contextual information related to the specific case and a party-based inquiry of meaning makes it more "subjective".[62]

This point will be further explored while examining relevant circumstances to be taken into account in the interpretation process.

It should be noted that the CISG, PICC, PECL and DCFR combine the "subjective" and "objective" theories by adopting a two-level inquiry which makes all "subjective" and "objective" data available in order to establish contractual meaning.

In conclusion, it can be said that when we take the notion of intent into account as a central notion of interpretation, three competing definitions of "contractual meaning" can be extracted. The most objective approach, which completely disregards the relevance of party intent, is, in this author's opinion, not compatible with the nature of the contractual relationship based on party autonomy. The degree of relevance of the intent, however, depends on how far the context is taken into account.

In this respect, while subjective approaches seeking the actual intent are always contextualist by nature, objective approaches focusing on the apparent intent, which objectify party intent by having recourse to the

---

60 KORNET, N., *Contract Interpretation and Gap-Filling: Comparative and Theoretical Perspectives*, Intersentia, Antwerpen-Oxford 2006, p. 275.

61 KACZOROWSKA, A., "*Règles uniformes d'interprétation d'un contrat international*", 68 Revue de droit international et de droit comparé 294 (1991), pp. 298–299.

62 On how objective and subjective theories relate with each other in modern legal systems see VOGENAUER, S., "*Interpretation of Contracts: Concluding Comparative Observations*" in *Contract Terms*, Andrew Burrows, Edwin Peel (eds.), Oxford University Press, Oxford July 2007, pp. 125–128 where the author makes a comparison of French and German Laws. See also, VOGENAUER, S., in *Commentary on the UNIDROIT Principles on International Commercial Contracts*, S. Vogenauer (ed.), Oxford University Press, Oxford 2015, Article 4.1, §§14 and 15.

reasonable person criterion, can vary significantly on that point as all depends on the construction of the reasonable person.

Although some preliminary elements in relation with the construction of this fictional person are provided in the first part of the Chapter 2 (party-based, more like a neutral third party, normative, descriptive etc.), only a concrete analysis of the context admitted to be relevant in a specific legal system (in our case in the CISG, PICC, PECL and DCFR) can better explain this notion. This will be conducted in the following section, where the inter-subjective interpretation method adopted by these instruments will be examined.

1.3.1. Subjective Theory of Interpretation and the CISG, PICC, PECL and DCFR

If we compare the formulation of Article 8 CISG with the formulations of the rules of Article 5:101 PECL, Article 4.1 PICC and Article II-8:101 of DCFR, we observe that in contrast to PECL, PICC and DCFR, CISG does not mention the interpretation of a "contract" and the "common intention of the parties". Instead, the rules of Article 8 are concerned with the unilateral interpretation of "a statement or conduct" of a party such as an offer, acceptance etc.

In the text of the Secretariat's Commentary, it is clarified that Article 8 is equally applicable to the interpretation of "the contract" when the contract is embodied in a single document. Analytically, the Convention treats such an integrated contract as the manifestation of an offer and an acceptance. Therefore, for the purpose of interpreting, the contract is considered to be the product of two unilateral acts.[63]

When we examine the above-mentioned rules on interpretation existing in CISG, PECL, PICC and DCFR, we see that the first test used in the interpretation process is a subjective one.

According to Article 8(1) CISG, "For the purposes of this Convention statements made by and other conduct of a party are to be interpreted

[63] The Secretariat Commentary, See, KRITZER, A.H., *Guide to Practical Applications of the United Nations Convention on Contracts for the International Sale of Goods*, Kluwer, Dewenter 1989, p. 122; Vogenauer explains that this is a repercussion of Germanic systems where individual 'declaration of intent' became the central constitutive building block of contractual interpretation under the influence of Pandectist writers, see VOGENAUER, S., "*Interpretation of Contracts*" in *The Max Planck Encyclopedia of European Private Law*, Vol. 1, Basedow, J., Hopt, K.J., Zimmermann, R., Stier, A. (eds.), Oxford University Press, Oxford 2012, p. 974.

according to his intent where the other party knew or could not have been unaware what that intent was".

The subjective test provided by the rule of Article 8(1) CISG which gives priority to the subjective intention of the party supplements the rule of Article 6 on the principle of freedom of contract. "As a result, there has been a codification of the decisive principles of world trade, which – despite the different nature of domestic economic systems – is based on market-economy principles".[64]

The rule of paragraph (1) emphasizes that the intent of a party would prevail if the other party knew or could not have been unaware what that intent was. So a party's actual understanding is only relevant to the extent that the other party shares this understanding or that it is recognizable to the other party.[65] Consequently, the reliance of the promisee is protected.[66]

The subjective test is also adopted in Article 5:101(1) and (2) PECL.[67] In the Comments on the PECL on Article 5:101, the principle of freedom of contract is underlined: it is stressed that in the system of PECL, the judge is

---

64 JUNGE, W., in *Commentary on the UN Convention on the International Sale of Goods (CISG)*, P. Schlechtriem (ed.), Oxford University Press, Oxford 1998, p. 69.

65 KORNET, N., *Contract Interpretation and Gap-Filling: Comparative and Theoretical Perspectives*, Intersentia, Antwerpen-Oxford 2006, p. 237. For applications of Article 8(1) see for instance, Germany, 27 November 2007, Federal Supreme Court (*Glass bottles case*), http://www.unilex.info/case.cfm?pid=1&do=case&id=1345&step=FullText; the seller knew or could not have been unaware of the real purpose of the contractual amendment proposed by the buyer; that is, to conceal the real purchase price to its customers in Russia. http://www.unilex.info/case.cfm?pid=1&do=case&id=1345&step=Abstract; Germany, 18 November 2008, Appellate Court, Brandenburg (*Beer case*), http://cisgw3.law.pace.edu/cases/081118g1.html. Jan Henning Berg (trans.). See also Arbitral award, case number: 8324 of 1995 of the ICC Court of Arbitration, Paris which held that Article 8(1) implies that the parties either already had strong business ties and knew each other well, or the statements and conduct of each could be known and decoded by the other party, http://cisgw3.law.pace.edu/cases/958324i1.html. Julia Hoffmann (trans.).

66 See NEUMAYER, K.H., MING, C., "Convention de Vienne sur les Contrats de Vente Internationale de Marchandises", F. Dessemontet (ed.), CEDIDAC No 24, Centre du droit de l'entreprise de l'Université de Lausanne, 1993, p. 111: "The Convention is governed by the principle of reliance", and fn 1; Article 8 "seems to place stronger emphasis on the recipient rather than the author of the expressions, which would give more weight to the 'objectified sense' of the expressions". Author's translation.

67 "(1) A contract is to be interpreted according to the common intention of the parties even if this differs from the literal meaning of the words. (2) If it is established that one party intended the contract to have a particular meaning, and at the time of the conclusion of the contract the other party could not have been unaware of the first party's intention, the contract is to be interpreted in the way intended by the first party".

encouraged to start by looking to see what the parties' common intention was at the time the contract was made, and submitted that this is normal "because the contract is primarily the creation of the parties and the judge should respect their intentions, expressed or implicit, even if their will was expressed obscurely or ambiguously".[68]

Thus, in case of conflict between the written document and the parties' common intention, the latter should prevail. Also, when the intent of a party differs from the wording and the other party knew or could not have been unaware of the real intent of his or her contractual partner, this other party cannot rely on the reasonable meaning of the words used in the writing, and the actual intent of his or her contractual partner prevails (paragraph 2).

The PICC also refers to the subjective test as the starting point of the interpretation process. In this regard, the Article 4.1(1) PICC[69] refers to the interpretation of contract (as does Article 5:101(1) PECL) whereas the Article 4.2(1)[70] is related to the interpretation of unilateral statements or conduct (as are Article 5: 101(2) PECL and Article 8 CISG).

In the comments of the PICC, it is underlined that the effect of the subjective test is that a contract term may be given a meaning which differs both from the literal sense of the language used and the meaning that a reasonable person would attach to it, to the extent that such a different understanding was common to the parties at the time of the conclusion of the contract.[71]

DCFR also adopts first a subjective inquiry of intent. According to Article II.–8:101(1) and (2),

> (1) A contract is to be interpreted according to the common intention of the parties even if this differs from the literal meaning of the words.
> (2) If one party intended the contract, or a term or expression used in it, to have a particular meaning, and at the time of the conclusion of the contract the other party was aware, or could reasonably be expected to have been aware, of the first party's intention, the contract is to be interpreted in the way intended by the first party.

---

68 *Principles of the European Contract Law, Parts I and II*, Prepared by The Commission on European Contract Law O. Lando, H. Beale (eds.), Kluwer Law International, The Hague 2000, p. 288.

69 "A contract shall be interpreted according to the common intention of the parties".

70 "The statements and other conduct of a party shall be interpreted according to that party's intention if the other party knew or could not have been unaware of that intention".

71 Comments on PICC 2016, Art. 4.1.

The formulation of this article is slightly different than that of the corresponding articles of former instruments, as the expression "could reasonably be expected to have been aware" is preferred instead of "could not have been unaware". This formulation renders the test of the DCFR article more objective concerning the inquiry of the awareness of the promise and I think is a better formulation.

Another point which should be emphasized is that in the application of the subjective test, all the relevant circumstances should be taken into account. A detailed analysis of these circumstances is made below in this chapter.

1.3.2. Objective Theory of Interpretation and the CISG, PICC, PECL and DCFR

1.3.2.1. In General

If the intention cannot be established by the application of the subjective test, the CISG,[72] PECL,[73] PICC[74] and DCFR[75] provide the

[72] Article 8(2): "If the preceding paragraph is not applicable, statements made by and other conduct of a party are to be interpreted according to the understanding that a reasonable person of the same kind as the other party would have had in the same circumstances". On this paragraph see for instance Austria, 23 January 2006, Oberlandesgericht [Appellate Court] Linz (*Auto case*), http://cisgw3.law.pace.edu/cases/060123a3.html. Jan Henning Berg (trans.). The combination of Article 8(1) and 8(2) provides for the requirements of a real intent. A mere hypothetical intent is not sufficient; Spain, 17 January 2008, Supreme Court (*Used automobiles case*), http://cisgw3.law.pace.edu/cases/080117s4.html. Lindsay J. Ramistella (trans.), Juan Manuel Falabella (ed.): Each party has equal status as a reasonable person in terms of Article 8(2). Switzerland, 12 December 2006, Canton Appellate Court, Thurgau (*Building materials case*), http://cisgw3.law.pace.edu/cases/061212s1.html. Veit Konrad (trans.), Jan Henning Berg (ed.). Article 8(2) has a larger field of application than article 8(1). On article 8(2) reflecting the "principle of reliance" see for instance Germany, 11 December 1996, Supreme Court (*Marzipan Case*), http://cisgw3.law.pace.edu/cases/961211g1.html. Thorsten Tepasse (trans.); Switzerland, 12 May 2006, Appellate Court Geneva (*Office furniture case*), http://cisgw3.law.pace.edu/cases/060512s1.html. Claire Chabat (trans.); Switzerland, 29 October 2003, Appellate Court Lugano, Cantone del Ticino (*Modular wall partitions case*); http://cisgw3.law.pace.edu/cases/031029s1.html. Joseph Gulino (trans.). On the "principle of reliance" and the CISG see also Switzerland, 11 October 2004, Canton Court Freiburg (*Chemical product case*), http://cisgw3.law.pace.edu/cases/041011s1.html. Dr. Andrea Vincze (trans.), Mariel Dimsey (ed.). In a number of cases the court applied article 8(2) after the application of Article 8(1) did not yield to a solution: Germany 16 July 2001 Appellate Court Köln (*Farm animals case*), http://cisgw3.law.pace.edu/cases/010716g1.html; United States, 18 January 2011, Federal District Court [New York] (*Hanwha Corporation v. Cedar Petrochemicals, Inc.*), http://cisgw3.law.pace.edu/cases/110118u1.html. In some other

application of the objective test of interpretation through the reasonable person standard.[76] In the comments on the PECL, it is submitted that the judge should not try to discover the intentions of the parties at any price and end up deciding what they were in an arbitrary way. But the use of the objective interpretation should not empower the judge to overturn the contract under the guise of interpretation and to go against the unequivocal will of the parties either.[77]

According to objective tests provided by the CISG, PECL and PICC, the contract or the statements or conduct of the parties shall be interpreted according to the meaning that reasonable persons of the same kind as the parties (for the interpretation of contracts) or the same kind as the other party (for the interpretation of the statements or conduct) would give to it in the same circumstances.[78]

---

cases the court directly applied Article 8(2): Germany, 27 December 1999, Appellate Court Dresden (*Chemical products case*), http://cisgw3.law.pace.edu/cases/991227g1.html; Serbia, 25 May 2001, Foreign Trade Arbitration Court attached to the Yugoslav Chamber of Commerce in Belgrade, Serbia (*Berries case*), http://cisgw3.law.pace.edu/cases/010525sb.html; Germany 25 January 2008, Appellate Court Hamburg (*Café inventory case*), http://cisgw3.law.pace.edu/cases/080125g1.html. Jan Henning Berg (trans.).

73 Article 5:101(3): "If an intention cannot be established according to (1) or (2), the contract is to be interpreted according to the meaning that reasonable persons of the same kind as the parties would give to it in the same circumstances".

74 Article 4.1(2): "If such an intention cannot be established, the contract shall be interpreted according to the meaning that reasonable persons of the same kind as the parties would give to it in the same circumstances" (on interpretation of contracts) and Article 4.2(2): "If the preceding paragraph is not applicable, such statements and other conduct shall be interpreted according to the meaning that a reasonable person of the same kind as the other party would give to it in the same circumstances" (on the interpretation of statement and conduct).

75 Article II.-8:101: "The contract is, however, to be interpreted according to the meaning which a reasonable person would give to it: (a) if an intention cannot be established under the preceding paragraphs; or (b) if the question arises with a person, not being a party to the contract or a person who by law has no better rights than such a party, who has reasonably and in good faith relied on the contract's apparent meaning".

76 DiMatteo calls this choice of rule as the inter-subjective theory of contract interpretation. See, DiMATTEO, L.A., "*False Dichotomies in Commercial Contract Interpretation*", 11(1) Int'l J. Trade L. & P'cy 27–43 (2012).

77 *Principles of European Contract Law, Parts I and II*, Prepared by The Commission on European Contract Law, O. Lando, H. Beale (eds.), Kluwer Law International, The Hague 2000, p. 289.

78 In the ICC Arbitration case no: 7331, it was held by the arbitrators that in interpreting statements of parties and provisions in contracts, it is generally accepted in international commercial law that the meaning of such statements and provisions is to be assessed on an objective basis, unless it can be shown that the parties had a contrary subjective understanding. It was emphasized by arbitrators that the Vienna

The expression of "the same kind as the other party" is said to be referring to "a person from the same background as the person concerned and engaged in the same occupation, the same trade activities for example".[79] Feltham states that the reference to a reasonable person of the same kind is intended to ensure that the statement of a tractor salesman from a developed country to a Nusquamian peasant is to be interpreted as it would be understood by the reasonable Nusquamian peasant.[80]

All relevant circumstances, whether intrinsic or extrinsic, are taken into account in order to determine the meaning that the reasonable person of the same kind as the contracting parties would understand.

Unlike the other instruments, DCFR only refers to the notion of "reasonable person" instead of "reasonable person of the same kind as the contracting parties". Thus, although the relevant circumstances to be taken into account in the construction of the reasonable person according to the DCFR are the same as for the other instruments, it seems that the reasonable person of DCFR is intended to be more objective.[81] This point will be developed further in this chapter.

It should be noted here that the adoption of the objective test via the reasonable person standard, as a second test for the interpretation of the contracts, seems to be necessary when considering the nature of the contracts generally governed by the CISG, PECL, PICC and DCFR.

In fact, the CISG and PICC are instruments which govern "international" commercial contracts and the main objective of the PECL which could also apply to the DCFR is in fact to respond to a growing recognition, as stated in the Comments on the PECL, "of the need for measures of harmonization to eliminate differences in national laws which are inimical to the efficient conduct of cross-border business within Europe".

The authors of the PECL also emphasized that such harmonization measures confer particular benefits on contracting parties carrying on business in different states, enabling them to contract with reference to a

---

Convention reflects these general international commercial principles. See the Editorial Remarks by Albert H. Kritzer on ICC Arbitration Case No. 7331 of 1994 (*Cowhides case*), http://cisgw3.law.pace.edu/cases/947331i1.html.

79 See the Legislative History of the CISG, Article 8, http://www.cisg.law.pace.edu/cisg/text/secomm/newsecomm/secomm-08.html.

80 FELTHAM, J., "*The United Nations Convention on Contracts for the International Sale of Goods*", J. Bus. L. 346 (1981) p. 349.

81 See HESEN G., HARDY R., "*Contract Interpretation, Interpretative Criteria*" in *Economic Analysis of the DCFR, The Work of the Economic Impact Group within the CoPECL Network of Excellence*, P. Larouche, F. Cihirico (eds.), Sellier, Munich 2010, p. 93.

set of rules which apply uniformly across the territories of various states, which are detached from any particular legal system, which are available in languages of which at least one is likely to be known to the parties, and which over time will become much more familiar to those who use them than the individual national laws of the various foreign countries in which they transact business.[82]

As parties to the contracts governed by these four instruments are generally situated in different countries, there is not much room for face-to-face transactions and parties' communications are generally separated by time and distance. The parties separated from each other generally rely on the written word and it is very difficult for a party to show that his or her contracting partner knew or could not have been unaware of his or her actual intention.

In the Comments on PICC Article 4.1(1) it is submitted that the practical importance of the test on subjective interpretation should not be over-estimated because of two reasons: First, parties to commercial transactions are unlikely to use language in a sense entirely different from that usually attached to it. Second, even in cases where such language would be adopted, it would be extremely difficult to prove ex *post* that this particular meaning was in fact shared by the other party at the time of the conclusion of the contract.[83]

In examining the objective tests of the CISG, PECL, PICC and DCFR, the main question that should be asked is: "Who is reasonable person in terms of these instruments?" Before examining contextual issues related to the construction of the reasonable person in detail, let us make some additional preliminary remarks on this question.

1.3.2.2. Reasonable Person in the CISG, PICC, PECL and DCFR

Article 7(1) CISG provides that in the interpretation of the CISG, regard is to be had to its international character and to the need to promote uniformity in its application and the observance of good faith in

82 *Principles of European Contract Law, Parts I and II*, Prepared by The Commission on European Contract Law, O. Lando, H. Beale (eds.), Kluwer Law International, The Hague 2000, p. xxi (Introduction).

83 See Comments on PICC 2016 Art. 4.1, In the same direction see also MURRAY, J.E., "*An Essay on the Formation of Contracts and Related Matters under the United Nations Convention on Contracts for the International Sale of Goods*", 8 Journal of Law and Commerce 11–51 (1988). See also VOGENAUER, S., "Interpretation of Contracts" in *The Max Planck Encyclopedia of European Private Law*, Vol. 1, Basedow, J., Hopt, K.J., Zimmermann, R., Stier, A. (eds.), Oxford University Press, Oxford 2012, p. 976.

international trade. This provision applies also to the interpretation of Article 8 CISG on contractual interpretation and to the reasonable person standard.

Honnold underlines that in international contracts, where parties are generally based in different language and legal settings, the problems intrinsic to language rise to a higher power. So, the party who makes a statement must avoid using obscure expressions or "faux amis" (which are the results of the use of different legal terms with different meanings in different legal cultures and mercantile terms with divergent meanings in different areas or settings).[84] He also acknowledges that the reasonable person test of Article 8(2) responds to the fact that "only the one who communicates has an opportunity to consider and choose among alternative modes of expression and takes account of a drafters opportunity to hide an unpleasant meaning inside his or her expressions" is consistent with the *contra proferentem* rule.[85]

Junge points out that in terms of the reasonable person test of Article 8(2), the "recipient's understanding" is applied in a generalized form, without reference to parties' actual intentions and insights, and that it is practically identical to the "generally accepted view". He adds that in international sale of goods transactions the relevant view is therefore that of a specialist who is aware of the practice in his trade sector, of the various types of sales contracts involved and of the related technical language, and is also familiar with the technical implementation of the transaction (form of dispatch, customs, formalities and payment methods) and the technical characteristics of the goods and their use.[86]

Kaczorowska is pessimistic on a uniform construction of the reasonable person standard in the field of international commercial transactions on the basis of "business common sense". She states that the CISG seems to believe that reasonable behavior in commercial matters would be the same all over the world although it is not the case in reality. She also points out that the Convention disregards the fact that the notion of reasonable person is vague, ambiguous and socially conditioned.[87]

---

84 HONNOLD, J.O., *Uniform Law for International Sales*, 3rd ed., Kluwer Law International, The Hague 1999, p. 118.

85 HONNOLD, J.O., *Uniform Law for International Sales*, 3rd ed., Kluwer Law International, The Hague 1999, p. 118.

86 JUNGE, W., in *Commentary on the UN Convention on the International Sale of Goods (CISG)*, P. Schlechtriem (ed.), Oxford 1998, p. 72.

87 KACZOROWSKA, A., "Règles uniformes d'interprétation d'un contrat international", 68 Revue de droit international et de droit comparé 294 (1991), p. 304.

As is rightly submitted by Perelman in the literature, what is reasonable is defined on a case-by-case basis with relation to values, aspirations, usages and beliefs in a given social environment. Thus, its application does not give a unique solution but a plurality of solutions.[88] Accordingly, it seems that any uniform construction in accordance with Article 7 of the reasonable person standard based on "business common sense" of the CISG seems to be very questionable, especially if one observes that its uniform application has not even been provided for in the system of national laws.[89]

Although notions like "generally accepted view" and "common business sense" may be of important guidance in the construction of the reasonable person in commercial contracts and in the quest for uniformity of application, in adopting such general approaches, the characteristics of the parties and the case should not be forgotten.[90] This is especially important when the availability of an internationally accepted common business sense is highly questionable, as mentioned above. The fact that the reasonable person is construed on a case-by-case basis, with consideration of the parties' characteristics and all the relevant circumstances, implies that the reasonable person of the CISG should take the international character of the transaction and the fact that parties are based in different languages and legal settings into account. I think that this result is in conformity with Article 7(1).

It should also be noted that the CISG does also not contain any definition of reasonableness and it is submitted that the definition provided by the PECL could be used in order to interpret CISG articles where a reference is made to this concept.[91]

The PECL recognize an express general duty of good faith and define the term reasonableness as "what persons acting in good faith and

---

88 PERELMAN, C., *Le Raisonnable et le Déraisonnable en Droit. Au-delà du Positivisme Juridique*, L.G.D.J., Paris 1984, p. 15.

89 See KACZOROWSKA, A., "*Règles uniformes d'interprétation d'un contrat international*", 68 Revue de droit international et de droit comparé 294 (1991), pp. 305–310.

90 After all, as Zeller rightly points out, "The CISG recognizes that in international trade, an effective contract must express the true intent of the parties and not an intent measured by the views of informed bystanders". See ZELLER, B., "*Determining the Contractual Intent of Parties under the CISG and Common Law-A Comparative Analysis*", 4(4) European Journal of Law Reform 633 (2002), p. 642. Accordingly, even when a "subjective intent" cannot be extracted, "objective intent" should be construed by referring to all relevant subjective elements of the case.

91 See overview of the comments on reasonableness. KRITZER A. (ed.), http://www.cisg.law.pace.edu/cisg/text/reason.html.

in the same situation as the parties would consider to be reasonable" (Article 1:302). This definition presupposes a duty to act in good faith and thus is consistent with the system of PECL although the PECL are criticized as using these two notions interchangeably, thus, as providing no difference between good faith and reasonableness.[92]

In order to be able to transfer this definition to the CISG, one should accept the existence of a duty of good faith in terms of the CISG. In accordance with their system, the PECL state expressly in Article 5:102 "good faith and fair dealing" as a relevant circumstance in the interpretation of contracts and the CISG does not.

Accordingly, different constructions of the reasonable person in terms of the CISG can be put forward, depending on the position taken on the recognition of an express duty of good faith by the CISG. If a literal reading of the Convention is adopted, it can be suggested that this position of the PECL would normally be susceptible to rendering the reasonable person of this instrument more normative than that of the CISG. If the Convention is not read literally, however, normative constructions of the reasonable person in terms of this Convention could become frequent in order to establish fairness in contractual relationships which could serve in time for the creation of an "autonomous reasonable person" in terms of the CISG, thereby minimizing reference to national laws in relation with good faith and fair dealing issues, and thus promote uniformity of application.

The PICC contain a general duty of good faith (Article 1.7), no definition of reasonableness and, unlike the PECL, do not state good faith as a relevant circumstance in the interpretation of contracts.

The DCFR contains also a general duty of good faith and fair dealing (Article III.–1:103) and a definition on reasonableness stating that "reasonableness is to be objectively ascertained, having regard to the nature and purpose of what is being done, to the circumstances of the case and to any relevant usages and practices" (Article I.–1:104). I think that this latter definition adopted by DCFR may more easily be transferred to the CISG than the definition proposed by the PECL.

---

92 See, BEALE, H., "*General Clauses and Specific Rules in the Principles of European Contract Law: The 'Good Faith' Clause*", in *General Clauses and Standards in European Contract Law, Comparative Law, EC Law and Contract Law Codification*, Stefan Grundmann, Denis Mazeaud (eds.), Kluwer Law Interational, 2006, pp. 216–217: Beale gives the example of Art. 9:201, where the comments refer to the principles of good faith and fair dealing when the test is one of reasonableness.

Finally, the DCFR, like the PECL, enumerates good faith and fair dealing as a relevant circumstance to be taken into account in the interpretation process (Article II.–8:102), as we will examine in detail in the coming section.

In this section, we tried to focus on methodological approaches to "interpretation as the ascertainment of the contractual meaning attached by the parties" in order to provide a theoretical framework.

In conclusion, it can be said that the uniform or harmonized instruments that we are referring in terms of this book, namely the CISG, PICC, PECL and DCFR all have recourse first to a subjective test of contract interpretation which considers all relevant contextual data in order to reveal actual intent. If this subjective test does not yield a solution, the objective test is applied in order to construe the presumed intent via the reasonable person criterion, again with recourse to all relevant contextual information. Thus, the reasonable person in terms of these instruments is highly party-based and far from being an objective third-party listener.

In order to be able to further understand how the "actual" intent of the subjective theory can be established or how the reasonable person of the objective theory can be construed in accordance with the provisions of the CISG, PECL, PICC and DCFR we will have to examine next the relevant circumstances playing a role in the interpretation process.

2. RELEVANT CIRCUMSTANCES

2.1. INTRODUCTION

The legal material that we are examining in this book adopts a highly contextual approach to contract interpretation and provides a non-exhaustive list of relevant circumstances to be applied in both objective and subjective tests. Accordingly, formalistic rules on contract interpretation such as the plain meaning rule, four corners rule and parol evidence rule are excluded by these instruments.

This choice should be seen as the result of the inter-subjective interpretation approach to contract interpretation adopted by the instruments discussed above, according to which the aim of the interpretation process is above anything else the determination of the subjective intent of the parties. Even where such an intent cannot be established and an objective interpretation technique is needed, all circumstances are taken into account in order to establish an objective intent which is aimed to correspond the best to the real life case even if circumstances of more general character may inevitably find more application, as the subjective test would already have been applied and not have yielded a solution.

At this point, the supplementing rule adopted by the CISG, PICC and PECL, according to which the reasonable person is construed as a fictional person in "the shoes of the actual parties", should be stated as playing a key role in this matter. Thus, in terms of these three instruments, all relevant contextual information will be applied to these real-life-similar constructions of law.

Although the DCFR adopts a more objective wording[93] concerning the construction of the reasonable person, this should not be understood as excluding the context related to the characteristics of the parties.[94]

As we will develop further below, the choice of a highly contextual interpretation approach can be explained primarily by the fact that these instruments are essentially provided as a response to the needs of growing cross-border business, which also means an increase in the number of intercultural relationships between people who generally speak different languages.

It should also be noted here that there are two higher level contexts which apply to the interpretation of "international commercial contracts", namely "commercial context" and "international context". One can suggest that these two contexts can be considered two competing contexts which may have competing needs; "predictability in commercial transactions" on one side and "ability to respond to problems related to cultural and linguistic divergences" on the other side.

From this point of view, as will be further explained, these instruments can be considered as giving more weight to the "internationality" of the contract than its "commercial character". This especially concerns the CISG and PICC because the PECL and DCFR not only apply to commercial contracts but also to consumer transactions. Before treating issues on contextualism and formalism let us first consider related articles in the CISG, PICC, PECL and DCFR.

---

93 See MANTYSAARI, P., *The Law of Corporate Finance: General Principles and EU Law, Volume II: Contracts in General*, Springer 2010, p. 87.

94 See DCFR Comments on Article II.–8:101.

2.2. RELATED ARTICLES

2.2.1. CISG

Article 8 CISG, after specifically mentioning that the context related to party characteristics should be taken into account in the construction of the reasonable person of the objective test (Article 8(2)) if the subjective test cannot yield a solution, provides further that in determining both the subjective intent of a party and the understanding a reasonable person would have had, due consideration is to be given to all relevant circumstances of the case, including the negotiations, any practices which the parties have established between themselves, usages and any subsequent conduct of the parties (Article 8(3)).[95] Accordingly, the list of relevant circumstances is not exhaustive and other elements can be taken into account by courts if they are considered to be relevant. In the Secretariat's Commentary on the draft counterpart of Article 8(3) it is suggested that in order to go beyond the apparent meaning of the words or the conduct of the parties, Article 7(3) [draft counterpart of CISG Article 8(3)] states that "due consideration is to be given to all relevant circumstances" of the case. The article "then goes on to enumerate some, but not necessarily all circumstances of the case which are to be taken into account."[96]

2.2.2. PICC

The PICC adopt the same position as the CISG. First, Article 4.1(2) states that if a common intention cannot be established; the contract shall be interpreted according to the meaning that reasonable persons "of the same kind" as the parties would give to it "in the same circumstances". Second, it is provided in Article 4.3 that in applying Article 4.1 on contract interpretation and Article 4.2 on the interpretation of statements and

95 For an overview of the rules contained in Article 8 see, for instance, Switzerland, 26 November 2008 Handelsgericht [Commercial Court] Aargau (*Fruit and vegetables case*), http://cisgw3.law.pace.edu/cases/081126s1.html. Jan Henning Berg (trans.); Arbitral award, case number 8324 of 1995 of the ICC Court of Arbitration, Paris. See also United States, 30 January 2001, Federal District Court [California] (*Supermicro Computer v. Digitechnic*), where the court states that Article 8 CISG required a mirror-image approach to contract negotiations, http://cisgw3.law.pace.edu/cases/010130u1.html.

96 Secretariat's Commentary on Article 7 of the 1978 Draft, which is the draft counterpart of Article 8. See, http://www.cisg.law.pace.edu/cisg/text/secomm/secomm-08.html.

other conduct, "regard shall be had to all the circumstances", including preliminary negotiations between the parties, practices which the parties have established between themselves, the conduct of the parties subsequent to the conclusion of the contract, the nature and the purpose of the contract, the meaning commonly given to terms and expressions in the trade concerned and the usages.

2.2.3. PECL

The PECL also have a similar approach. In their subjective test, they stresses harder their rejection of formalistic interpretation, stating that the contract is to be interpreted according to the common intention of the parties "even if it differs from the literal meaning of the words" (Article 5:101(1)).

The reasonable person is once more construed as a fictional person of the same kind as the parties in the same circumstances (Article 5:101(2)). And finally, it provides that in interpreting the contract, regard shall be had, in particular, to the circumstances in which it was concluded, including the preliminary negotiations, the conduct of the parties, even subsequent to the conclusion of the contract, the nature and purpose of the contract, the interpretation which has already been given to similar clauses by the parties and the practices they have established between themselves, the meaning commonly given to terms and expressions in the branch of activity concerned, and the interpretation similar clauses may already have received, usages and good faith and fair dealing (Article 5:102).

2.2.4. DCFR

Like PECL, DCFR also stresses specifically in its subjective test that any commonly intended meaning overrides the literal meaning of the contractual language (Article II.–8:101(1)). Differently from the previous instruments, however, it does not mention that the reasonable person would be of the same kind as contracting parties in the same circumstances (third paragraph). The context to be taken into account in the establishment of a subjective or objective meaning is, however, similar to previous instruments which give a non-exhaustive list of elements.

Indeed according to Article II.–8:102 on relevant matters, in interpreting the contract, regard may be had, in particular, to the circumstances in which it was concluded, including the preliminary negotiations, the conduct of the parties, even subsequent to the conclusion of the contract, the interpretation which has already been given by the parties to terms or expressions which are the same as, or similar to, those used in the contract and the practices they have established between themselves, the meaning commonly given to such terms or expressions in the branch of activity concerned and the interpretation such terms or expressions may already have received, the nature and purpose of the contract, usages and good faith and fair dealing.

Thus, in the DCFR the reasonable person is not specified as being of the same kind as the other party in the same circumstances, although all relevant circumstances are accepted as context. The Comments on Article II.–8:101 DCFR clarify this difference of wording.

Accordingly, "a reasonable person would, of course, take into account the objective circumstances in which the contract was concluded and the nature of the parties between whom it was concluded".[97] Thus, it would not be wrong to suggest that the difference between this article and corresponding CISG, PICC and PECL articles is purely cosmetic.

3. AN EXAMINATION OF THE RELEVANT CIRCUMSTANCES STATED IN CISG, PICC, PECL AND DCFR

All four instruments provide, thus, a non-exhaustive list on contextual elements. The circumstances which are enumerated in those lists can be classified in two sub-categories as "those related with the particular relationship which exists between the parties" and "others of general character", as suggested in the comments on the PICC, which underline that although in principle all circumstances may be relevant in a given case, first category circumstances – such as preliminary negotiations, practices established between the contracting parties and subsequent conduct – are likely to have a greater weight in the application of the subjective test, while the second category circumstances – such as the nature and purpose of the contract, the meaning commonly given to terms and expressions in the trade concerned and usages – are important primarily, although not exclusively, in the application of the reasonableness test.[98]

---

97 DCFR Comments on Article II.–8:101.

98 UNIDROIT Principles of International Commercial Contracts 2016, Comments on Article 4.3.

3.1. PRELIMINARY NEGOTIATIONS

The admissibility of preliminary negotiations as a relevant circumstance to discover the meaning of a contract is generally rejected in common law countries. In the leading case of *Investors Compensation Scheme Limited v. West Bromwich Building Society*, after stating that interpretation should be made with due consideration to all the background knowledge which would reasonably have been available to the contracting parties in the situation in which they were at the time of contracting, Lord Hoffman explains that the law excludes from the admissible background the previous negotiations of the parties and their declarations of subjective intent. According to Lord Hoffman, these are only admissible in an action for rectification, and thus "the law makes the distinction for reasons of practical policy and, in this respect only, legal interpretation differs from the way we should interpret utterances in ordinary life". He finally emphasizes that the boundaries of this exception are in some respects unclear, without further discussing these boundaries in the circumstances of the case.[99]

There are, in fact, a number of practical policy reasons which can be shown in order to explain this exclusion of the English Law. First, there is a fear that the admission of preliminary negotiations as relevant context would create greater uncertainty of outcome in disputes and would increase significantly the litigation costs.[100] Second, it is put forward in the literature that statements made by the parties during the negotiation process mostly reflect one-sided expectations of the parties that are only

99 [1998] 1 W.L.R. 896.

100 See *Chartbrook v. Persimmon*, [2009] UKHL 38, [2009] 1 A.C. 1101 [36]–[38]. See also KÖTZ, H., "*Interpretation of Contracts*" in *European Contract Law*, 2nd ed., Gill Mertens and Tony Weir (trans.), Oxford University Press, Oxford 2017, p. 95, fn. 19. For a transfer of the reasoning of this case to the context of oral modifications see WAGNER-VON PAPP, F., "*European Contract Law: Are No Oral Modification Clauses Not Worth the Paper They Are Written On?*", 63(1) C.L.P. 511–596 (January 2010). KÖTZ, H., "*Interpretation of Contracts*" in *European Contract Law*, 2nd ed., Gill Mertens and Tony Weir (trans.), Oxford University Press, Oxford 2017, p. 95, fn 19; See also United Kingdom, 18 December 2006, Court of Appeal (Civil Division) (*The Square Mile Partnership Ltd. v. Fitzmaurice McCall Ltd.*), http://cisgw3.law.pace.edu/cases/061218uk.html. Compare this decision with *ProForce Recruit Ltd v. Rugby Group Ltd.*, United Kingdom, 17 February 2006, Court of Appeal (Civil Division). In support of a formalistic approach to reduce transaction costs see for instance BERNSTEIN, L., "*Private Commercial Law in the Cotton Industry: Creating Cooperation Through Rules, Norms and Institutions*", 99 Mich. L. Rev. 1724 (2001) pp. 1735–1744; SCHWARTZ, A., SCOTT, R.E., "*Contract Interpretation Redux*", 119 Yale L.J. pp. 926–964 (2010).

meant to be subject to contract, and that will later be replaced by the mandatory wording of the contract itself.[101] Third, it is supported that the law does not wish to encourage parties to make self-serving statements during the negotiation process in order to present them as evidence in case of litigation.[102]

Zeller criticizes this approach by stating that "utterances in ordinary life" are in many cases the foundation of a business relationship which leads to a contractual relationship.[103] In the same direction, McKendrick points out that, as courts now state that they should seek to adopt an interpretation advancing the commercial purpose which the parties had in mind, pre-contractual negotiations may provide very good evidence as to what was the commercial purpose of the parties.[104] It should also be noted that it is possible to adopt a moderate approach on the matter without rejecting recourse to preliminary negotiations as such. Consequently, it is put forward in the literature that in the light of the policy arguments cited above, preliminary negotiations could be accepted as relevant circumstances with necessary reservation on their evidentiary value.[105]

Some examples of the application of preliminary negotiations follow.

A contract for the writing of a book indicates that the book should consist of "about 300 pages". During their negotiations the publisher assures the writer that an approximate indication of the number of pages was necessary for administrative reasons and that the writer could exceed it, substantially if need be. The writer submits a manuscript of 500 pages. In interpreting the meaning of "about 300 pages" due consideration should be given to these preliminary negotiations.[106]

---

101 See KÖTZ, H., "*Interpretation of Contracts*" in *European Contract Law*, 2nd ed., Gill Mertens and Tony Weir (trans.), Oxford University Press, Oxford 2017, p. 95, fn. 19.

102 See McKENDRICK, E., "*The Interpretation of Contracts: Lord Hoffmann's Restatement*" in *Commercial Law and Commercial Practice*, Sarah Worthington (ed.), Hart Publishing, Oxford/Portland OR, 2003, p. 155.

103 ZELLER, B., "*Determining the Contractual Intent of Parties under the CISG and Common Law-A Comparative Analysis*", 4(4) European Journal of Law Reform 629 (2002), p. 640.

104 See McKENDRICK, E., "*The Interpretation of Contracts: Lord Hoffmann's Restatement*" in *Commercial Law and Commercial Practice*, Sarah Worthington (ed.), Hart Publishing, Oxford/Portland OR, 2003, p. 155.

105 See KÖTZ, H, "*Interpretation of Contracts*" in *European Contract Law*, Gill Mertens and Tony Weir (trans.), Oxford University Press, 2nd ed., 2017, p.95. In the same direction, see also McKENDRICK, E., "*The Interpretation of Contracts: Lord Hoffmann's Restatement*" in *Commercial Law and Commercial Practice*, Sarah Worthington (ed.), Hart Publishing, Oxford/Portland OR, 2003, p. 155.

106 See, UNIDROIT Principles of International Commercial Contracts 2016, Comments on Article 4.3.

One of the parties defines, in the course of negotiations, a term that would be incorporated in the future contract in a letter. The other party has not contested this interpretation even when opportunity arose. The judge will consider the preliminary negotiations even if the contract embodies a merger clause.[107]

The reference to preliminary negotiation means that all documents prior to the conclusion of the contract and oral evidence of negotiations are among the circumstances to be taken into account in the interpretation process.[108]

3.2. THE CONDUCT OF THE PARTIES EVEN SUBSEQUENT TO THE CONTRACT

As is submitted in the literature, interpretation is frequently inference from the conduct of contracting parties preceding and/or following the conclusion of the contract, because they have certain views on what the contract or its clauses mean and they behave accordingly.[109] It is, thus, interesting to see that recourse to subsequent conduct in interpreting contracts is a highly controversial matter.

Farnsworth underlines that the reference to subsequent conduct permits a party to rely on what is sometimes called "course of performance" or "practical construction", in which the behavior of the parties over repeated occasions of performance is used in determining their understanding of the contract. He also acknowledges that the reference by Article 8(3) CISG to subsequent conduct is of special

---

107 See, *Principles of European Contract Law, Parts I and II*, O. Lando, H. Beale (eds.), Kluwer Law International, 2000 pp. 291–292. Another very significant example is provided by Leonhard. See LEONHARD, C., "*Beyond the Four Corners of a Written Contract: a Global Challenge to U.S. Contract Law*", 21 Pace Int'l L. Rev. 1 (2009). In this example, the applicable law was US Law, and formalistic rules rejecting recourse to preliminary negotiations applied. Under the system of the CISG, PECL, PICC and DCFR the preliminary negotiations would be considered by the court.

108 See VOGENAUER, S., in *Commentary on the UNIDROIT Principles on International Commercial Contracts*, Stefan Vogenauer (ed.) Oxford University Press, Oxford 2015, Article 4.3, §5. See also, Arbitral Award of 3 March 2010, *Ioannis Kardassopoulos v. Republic of Georgia*, ISCID case no. ARB/05/18 and ARB/07/15, https://www.italaw.com/sites/default/files/case-documents/ita0445.pdf.

109 EORSI, G., "*General Provisions*" in *International Sales: The United Nations Convention on Contracts for the International Sale of Goods*, N.M. Galston, H. Smit (eds.), Matthew Bender, New York 1984, Ch. 2, paras. 2-1 to 2-36, paras. 2-14, 2-15.

importance because, although some legal systems allow this use of subsequent conduct, not all systems do.[110]

Indeed, from a comparative law perspective, while for instance the United States Uniform Commercial Code, Article 2-208(1) accepts recourse to subsequent conduct by stating that a "course of performance accepted or acquiesced in without objection shall be relevant to determine the meaning of the agreement", English law has traditionally been hostile to evidence in relation to subsequent conduct.[111] Accordingly, in English law subsequent conduct has traditionally been considered to be irrelevant, together with preliminary negotiations, as suggested by Lord Wilberforce who stated that "[i]t is one and the same principle which excludes evidence of statements, or actions, during negotiations at the time of the contract, or subsequent to the contract".[112]

Liao claims that, as a contract is to be interpreted at the time it was made, subsequent conduct which simply did not exist at that time cannot be referred to as a relevant circumstance to be taken into account.[113] McLauchlan criticizes this approach by stating that this is rather like arguing that, since the real element of the crime of murder must be determined at the time the homicide was committed, no regard can be paid to a subsequent confession because it simply did not exist at the relevant time.[114]

It should, however, be emphasized that reference to subsequent conduct should not be understood as covering all conduct of the parties

---

110 FARNSWORTH, A. "*Article 8*" in *Commentary on the International Sales Law*, C.M. Bianca, M.J. Bonell (eds.), Giuffrè, Milan 1987, pp. 95–102. Reproduced with permission of Dott. A Giuffrè Editore, S.p.A., p. 100.

111 See HONNOLD J.O., *Uniform Law for International Sales under the 1980 United Nations Convention*, 3rd ed., Kluwer Law International, The Hague 1999, pp. 115–123, p. 123.

112 See *L. Schuler AG v. Wickman Machine Tool Sales Ltd.* [1974] A.C. 235, 261; see also McMEEL, G., "*Prior Negotiations and Subsequent Conduct: The Next Step Forward for Contractual Interpretation?*", 119 LQR 272 (2003), p. 278; see also LIAO, J., "*The Role of Subsequent Conduct in Contract Interpretation*", 11 N.Z.B.L.Q. 66 (2005).

113 LIAO, J., "*The Role of Subsequent Conduct in Contract Interpretation*", 11 N.Z.B.L.Q. 66 (2005).

114 See MCLAUCHLAN, D.W., "*In Defence of a Role for Subsequent Conduct in Contract Interpretation*", 12 N.Z.B.L.Q. 30 (2006); see also the notion of dynamic principles of contract law in EISENBERG, M.A., "*The Emergence of Dynamic Contract Law*", 88 Cal. L. Rev. 1743 (2000), p. 1762: On the time of contract formation Eisenberg highlights the emergence of dynamic principles of contract law whose application does not depend solely on what occurred at the moment where contract was formed and which turn on the "moving stream of events that precedes, follows or constitutes the formation of the contract".

subsequent to the conclusion of the contract. For that matter, such conduct can be relevant in cases when a party relies on the other party's subsequent conduct in order to determine its intention at the time of contracting and in cases of common subsequent conduct.[115] It would be illogical, however, to allow a party to rely on its own subsequent conduct in order to render contractual language ineffective.[116]

That said, subsequent conduct can be an important indicator as to the meaning of the contract and is particularly relevant in terms of long-term contracts which involve "complex performance and are 'evolutionary' in nature".[117]

An illustration provided in the Comments on the PECL gives the example of such possibility: A German manufacturer of office supplies has engaged a representative to represent itself in a given area. The contract is for six years but it may be terminated without notice if the representative commits a serious non-performance of his obligations. One of these obligations is to visit each of 20 universities in the area "every month". Assuming that this obligation applies only to the months, in the country concerned, when the universities are open and not to the vacations, the representative only visits each one 11 times a year, and the manufacturer knows this from the accounts which are submitted by the representative. After four years, the manufacturer purports to terminate the contract for serious non-performance. Its behavior during the four years since the conclusion of the contract leads to the interpretation that the phrase "every month" must be interpreted as applying only to the months when universities are active.[118]

In the Austrian case of 10 November 1994, Supreme Court (*Chinchilla furs case*),[119] the Buyer's view that the order of a "larger amount of

---

115 See LAUTENSCHLAGER, F., "*Current Problems Regarding the Interpretation of the Statements and Party Conduct under the CISG – The Reasonable Third Person, Language Problems and Standard Terms and Conditions*", 11(2) Vindobona Journal of International Commercial Law & Arbitration 259 (2007), pp. 265–269.

116 See LAUTENSCHLAGER, F., "*Current Problems Regarding the Interpretation of the Statements and Party Conduct under the CISG – The Reasonable Third Person, Language Problems and Standard Terms and Conditions*", 11(2) Vindobona Journal of International Commercial Law & Arbitration 259 (2007), pp. 265–269.

117 UNIDROIT Principles of International Commercial Contracts 2016, Comments on Article 4.3.

118 See, *Principles of European Contract Law, Parts I and II*, O. Lando, H. Beale (eds.), Kluwer Law International, The Hague 2000 p. 292. See also the dental practice example provided by McLauchlan: McLAUCHLAN, D.W., "*In Defence of a Role for Subsequent Conduct in Contract Interpretation*", 12 N.Z.B.L.Q. 30 (2006).

119 http://cisgw3.law.pace.edu/cases/941110a3.html. Martin Eimer (trans.), Translation edited by Ruth M. Janal.

chinchilla furs" lacked the necessary precision of the quantity of the goods was rejected because the buyer took delivery of the furs that he sold, except for a small number, without raising any objection as to the quantity of the goods delivered. Therefore, based on the later conduct of the parties, it was assumed that the order of a "larger amount of furs" was to be seen as sufficiently definite.

In the French case of 26 April 1995, Appellate Court Grenoble (Enterprise *Alain Veyron v Ambrosio*),[120] it was held that taking delivery of the goods without challenging, in a precise manner, their sale price could have been interpreted by the other contracting party, pursuant to Article 8(2) and (3), as an indication of acceptance of the price.

In the Russian Arbitration no. 224/1993 of 6 April 1994,[121] concerning the currency in which payment ought to have been made in terms of the contract, the tribunal held that the fact that respondent (who later changed the terms of the letter of credit) had initially opened the letter of credit in US Dollars could serve as evidence that he has based himself on US Dollars.

In the Belgian case of 25 January 2005, Commercial Court Tongeren (*Scafom International BV & Orion Metal BVBA v. Exma CPI SA*),[122] the Court gave an overview of the type of conduct which can be relevant in the determination of whether a statement and/or conduct may count as an acceptance. Accordingly, the Court suggested that when determining whether statements or other conduct counts as an acceptance, Articles 8 and 9 CISG should be taken into account. Generally, this is conduct that implies the performance of the contract, or that prepares for the performance, i.e., payment, acceptance of the goods without protest (possibly followed by processing) by the buyer, the start of production, or the sending of (part of) the goods by the seller. The Court also stated that the statement or conduct of the other party must indicate assent to the offer. The mere confirmation of receipt of the offer, or the indication of the other party that this interested him was not sufficient according to the Court.

---

120 http://cisgw3.law.pace.edu/cases/950426f1.html. Charles Sant 'Elia (trans.).

121 See SAIDOV, D., "*Cases on CISG Decided in the Russian Federation*" 7(1) Vindobona Journal of International Commercial Law and Arbitration 1–62 (2003), section 3.6 at fn. 87. http://cisgw3.law.pace.edu/cases/940406r1.html.

122 http://cisgw3.law.pace.edu/cases/050125b1.html. Thorsten Tepasse (trans.), Kristof Cox (ed.).

Similarly in an Austrian case,[123] the Court underlined that acceptance is a declaration of intent that can be communicated expressly or impliedly. According to the Court, the implied, indirect declaration of consent by the offeree is established through a certain action which earnestly and unquestionably expresses its consent and intent to be bound. Relevant in that respect is, under Article 8 CISG, the reasonable understanding of an objective third person taking into account all circumstances of the individual case and thus the objective meaning of a declaration. Examples of such conduct might be: acceptance of the goods; payment of the purchase price; sending of an invoice or its signing by the buyer.

3.3. OTHER RELEVANT CIRCUMSTANCES

As is noted below, according to Article 5:102 PECL, "the interpretation which has already been given to similar clauses by the parties and the practices they have established between themselves" (paragraph (d)), "the meaning commonly given to terms and expressions in the branch of activity concerned and the interpretation similar clauses may already have received" (paragraph (e)) and "usages" (paragraph (f)) are shown among the relevant circumstances to be taken into account in contract interpretation.

It should also be noted that according to Article 1:105 PECL,

(1) The parties are bound by any usage to which they have agreed and by any practice they have established between themselves.
(2) The parties are bound by a usage which would be considered generally applicable by persons in the same situation as the parties, except where the application of such usage would be unreasonable.

Similarly, in the UNIDROIT Principles, Article 4.3 refers to usages and practices established between the parties and to the meaning commonly given to terms and expressions in the trade concerned, as relevant circumstances to be taken into account for the interpretation of contracts, be it according to common intention of the parties or the understanding

123 Austria, 23 March 2005, Oberlandesgericht [Appellate Court] Linz (*Conveyor band case*), http://cisgw3.law.pace.edu/cases/050323a3.html. Jan Henning Berg (trans.).

of reasonable persons of the same kind as the parties being in the same circumstances.

Moreover, according to Article 1.9 PICC,

> (1) The parties are bound by any usage to which they have agreed and by any practices which they have established between themselves.
> (2) The parties are bound by a usage that is widely known to and regularly observed in international trade by parties in the particular trade concerned except where the application of such a usage would be unreasonable.

In Article II.–8:102 on relevant matters, DCFR also states that "the interpretation which has already been given by the parties to terms and expressions which are the same as, or similar to, those used in the contract and the practices they have established between themselves" (paragraph (c)), "the meaning commonly given to such terms or expressions in the branch of activity concerned and the interpretation such terms and expressions may already have received" (paragraph (d)) and "usages" (paragraph (f)) among the relevant circumstances to be taken into account in contract interpretation, and according to Article II.–1:104,

> (1) Parties are bound by any usage to which they have agreed and by any practice they have established between themselves.
> (2) The parties are bound by a usage which would be considered generally applicable by persons in the same situation as the parties, except where the application of such usage would be unreasonable.
> (3) This article applies to other juridical acts with any necessary adaptations.

CISG, Article 8(3) refers also to usages and practices which the parties have established between themselves as relevant circumstances to be taken into account in determining the intent of a party or the understanding of a reasonable person. Article 9 CISG deals with usages and practices which the parties have established between themselves. According to this article,

> (1) The parties are bound by any usage to which they have agreed and by any practices which they have established between themselves.
> (2) The parties are considered, unless otherwise agreed, to have impliedly made applicable to their contract or its formation a usage of which the parties knew or ought to have known and which in international trade is widely known to, and regularly observed by, parties to contracts of the type involved in the particular trade concerned.

3.3.1. Practices Established between the Parties

With reference to Comments on Article 1:105 PECL the definition of a practice established between the parties in terms of this instrument can be given as conduct "arising from the sequence of previous conduct to a particular transaction or a particular kind of transaction between the parties" which can be "fairly regarded as a common understanding." If the requirements set forth in this definition are fulfilled, the conduct may be used either to interpret the words and expressions of the contract (and lend a special meaning to words and expressions which the parties use) or to create rights and duties in terms of the PECL.[124] This second use of practices will be examined in Chapter 4 on gap-filling.

An illustration is provided in the Comments on Article 5:102 on relevant circumstances in contract interpretation, in which parties A and B have made a franchise contract. In a clause of the contract, it is provided that B shall pay for goods that he receives from A within "ten days". For a three-month period, B pays within "ten working days". After three months, A demands payment within "ten days including holidays". The practice adopted between the parties indicates that this is not the correct interpretation of the contractual clause.[125]

Such a practice may also vary the terms of the initial agreement between the parties and create other mutual rights and obligations. The following illustration is given in order to illustrate such a possibility. Accordingly, B, after having been called a few times to fill A's oil tank, filled the tank for more than five years without having been called so that A, whose factory is dependent on the oil, never runs out of oil. A always paid B not later than 90 days after receipt of the oil. The initial agreement between the parties that B should only fill the tank when called upon has been changed by their practice; a duty on B to see to it that the tank never runs out of oil has been created.[126]

The definition of a practice established between the parties is not given in the Comments on Article 1.9 PICC. It is submitted, however, that the question whether a particular practice can be deemed to be

---

124 See, *Principles of European Contract Law, Parts I and II*, O. Lando, H. Beale (eds.), Kluwer Law International, The Hague 2000 p. 104.

125 *Principles of European Contract Law, Parts I and II*, O. Lando, H. Beale (eds.), Kluwer Law International, The Hague 2000 p. 292.

126 *Principles of European Contract Law, Parts I and II*, O. Lando, H. Beale (eds.), Kluwer Law International, The Hague 2000 p. 105.

established between the parties will be answered with regard of the circumstances of the case, "but behavior on the occasion of only one previous transaction between the parties will not normally suffice".[127] The authors of the Principles emphasize in the Comments on Article 4.3 that the practices established between the parties are particularly relevant in interpreting long-term contracts.[128] It is, indeed, logical that the long-term character of the contract paves the way for practices to be established between the parties during the course of performance.

The following example is given in order to show the relevance of practices established between the parties for the purposes of interpretation of the contract. Accordingly, if parties conclude a number of contracts in which the price is always expressed in "Canadian Dollars", when one of them makes a new offer indicating the price in "Dollars", the price in the offer should be interpreted as referring to "Canadian Dollars".[129]

In another illustration, if a party accepted claims for defects in the goods as much as two weeks after their delivery, it cannot object when the other party gives another notice a fortnight after another delivery, as the two-week notice became a practice established between them.[130]

The CISG does not give the definition of a practice established between the parties either. The definition of such a practice in terms of this instrument is given by scholars.

On this matter, Ferrari writes that "practices within the meaning of the CISG are manners of conduct that are regularly observed by or have been established between the parties to a specific transaction, whichever the case may be".[131]

According to Bonell, "practices which the parties have established between themselves" means a course of dealing adopted by the individual parties. For this purpose, except for the case in which a party expressly excludes their application for the future, courses of dealing are automatically applicable not only to supplement the terms of the

---

127 UNIDROIT Principles of International Commercial Contracts 2016, Comments on Article 1.9.

128 UNIDROIT Principles of International Commercial Contracts 2016, Comments on Article 4.3.

129 UNIDROIT Principles of International Commercial Contracts 2016, Comments on Article 4.3.

130 UNIDROIT Principles of International Commercial Contracts 2016, Comments on Article 1.9.

131 FERRARI, F., "*Trade Usage and Practices Established Between the Parties under the CISG*", 5 I.B.L.J. 571 (2003), p. 572.

contractual agreement but also, pursuant to Article 8, to help determine the parties' intent. Bonell points also out that this almost literally corresponds with §1-205 of the United States Uniform Commercial Code whereby a course of dealing, defined as "a sequence of previous conduct between the parties to a particular transaction which is fairly to be regarded as establishing a common basis of understanding for interpreting their expressions and other conduct", serves the purpose "to give particular meaning to and supplement or qualify terms of an agreement".[132]

It is also submitted in the literature that a practice is involved if in an individual relationship between two parties, the parties act in a similar way under similar circumstances. Thus, a business relation lasting for some time is a necessity for the origin of a practice.[133] In terms of Article 9(1) CISG, the individual practice established between the parties to a given contract is relevant rather than the general practice which can be observed.[134]

The binding force of practices established between the parties can generally be explained by the fact that they create expectations on contracting parties based on the previous conduct.

Accordingly, Honnold underlines that under Article 9(1) the parties are bound by the "practices which they have established between themselves" and that "practices" are established by a course of conduct that creates an expectation that this conduct will be continued. Article 8(2) provides that the "conduct of a party" is to be "interpreted according to the understanding that a reasonable person of the same kind as the other party would have had in the same circumstances." As a result, under Article 9(1) a course of conduct by a party in past transactions may create an expectation by the other party that will bind the first party in

---

132 BONELL, M.J., in *Commentary on the International Sales Law*, C.M. Bianca, M.J. Bonell (eds.), Giuffrè Milan 1987, pp. 103–115. See also LOOKOFSKY, J., "*The 1980 United Nations Convention on Contracts for the International sale of Goods, Article 9 Commercial Custom and Usages*", http://www.cisg.law.pace.edu/cisg/biblio/loo9.html. See also, ESSER, M., "*Commercial Letters of Confirmation in International Trade: Austrian, French, German and Swiss Law under the 1980 Sales Convention*", 18 Georgia Journal of International and Comparative Law 427, (1988), pp. 450–451. For the similarity between the CISG and the UCC, see also the U.S. District Court, (S.D.N.Y. April 6, 1998) *Calzaturificio Claudia s.n.c. v. Olivieri Footwear Ltd.*, http://www.unilex.info/case.cfm?id=336.

133 BOUT, P.X., "*Trade Usages: Article 9 of the Convention on Contracts for the International Sale of Goods*", http://www.cisg.law.pace.edu/cisg/biblio/bout.html.

134 See FERRARI, F., "*Trade Usage and Practices Established Between the Parties under the CISG*", 5 I.B.L.J. 571 (2003), p. 572.

a future contract. Exceptions to this rule are cases where he notifies the other party of a change before the other party enters into a new contract and cases where further reliance may become unreasonable because of the changed circumstances. Honnold, thus, points out that the reference in Article 9(1) to practices established by the parties is one example of many situations in which binding expectations may be based on conduct.[135]

Thus, if the circumstances of the case will lead to the conclusion that the expectation of a particular behavior based on previous cases is not justified, the practice will not apply.[136]

It is also submitted in the literature that the binding force of practices established between the parties is in accordance with the principle of good faith and the prohibition of *venire contra factum proprium*.[137]

The practice established between the parties may not only be relevant in dealing with minor questions such as the interpretation of a specific clause of a contract on time requirements, as in the above-mentioned illustration, but also in the determination of the entire content of the contract, as in the case of incorporation of a party's general conditions contained in separate writing into the contract with reference to previous practices established between the parties.[138]

The following court decisions may be cited as related to the practices established between the parties in terms of the CISG.

In a Dutch decision,[139] the Court held that the fact that in "subsequent acknowledgments" reference has been made to the seller's general conditions (also printed on the back of these documents) does not mean that those conditions that were communicated after the conclusion of this contract apply. The Court further stated that in that respect, it is

---

135 HONNOLD J.O., *Uniform Law for International Sales under the 1980 United Nations Convention*, 3rd ed., Kluwer Law International, The Hague 1999, p. 126. See also CHAN LENG SUN, "*Interpreting an International Sale Contract*", http://www.cisg.law.pace.edu/cisg/biblio/sun1.html.

136 BOUT, P.X., "*Trade Usages: Article 9 of the Convention on Contracts for the International Sale of Goods*", http://www.cisg.law.pace.edu/cisg/biblio/bout.html.

137 FERRARI, F., "*Trade Usage and Practices Established between the Parties under the CISG*", 5 I.B.L.J. 571 (2003), p. 572.

138 See BONELL, M.J., in *Commentary on the International Sales Law*, C.M. Bianca, M.J. Bonell (eds.), Giuffrè, Milan 1987, pp. 103–115. See also ESSER, M., "*Commercial Letters of Confirmation in International Trade: Austrian, French, German and Swiss Law under the 1980 Sales Convention*", 18 Georgia Journal of International and Comparative Law 427 (1988), pp. 450–451.

139 Netherlands, 17 March 2004, District Court Arnhem (*Sluiter Ellwood II et al. v. Blumenerdenwerk Stender GmbH*), http://cisgw3.law.pace.edu/cases/040317n1.html. Vasiliki Mitria (trans.).

first important that the parties had done no business with each other before, so that no one can think that a commercial practice existed between them which would allow the silent acceptance of the validity of the seller's general conditions (Article 9 CISG).

In an Austrian case,[140] the Trial Court held that an established business relationship existed between seller and buyer. During the period between 24 January and 10 June 2002 a total of 11 invoices or confirmation letters, respectively, were exchanged between the parties. All of them contained the same place of payment and competent tribunal. In addition to this, these documents contained several references to terms of delivery (Incoterms), such that the same place was agreed upon as place of performance. The Appellate Court reversed this decision, holding that between 11 invoices only three of them were order confirmations, which does not justify established practice.

In a Dutch arbitration case,[141] the Court found that the buyer had continued with the practice developed between him and the seller to sign the faxed copy of the confirmation. Accordingly, pursuant to Article 9(1) CISG, regard was to be had to such practices developed between parties and such practices are binding. In the circumstances of the case, the buyer had not deviated from this practice once nor had he informed the seller after receipt of the General Conditions that he did not wish the application of these conditions or wished to apply his own general conditions, if any. Thus, the Court ruled that by not informing the seller that he did not accept the General Conditions, the buyer created in any case the expectation that he agreed to the application of the General Conditions.

In the Austrian case of 23 March 2005,[142] the Appellate Court of Linz ruled that the CISG does not impose particular requirements for the incorporation of standard terms into contracts of sale. Accordingly, the corresponding rules must be developed from CISG Article 14 et seq., which govern the conclusion of a contract. The Court emphasized that therefore, standard terms will become part of the contract only if they form part of the offer according to the offeror's intent, as far as it is objectively recognizable (Article 8(1) and (2) CISG), and that this

140 Austria, 14 December 2004, Supreme Court (*Laser devices case*), http://cisgw3.law.pace.edu/cases/041214a3.html. Daniel Fritz (trans.), Todd Fox (ed.).

141 Netherlands, 10 February 2005, Netherlands Arbitration Institute (interim award), http://cisgw3.law.pace.edu/cases/050210n1.html.

142 Austria 23 March 2005 Oberlandesgericht [Appellate Court] Linz (*Conveyor band case*) http://cisgw3.law.pace.edu/cases/050323a3.html. Jan Henning Berg (trans.).

can also happen impliedly or might result from negotiations between the parties or from practices that have been established between them.

In a Russian Arbitration award,[143] it was held that while performing the contract, the seller not only committed numerous over-deliveries in respect of individual items mentioned in the specifications contained in the supplements to the contract, but also delivered goods that were not covered by these specifications at all. Since these goods had been duly accepted and paid for by the buyer, in accordance with Article 39 CISG, the buyer lost its right to rely on a lack of conformity of the delivered goods with the provisions of supplements to the contract. With reference to Article 9 CISG, the Court ruled that all the goods delivered by the seller and accepted by the buyer were to be taken into consideration while calculating the total amount of goods delivered by the seller under the contract.

In a Chinese arbitration award,[144] the seller claimed that the buyer had failed to perform the obligation to notify it under the contract in appointing the port of shipment, the carrier, and the detailed delivery time, while the buyer alleged that the contract was not the first transaction between the parties, and the parties had confirmed details of the transaction by telephone in their previous transactions. The Court, with reference to Article 9(1) of the CISG, according to which, "The parties are bound by any usage to which they have agreed and by any practices which they have established between themselves", held that as at the hearings, the parties confirmed that they had mostly communicated the transactional details over the phone, the seller's refusal to perform the contract should not be supported or excused.

3.3.2. Usages on which the Parties Agreed

As can be observed from the related articles of the PECL, PICC, DCFR and CISG, a distinction is made between two types of usage: 1) Usages on

143 Russia, 13 April 2006, Arbitration proceeding 105/2005, http://cisgw3.law.pace.edu/cases/060413r1.html. Alexander Morari (trans.).

144 China, 9 January 2008, CIETAC Arbitration proceeding (*Metallic silicon case*), http://cisgw3.law.pace.edu/cases/080109c1.html. Jing Li (trans.), Xiangyu Huang (ed.). As other examples see also ICC Court of Arbitration Paris, No. 8611, where the delivery of the machinery spare parts became a practice between parties, http://www.unilex.info/case.cfm?id=229. See also the Canadian decision of *Mazzetta Company, l.l.c. v. Dégust-Mer inc.*, 2011 QCCA 717 (CanLII), http://canlii.ca/s/6k505.

which the parties agreed upon; and 2) Usages applicable in the absence of an agreement between the parties.

The rules on the application of the first type of usage are drafted in the same way in the PECL, PICC, DCFR and the CISG. Accordingly, the first paragraph of Article 1:105 PECL deals with the first type of usages, applicability of which stems from the express or implicit wording of the contract. Definition of usages in terms of the PECL is given in the Comments. In this respect, "a usage may be described as a course of dealing or line of conduct which is and for a certain period of time has been generally adopted by those engaged in trade or in a particular trade."[145]

The first paragraph plays an important role only if the trade usage in question is normally inapplicable because it does not fulfill the general applicability test provided in the second paragraph. The second test existing in the second paragraph, namely the reasonableness test, applies also to usages agreed upon by the parties.[146] Thus, a usage, application of which would be unreasonable in the circumstances of the case, will not operate even in the presence of an express agreement of the parties concerning its application.

An illustration is given on this matter.[147] Accordingly, A, who operates in Copenhagen and has bought a commodity in Hamburg, resells it to B, his fellow townsman. In their contract, the parties agree to have the local usages of the Hamburg Commodity Exchange apply, which will then bind both of them.

The PICC does not give the definition of a "usage". If the usage is applicable by virtue of the first paragraph of Article 1.9, no other criteria or requirements are needed except that the usage should be agreed upon by the parties.[148] As is set forth in the Comments, the first paragraph is a mere application of the principle of freedom of contract.

Accordingly, it is submitted that the parties may stipulate the application of any usage, including a usage developed within a trade sector to which neither party belongs, or a usage relating to a different type of contract.

---

145 *Principles of European Contract Law, Parts I and II*, O. Lando, H. Beale (eds.), Kluwer Law International, The Hague 2000, p. 104.

146 *Principles of European Contract Law, Parts I and II*, O. Lando, H. Beale (eds.), Kluwer Law International, The Hague 2000, p. 105.

147 *Principles of European Contract Law, Parts I and II*, O. Lando, H. Beale (eds.), Kluwer Law International, The Hague 2000, p. 105.

148 This does not mean, of course, that the usage is not subject to the requirements of good faith and fair dealing.

It is even possible that the parties may agree on the application of what sometimes are misleadingly called usages, such as a set of rules issued by a particular trade association under the title of "usages", but which only in part reflects established general lines of conduct.[149]

Considering the Comments of the Secretariat, the history of the provision and some of the scholarly comments on the issue, it can be said that Article 9(1) of the CISG applies only when there is an express agreement between the parties to the contract, and it is the second paragraph which covers the cases where usages are implicitly taken into consideration.[150] It is, however, submitted by different authors and supported by a court decision that the agreement between the parties in terms of Article 9(1) may also be implicit.[151]

In this respect, Bonell states that this would be the case where the parties, with respect to particular issues related to the formation or the performance of the contract, deliberately act in conformity with a local usage or a usage within a given trade, or where the statement of one party customarily can be interpreted as an implied reference to that usage and the other party failed to expressly object to it. He points out that the applicability of the usage in such a case should be decided by the application of the interpretation rules contained in Article 8 and that the real intent of the parties should be inquired into.[152]

According to Pamboukis, the fact that the Vienna Convention has omitted the reference "expressly or impliedly" made in Article 9(1) of the Convention relating to a Uniform Law on the International Sale of Goods (ULIS) should limit the creative interpretation of the parties' agreement by adjudicators even if nothing in the Convention prohibits

---

149 UNIDROIT Principles of International Commercial Contracts 2016, Comments on Article 1.9.

150 See the text of Secretariat Commentary on Article 7 of the 1978 Draft Counterpart of Article 9. http://www.cisg.law.pace.edu/cisg/text/secomm/secomm-09.html. EORSI, G., "*General Provisions*" in *The United Nations Convention on Contracts for the International Sale of Goods*, N.M. Galston, H. Smit (eds.), Matthew Bender, New York 1984, Ch. 2, paras. 2-23–2-24; LOOKOFSKY, J., "*Article 9 Commercial Custom and Usage*" in *The 1980 United Nations Convention on Contracts for the International Sale of Goods*, http://www.cisg.law.pace.edu/cisg/biblio/loo9.html.

151 See HUBER, P., "*Some Introductory Remarks on the CISG*", http://www.cisg.law.pace.edu/cisg/biblio/huber-09.html; BONELL, M.J. in *Commentary on the International Sales Law*, C.M. Bianca, M.J. Bonell (eds.), Giuffrè, Milan 1987, pp. 103–115; FERRARI, F., "*Trade Usage and Practices Established between the Parties under the CISG*", 5 I.B.L.J. 571 (2003), p. 572; Austria, 21 March 2000, Supreme Court (*Wood case*), http://cisgw3.law.pace.edu/cases/000321a3.html.

152 BONELL, M.J., in *Commentary on the International Sales Law*, C.M. Bianca, M.J. Bonell (eds.), Giuffrè, Milan 1987, p. 107.

a tacit agreement to make a usage applicable to the contract. Thus, "the assumption that there is implied agreement must not be stretched too far because paragraph 2 would lose its function and the additional requirements mentioned in this paragraph would be evaded".[153] The agreement of the parties according to Article 9(1) may be through their negotiations or in their course of dealing.[154]

The definition of the usage is not provided by the CISG and recourse to national law would be inconsistent with its uniform application and international character. An autonomous definition of usage in terms of the CISG is given by Ferrari. Accordingly, the term "usage" includes all those actions or modes of behavior which are generally and regularly observed in the course of business transactions in a specific area of trade or at a certain trade centre.[155]

While the second paragraph of Article 9 sets forth specific criteria for the application of a trade usage on which parties did not agree, the usages that are applicable by virtue of the first paragraph are not subject to these requirements. Thus, local or regional usages that are not widely known may also apply if it is the parties' real intention to be bound by them.[156]

3.3.3. *Usages not Agreed Upon*

For usages not agreed upon by the parties to be applicable, Article 1:105 PECL (like Article II-1.104 DCFR) brings two requirements. First, the usage must be considered applicable by persons in the same situation as the parties, and second, it must not be unreasonable.

According to the first requirement, "the usage must be so well established and have general application among those engaged in the trade that persons in the same situation as the parties would consider it applicable".[157] Such a usage, be it local, national or international (meaning

153 PAMBOUKIS, Ch., "*The Concept and Function of Usages in the United Nations Convention on the International Sale of Goods*", 25 Journal of Law and Commerce 107 (2005–2006), pp. 112–113.

154 SCHLECHTRIEM, P., *Uniform Sales Law, The UN Convention on Contracts for the International Sale of Goods*, Manz, Vienna 1986, p. 40.

155 FERRARI, F., "*Trade Usage and Practices Established between the Parties under the CISG*", 5 I.B.L.J. 571 (2003), p. 572.

156 FERRARI, F., "*Trade Usage and Practices Established between the Parties under the CISG*", 5 I.B.L.J. 571 (2003), p. 572.

157 *Principles of European Contract Law, Parts I and II*, Kluwer Law International, The Hague 2000, p. 105.

that either the usage applies to contracts between parties having their place of business in different states or it operates in both states) may be applicable to all or several trades or to only one particular trade.[158]

According to the second requirement, the application of the usage must not be unreasonable. Although "commercial acceptance by regular observance by business people" may be considered evidence for reasonableness of the usage, it is up to the court to decide whether, in a specific case, it would be reasonable to apply a usage.[159]

Similarly to the PECL and the DCFR, the PICC also contain two requirements for the application of a usage without agreement of the parties. Accordingly, a usage, in order to be applied by virtue of the second paragraph should be first widely known to and regularly observed in international trade by parties in the particular trade concerned. Thus, in terms of the PICC the classification of being "widely known and regularly observed by parties in the particular trade concerned" is supplemented by the additional requirement of internationality of the usage in order to avoid usages developed for domestic transactions applying also to international contracts.[160]

The difference between the wordings of Article 1.9 PICC and the related articles of the PECL and DCFR can be explained by the fact that the PICC, like the CISG, apply only to international contracts. It is not, however, impossible that a local usage applies in terms of Article 1.9(2).

It should be noted that two exceptions are given in the Comments: first, such a usage may belong to a certain commodity exchange, trade exhibition or port and be followed by foreigners as well; and second, a businessperson who entered into a number of similar contracts in a particular foreign country may be bound by usages existing in this country.[161]

As mentioned above in order to be applicable, the application of the usage needs not to be unreasonable. This test can only be evaluated on a case-by-case basis by taking the relevant circumstances into account. The illustration below, given in the Comments on the article, shows such a possibility.

---

158 *Principles of European Contract Law, Parts I and II*, Kluwer Law International, The Hague 2000, pp. 105–106.

159 See *Principles of European Contract Law, Parts I and II*, Kluwer Law International, The Hague 2000, p. 106.

160 UNIDROIT Principles of International Commercial Contracts 2016, Comments on Article 1.9.

161 UNIDROIT Principles of International Commercial Contracts 2016, Comments on Article 1.9. Compare also with illustrations in the Comments on Article 1:105 PECL.

Accordingly, a usage exists in a commodity trade sector according to which the purchaser may not rely on defects in goods if they are not duly certified by an internationally recognized inspection agency. When a buyer takes over the goods at the port of destination, the only internationally recognized inspection agency operating in that port is on strike and to call another from the nearest port would be excessively costly. The application of the usage in this case would be unreasonable and the buyer may rely on the defects it has discovered even though they have not been certified by an internationally recognized inspection agency.[162]

According to Article 9(2) CISG,

> the parties are considered, unless otherwise agreed, to have impliedly made applicable to their contract or its formation a usage of which the parties knew or ought to have known and which in international trade is widely known to, and regularly observed by, parties to contracts of the type involved in the particular trade concerned.

The wording of this article departs from the wordings of the related articles of the PECL, PICC and DCFR. When CISG Article 9(2) relies on the implied intention of the parties, Articles 1:105(2) PECL, 1.9(2) PICC and II-1:104(2) DCFR treat usages as legal norms applicable independently of the volition of the parties.[163]

Indeed, in terms of Article 9(2) a usage is applicable to the extent that the parties can "be considered to have impliedly made applicable to their contract" and for this purpose it is necessary that "the parties knew or ought to have known" of the usage.

This requirement of knowledge is criticized for being susceptible to leaving doubts on whether newcomers in a branch of trade or outsiders can be considered to be bound by a usage.[164]

According to Bonell, although from this wording it can be deduced that the application of a trade usage by virtue of Article 9(2) necessitates an intention of the parties to incorporate the usage inside the contract, the difference between Article 9(2) CISG and Article 1.9(2) PICC is

---

162 UNIDROIT Principles of International Commercial Contracts 2016, Comments on Article 1.9.

163 See the Comments on Article 1:105 PECL, note 4a. *Principles of European Contract Law, Parts I and II*, Kluwer Law International, The Hague 2000.

164 See the Comments on Article 1:105 note 4b, *Principles of European Contract Law, Parts I and II*, Kluwer Law International, The Hague 2000.

purely cosmetic. He points out that, in cases where the usage applies because one party or both parties ought to have known its existence, it is the law itself which confers binding force on the usage and amounts to a legal fiction to explain its application on the basis of an implied agreement.[165]

It is necessary, in order for a trade usage to be applicable by virtue of Article 9(2), that two conditions come together. First, a usage must be widely known and regularly observed in the particular international trade concerned. Thus, like Article 1.9(2) PICC and unlike Articles 1:105(2) PECL and II-1:104(2) DCFR, Article 9(2) CISG only applies to international usages. The remarks which have been made above concerning the internationality of the trade usage in terms of Article 1.9(2) PICC are also valid for usages applicable in terms of Article 9(2) CISG.

Indeed, according to an Austrian decision,[166] the provision of Article 9(2) is supposed to prevent usages, which so far have evolved only for internal sales, being applied in trade with foreign parties to a contract. The Court further emphasized that the wording of Article 9(2) CISG does not mean, however, that in the future, purely national or local usages can find no application for the interpretation and supplementation of contracts without an explicit reference by the parties. Thus, it is possible to presume an exception for usages which are in force at certain stock markets, trade fairs or deposit sites, as long as the usage is also regularly observed there in trade with foreigners. Furthermore, according to the Court, the possibility does not seem to be excluded that a foreign tradesman, who is constantly active in another country and has already formed a number of transactions there, is bound by national usages. In the light of these explanations the Court ruled that it cannot be excluded that the buyer – under the presumption that it was constantly active in Italy and had already concluded a number of similar contracts – was bound by possible Italian usages.

Second, the parties either must have known or ought to have known about the usage at the time of conclusion of the contract. Concerning the geographic scope of the knowledge it is generally supported that a party may be bound by a usage if it either has its place of business in

---

165 BONELL, M.J., *An International Restatement of Contract Law*, Transnational Publishers, New York 2005, p. 99.

166 Austria, 9 November 1995, Appellate Court Graz (*Marble slabs case*), http://cisgw3.law.pace.edu/cases/951109a3.html. Ruth M. Janal (trans.). Translation edited by Todd Fox.

the geographical area where the usage is applicable or permanently deals within the area where the usage is applicable.[167]

In the Comments on Article 5:102 PECL on relevant circumstances it is submitted that the usage referred to in the article is in principle that which is current at the place where the contract is made.[168]

As stated above, the PECL and the DCFR, the PICC, and the CISG provide different conditions to come together in order to make a usage not agreed upon by the parties applicable.

It is clear that regardless of the purpose for which recourse is had to the usage, the definition and characteristics of an applicable "usage" in terms of the PECL and PICC stay the same. Thus, a usage which applies in the interpretation of a contractual clause governed by the PECL needs to fulfill the requirements set out in Article 1:105(2).[169] Similarly, the criteria laid down in Article 1.9(2) PICC apply for recourse to usages for all purposes expressly indicated in the Principles, including the "interpretation of contracts".[170]

The subject is, however, controversial concerning the application of the criteria set forth in Article 9(2) CISG on the purposes of interpretation. According to Eorsi, Article 9 CISG on usages restricts binding usages to the type involved in the particular trade concerned but the question arises whether the term under Article 8(3) has the same sphere of application as in Article 9. On this matter, he points out that Article 9 is addressed specifically to usages and, by its location in Chapter II, constitutes one of the General Provisions which apply throughout the Convention, but it has been argued that as the function of usages in Article 8(3) differs from that of usages in Article 9, national and local usages may also be considered in determining party intent, notwithstanding the fact that under Article 9 usages must be international. He concludes that this argument seems to be correct since it would be foolish to restrict the possibilities of interpretation. Thus, "It could not serve any good purpose to prohibit the tribunal from giving due consideration to

---

167 FERRARI, F., "*Trade Usage and Practices Established between the Parties under the CISG*", 5 I.B.L.J. 571 (2003), p. 574; Austria, 21 March 2000, Supreme Court (*Wood case*), http://cisgw3.law.pace.edu/cases/000321a3.html. Veit Konrad (trans.), Jan Henning Berg (ed.).

168 *Principles of European Contract Law, Parts I and II*, Kluwer Law International, The Hague 2000, p. 293.

169 *Principles of European Contract Law, Parts I and II*, Kluwer Law International, The Hague 2000, p. 292.

170 UNIDROIT Principles of International Commercial Contracts 2016, Comments on Article 1.9.

any kind of usage or anything else that could be helpful in interpreting the contract."[171]

Sharing the same opinion, Schlechtriem points out that the usages to be considered when discovering the intended and/or objective meaning of a statement presumably include, in contrast to those mentioned in Article 9(2), usages which are only local, national, or followed by a particular group of business people. So, it is important to note that the function of Article 8(3) is different from that of Article 9(2): it does not address gap-filling of the contract, but rather the interpretation of a party's statements. According to Article 8(3), for interpretation purposes particular circumstances are important, including usages that are possibly significant only to a party making the statements or to a reasonable person in the shoes of the addressee. Thus, a German who remains silent after having received a letter of confirmation can be understood to have expressed approval, regardless of whether Article 9(2) includes the German customs pertaining to letters of confirmation.[172]

Bonell, who does not share this opinion, states that in interpreting the statements of the parties, only usages which fulfill the requirements of Article 9(2) may be employed.[173]

As Article 8 focuses on the understanding of the recipient in the interpretation of statements and conduct both in subjective and objective tests, an inquiry concerning the subjective intent of a party based on a local usage existing in that party's place of business can only be relevant to the extent that the other contracting party knew or could not have been unaware what that intent was (subjective test) or to the extent that the reasonable person of the same kind as the other party in the same circumstances could have understood what that intent was (objective test).

This may be the case, for instance, if the recipient has entered into several contractual relationships before in the place of business of the party relying on a local usage or if the foreigners doing business in that particular place (seaport, etc.) follow the local usage.

---

171 EORSI, G., "*General Provisions*" in *The United Nations Convention on Contracts for the International Sale of Goods*, N.M. Galston, H. Smit (eds.), Matthew Bender, New York 1984, Ch. 2, "General Provisions", paras. 2-23–2-24.

172 SCHLECHTRIEM, P., *Uniform Sales Law, The UN Convention on Contracts for the International Sale of Goods*, Manz, Vienna 1986, p. 40.

173 BONELL, M.J., in *Commentary on the International Sales Law*, C.M. Bianca, M.J. Bonell (eds.) Giuffrè, Milan 1987, p. 107.

As stated above, in such cases the local usage can also be binding, on a liberal reading of Article 9(2), taking the purpose of the article into account.[174] Thus, it seems that it is not necessary to make a distinction between trade usages applicable in terms of CISG for interpretation purposes (Article 8(3)) and those that are applicable for other purposes (Article 9(2)). This approach also coincides with the view expressed in the Comments on Article 1.9(2) PICC that only requires that the usage be widely known and regularly observed in international trade, which is a condition for the application of any usage (at international, national or local level).

If the recipient or the circumstances of the case do not have such characteristics, then other relevant circumstances – such as preliminary negotiations, subsequent conduct or practices established between the parties – need to be present in order to interpret a statement in accordance with the local usage existing in a party's place of business.

Some examples of court decisions on usages in terms of Article 9 are as follows:

In an ICC Arbitration Award,[175] it was held that the revision of the contractual price was a usage in the given trade of minerals. According to the court, there was no market price in the common sense of the term; that is to say, a price determined in a market like the London Metal Exchange or any other analogous institution and varying according to the offer and the demand, but rather a reference price which results from the annual negotiations between the Japanese steelworkers and the Australian and South African miners. It was that price which was serving as a reference for professionals (miners and transformers) and which would enable each and every one to fix their own contractual price. The parameters generally used were the cost of transport, the quality of the mineral, the quantities bought, and the links between each of them which could result in a linking clause establishing a relationship between the price of the finished product and that of the mineral.

In a German case,[176] the Court held that according to German case law, a clause stipulating "net" or "net cash" payment therefore constituted an exclusion of set-off by trade usage.

---

174 See the Austrian *Marble slabs* case (n. 166 above). Compare this decision with the Comments on Article 1.9 PICC.

175 ICC Arbitration Case No. 8324 of 1995 (*Magnesium case*), http://cisgw3.law.pace.edu/cases/958324i1.html. Julia Hoffmann (trans.).

176 Germany, 5 October 1998, Appellate Court Hamburg (*Circuit boards case*), http://cisgw3.law.pace.edu/cases/981005g1.html. Ruth M. Janal (trans.), Camilla Baasch Andersen (ed.).

3.3.4. *Interpretation Already Given to Similar Clauses by the Parties*

Interpretation given by the parties to similar clauses is also an important indicator of contractual meaning. In cases where such an interpretation can be established, it should be preferred over any customary usage of the words.

Indeed, in a US Court decision,[177] by applying the CISG, the lower judge held that "evidence of the parties' interpretation of the term in their course of dealings trumped evidence of the term's customary usage in the industry", and that the buyer was obligated to purchase all compound delivered pursuant to the contract and was condemned to pay the price. The buyer appealed, arguing that under the CISG, a term in a contract should be interpreted according to its customary usage "unless the parties have expressly agreed upon another usage". The appellate court, however, affirmed the judgment of the lower court.

3.3.5. *The Meaning Commonly Given to Terms and Expressions in the Trade Concerned*

The difference should also be made between "the meaning commonly given to terms and expressions in the trade concerned" and "the usages", which are both among relevant circumstances to be taken into account in interpretation process in the light of the PECL, PICC and DCFR.

Although it seems that these two concepts seem to be the same, while usages apply only if they meet the requirements laid down in related articles on usages and practices,

> the meaning commonly given to terms and expressions in the trade concerned can be relevant even if it is peculiar to a trade sector to which only one or even, neither party belongs, provided that the expression or term concerned is one which is typical in that sector.[178]

Two examples are provided in the Comments on the PICC in order to show the difference between the two concepts. In the first example,

---

177 *Treibacher Industrie, A.G. v. Allegheny Technologies, Inc.* United States, 12 September 2006, Federal Appellate Court [11th Circuit], http://cisgw3.law.pace.edu/cases/060912u1.html. Abstract by John H. Rooney Jr.

178 UNIDROIT Principles of International Commercial Contracts 2016, Comments on Article 4.3.

parties conclude a contract for the sale of a cargo of oil at a price of 80 USD per barrel. The parties subsequently disagree on the size of the barrel to which they had referred. In the absence of any indications, the understanding of the party who intended a barrel of 42 standard gallons prevails, as in the international trade it is a usage to measure barrels in standard gallons.

In the second example the contract contains the standard term "whether in berth or not". When it subsequently emerges that the parties attached different meanings to the term, preference should, in the absence of any indication to the contrary, be given to the meaning commonly attached to it in the shipping trade, since the term is typical in the shipping trade.[179]

3.4. THE NATURE AND THE PURPOSE OF THE CONTRACT

The nature and the purpose of the contract are of significant help, especially in order to determine the content of party obligations in a contract. The nature of the contract refers to the terms typically contained by certain types of contract (sale, construction etc.) that provide important indications of the legal consequences aimed for by the parties.[180] Similarly, the purpose of the contract refers to "what parties in transactions such as the one in question typically intend to achieve".[181]

The illustration submitted in the Comments on the PECL can be cited in this respect:

> The manager of a large real estate development makes a fixed price contract with a gardening company for the maintenance of the "green spaces". The manager later complains that A has not repaired the boundary wall. The contract cannot be interpreted as covering this as it is a contract for gardening.[182]

---

179 UNIDROIT Principles of International Commercial Contracts 2016, Comments on Article 4.3.

180 See MALEVILLE, M.H., *Pratique de l'Interprétation des Contrats, Etude Jurisprudentielle*, Publications de l'Université de Rouen, No. 164, Rouen 1991, pp. 266–267; VOGENAUER, S., in *Commentary on the UNIDROIT Principles on International Commercial Contracts*, Stefan Vogenauer (ed.), Oxford University Press, Oxford 2015, Article 4.3, p. 591.

181 VOGENAUER, S., in *Commentary on the UNIDROIT Principles on International Commercial Contracts*, Stefan Vogenauer (ed.), Oxford University Press, Oxford 2015, Article 4.3, pp. 591–592.

182 *Principles of European Contract Law, Parts I and II*, O. Lando, H. Beale (eds.), Kluwer Law International, The Hague 2000, p. 292.

3.5. GOOD FAITH AND FAIR DEALING

All legal instruments except the CISG recognize expressly a general duty to act in good faith.[183] In addition the PECL and DCFR state good faith and fair dealing as a relevant circumstance to determine the meaning of contractual clauses. Thus, it can be supported that for these instruments good faith and fair dealing is not only an overriding principle that can alter the already established meaning of the contract based on contractual clauses and surrounding facts, but also an element which is used in the establishment of that contractual meaning in the first place.[184]

We will examine the principle of good faith and fair dealing and discuss in detail the position of the CISG on this matter which is highly controversial. But first, it should be useful to discuss further the highly contextual interpretation approach adopted by these instruments in comparison with textualist and formalistic approaches which are generally highlighted in the commercial context.

4. CONTEXTUALISM v. FORMALISM

4.1. FORMALISTIC RULES AND THE CISG, PICC, PECL AND DCFR

In the light of the analysis of the set of rules provided by these instruments and before making a critical and practical analysis in order to better understand the outcome of these rules, it is important to emphasize that the CISG, PECL, PICC and DCFR reject formalistic interpretation rules such as the plain meaning rule, four corners rule and parol evidence rule in contract interpretation, by adopting a contextual approach.

The plain meaning rule provides that in ascertaining the meaning of contractual clauses, the plain and ordinary meanings of the words should be adopted. The four corners rule suggests that in ascertaining the legal significance and consequences of the document, the parties and the court can only examine its own language and all matters

---

183 See Articles 1:201 PECL, 1.7 PICC, III.-1:103 DCFR.

184 Mantysaari describes this choice as a shortcut; see MANTYSAARI, P., *The Law of Corporate Finance: General Principles and EU Law, Volume II: Contracts in General*, Springer 2010, p. 86.

encompassed within it. Extraneous information concerning the document that does not appear in it – *within its four corners* – cannot be evaluated.[185] Thus, if the text is not ambiguous, there is no need to go beyond the four corners of the document and take extrinsic evidence into account.[186]

The parol evidence rule is designed "to preserve the integrity of written contracts by refusing to allow the admission of oral statements or previous correspondence to contradict the written agreement".[187] Thus, *if a contract is completely integrated in writing*, the writing becomes the exclusive statement of the terms of the contract, and prior oral or written statements cannot be used to add to or modify the writing.[188]

In English law, the parol evidence rule involves a rebuttable presumption that the writing was intended to include all the terms of the contract. English courts first examine the writing to determine whether it was meant to serve as a true record of the contract.

In US law, the parol evidence rule operates in two steps. First, the court examines whether the writing was "integrated" – in other words, was intended to represent the final expression of the terms it contains. Accordingly, writing signed by the parties and containing detailed specifications will usually be found to be integrated. If the writing is integrated, neither party may introduce parol evidence to "contradict" the terms of the writing. The second step consists of examining whether the integrated document is "completely integrated" or not. If the document is intended to be completely integrated, parol evidence may not be introduced either "to contradict" or "to supplement" the contractual terms.[189]

Farnsworth explains the policy reasons behind the adoption of the parol evidence rule. Accordingly, the rule simplifies the administration of the resulting contract and facilitates the resolution of disputes by

---

185 http://legal-dictionary.thefreedictionary.com/four+corners. For leading cases see for instance, *Becky Jo Hartell v. Roy Joseph Hartell*, KY Supreme Court, 2007-CA-000498, *Howard Thompson and Aileen Thompson et al. v. Walter Sullivan and Effie Sulllivan et al.* KY Supreme Court, 1995-CA-001813.

186 See for instance, KY Supreme Court 2007-CA-000498, KY Supreme Court 1995-CA-001813.

187 See DiMATTEO, L., *The Law of International Contracting*, Kluwer Law International, The Hague 2000.

188 See FARNSWORTH, E.A., "*The Interpretation of International Contracts and the Use of Preambles*", 3/4 I.B.L.J. (2002) 271–279.

189 See "*CISG Advisory Council Opinion No. 3: Parol Evidence Rule, Plain Meaning Rule, Contractual Merger Clause and the CISG*", 17 Pace Int'l L. Rev. 61 (2005).

excluding from the scope of the agreement the matters that were "raised and dropped or even agreed upon and superseded during the negotiations".[190]

However, as is clearly established by the wording of Article 8 CISG, extrinsic evidence is admissible and that the parol evidence rule is not adopted by the Convention. This point made the autonomous interpretation and application of Article 8 by the courts of the countries where the rule is applicable an important issue. The following cases need particularly to be cited on this matter.

In *Filanto v. Chilewich* in 1992, the Federal District Court of New York stated (in the footnotes of the case) that the CISG rejected the parol evidence rule.[191]

In *Beijing Metals v. American Business Center* case of 1993,[192] where the Court held that "It is unnecessary to determine whether to apply Texas domestic law or to apply the CISG because our discussion is limited to application of the parol evidence rule (which applies regardless)", however, the parol evidence rule was applied.

In *MCC-Marble Ceramic Center v. Ceramica Nuova D'Agostino* in 1998,[193] the *Beijing Metals* case above was cited but not followed by the Court. The decision is one of the leading decisions on this matter. The Court first observed that the parol evidence rule, contrary to its title, is a substantive rule of law, not a rule of evidence, because it does not purport to exclude a particular type of evidence as an "untrustworthy or undesirable" way of proving a fact, but rather prevents a litigant from attempting to show "the fact itself" – the fact that the terms of the agreement are other than those in the writing.

The Court observed, moreover, that the CISG itself contains no express statement on the role of parol evidence, but found that the drafters of the CISG were comfortable with the concept of permitting parties to rely on oral contracts and that Article 8(3) of the CISG expressly directs courts to give due consideration to all relevant circumstances of the case, including preliminary negotiations, to determine the intent of the parties.

---

190 See FARNSWORTH, E.A., *Contracts*, Little, Brown Co., New York 1982, §7.2, p. 451.

191 United States, 14 April 1992, Federal District Court [New York] (*Filanto v. Chilewich*), http://cisgw3.law.pace.edu/cases/920414u1.html.

192 United States, 15 June 1993, Federal Appellate Court [5th Circuit] (*Beijing Metals v. American Business Center*), http://cisgw3.law.pace.edu/cases/930615u1.html.

193 United States, 29 June 1998, Federal Appellate Court [11th Circuit] (*MCC-Marble Ceramic Center Inc. v. Ceramica Nuova D'Agostino S.p.A.*), http://cisgw3.law.pace.edu/cases/980629u1.html.

The Court emphasized that, given Article 8(1)'s directive to use the intent of the parties to interpret their statements and conduct, Article 8(3) is considered to be a clear instruction to admit and consider parol evidence regarding the negotiations to the extent that they reveal the parties' subjective intent.

The Court also explained that although jurisdictions in the United States have found the parol evidence rule helpful to promote good faith and uniformity in contract, a wide number of other states, party to the CISG, have rejected the rule in their domestic jurisdictions. It was further underlined by the Court that, as one of the primary factors motivating the negotiation and adoption of the CISG was to provide parties to international contracts for the sale of goods with some degree of certainty as to the principles of law that would govern potential disputes, and to remove the previous doubt regarding which party's legal system might otherwise apply, courts applying the CISG cannot upset the parties' reliance on the Convention by substituting familiar principles of domestic law when the Convention requires a different result.

The Court then rejected the parol evidence rule on the basis of the provision of Article 8(1) which permitted the inquiry into the parties' subjective intent.

In the US Federal District Court decision of 23 August 2006[194] the same reasoning was followed and the Court held that the CISG, unlike American contract law, includes no parol evidence rule, and allows all relevant information into evidence, even if it contradicts the written documentation, noting that Article 8(1) "requires a court to consider evidence of the parties' subjective intent" and that Article 8(3) "is a clear instruction to admit and consider parol evidence regarding the negotiations to the extent they reveal the parties' subjective intent".

In another leading US case,[195] the parol evidence rule was also rejected but this time on the basis of both Article 8(1) and (2). Accordingly, the

194 United States, 23 August 2006, Federal District Court [New York] (*TeeVee Tunes, Inc. et al v. Gerhard Schubert GmbH*), http://cisgw3.law.pace.edu/cases/060823u1.html. See also United States, 6 July 2010, District Court [Colorado] (*Alpha Prime Development Corporation, Plaintiff, v. Holland Loader*), http://cisgw3.law.pace.edu/cases/100706u1.html.

195 United States, 29 January 2010, Federal District Court [Pennsylvania] (*ECEM European Chemical Marketing B.V. v. The Purolite Company*), http://cisgw3.law.pace.edu/cases/100129u1.html. On parol evidence rule see also United States, 26 March 2009, Federal District Court [Ohio] (*Miami Valley Paper, LLC v. Lebbing Engineering & Consulting GmbH*), http://cisgw3.law.pace.edu/cases/090326u1.html. "The CISG contains no parol evidence rule, but allows the Court to consider statements or conduct of a contracting party to establish, modify, or alter the terms of a contract."

Court concluded that regardless of whether Article 8(1) or (2) is applicable, the CISG allows all evidence of the parties' intent to be admitted to interpret the terms of the agreement. The Court concluded that an inquiry regarding whether writing is fully or partially integrated has little meaning under the CISG and courts are therefore less constrained by the "four corners" of the instrument in construing the terms of the contract. Consequently, the Court did not preclude extra-textual evidence of negotiations or agreements made prior to the contract pertaining to the scope of the parties' rights and obligations under it.

4.2. AN ANALYSIS OF THE CONTEXTUALIST APPROACH ADOPTED BY THE CISG, PICC, PECL AND DCFR

4.2.1. The Controversy

When we examine the rules on interpretation contained in the CISG, PICC, PECL and DCFR, we see that they all take a very important common position, which is rejection of formalism and promotion of contextualism in interpretation of international commercial contracts. One can put forward that this may be explained by the fact that these instruments were more influenced by civil law approaches than common law traditions. This author is of the opinion, however, that such an argument falls short to explain such a consistency in the choice of these four instruments, which are in fact different from each other in many ways, including nature and time.[196]

From a comparative law perspective, it can be supported that interpretation of international commercial contracts is a less controversial topic than before, as globalization has showed its effects and brought different systems closer to one another, especially with the success of the CISG and PICC as international instruments as "better law".[197]

---

196 While CISG (1980) is an international convention on the international sale of goods, the PICC (2016) is a non-binding instrument of unification or harmonization, considered to be a formulation of the "*lex mercatoria*", conceived by lawyers who are experts in the fields of international law and international trade law. The PECL (2000), which is also a non-binding instrument, was prepared by a commission composed of lawyers from all Member States of the European Union, and the DCFR (2009) is an academic, not politically authorized, text which is the fruit of the European Commission's 2003 Action Plan for European Contract Law. The last two instruments apply not only to commercial contracts.

197 See note 198 below.

The differences in different legal systems are considered less and less present and seen as more apparent than real.[198]

In the opinion of the present author, the controversy in the field of interpretation of international commercial contracts does not lie in the differences of interpretative approaches adopted in different legal systems. Instead, it lies in the autonomous special setting of international commercial contracts and can only be better understood based on this specific context.

4.2.2. A Classification of the "Contexts"

Before examining the notion of context it should be underlined that the term "context" is a very complex term, which can both be "ambiguous" and "vague", according to the "context" where it applies.[199]

---

198 On this matter, see VOGENAUER, S., "*Interpretation of Contracts: Concluding Comparative Observations*" in *Contract Terms*, A. Burrows, E. Peel (eds.), Oxford University Press, Oxford July 2007, pp. 125–128 where the author makes a comparison of French and German Laws. See also, VOGENAUER, S. in *Commentary on the UNIDROIT Principles on International Commercial Contracts*, Stefan Vogenauer (ed.), Oxford University Press, Oxford 2015, Article 4.1, §§14 and 15. For the terminology of "better law" and the differences being more apparent than real see HERBOTS, J.H., "*What Precisely is Interpretation?*" in *Elgar Encyclopedia of Comparative Law*, 2nd ed., Jan M. Smits (ed.), Edward Elgar, Cheltenham 2012, pp. 421–448.

199 For the notion of ambiguity, see for instance, LEWISON, K., *The Interpretation of Contracts*, Sweet & Maxwell, London 2004, pp. 241–242; FARNSWORTH, E.A., "*'Meaning' in the Law of Contract*", 76 Yale L.J. 953 (1967), p. 960; Lord Atkinson in *Watcham v. Attorney-General of the East African Protectorate* [1919] A.C. 533; Lord Wrenbury in *Great Western Railway v. Bristol Corp.* (1918) 87 L.J. Ch. 414; McMEEL, G., "*The Construction of Contracts*", 3rd ed., Oxford University Press, Oxford 2017, pp. 63–66; CHOMSKY, N., *Aspects of the Theory of Syntax*, MIT Press, Cambridge MA 1965, p. 21; SOLAN, L.M., "*Pernicious Ambiguity in Contracts and Statutes*", 79 Chicago-Kent Law Review 859 (2004), p. 859 et seq.; MALEVILLE, M.H., *Pratique de l'Interprétation des Contrats, Etude Jurisprudentielle*, Publications de l'Université de Rouen, No. 164, Rouen 1991, p. 27; QUINE, W., *Word and Object*, MIT Press, Cambridge MA 1964, para. 18, 27, 28. For the notion of vagueness and the distinction between the two concepts see for instance McMEEL, G., *The Construction of Contracts*, 3rd ed., Oxford University Press, Oxford 2017, p. 63; FARNSWORTH, E.A., "*'Meaning' in the Law of Contract*", 76, Yale L.J. 953; CHRISTIE, G.C., "*Vagueness and Legal Language*", 48 Minn. L. Rev. 885 (1963–1964); QUINE, W., *Word and Object*, 1964, para 17. See Leyhane who states that there are two types of ambiguity: (1) The contractual clause has more than one meaning; and (2) The contractual clause has no clear meaning. LEYHANE, J., "*The Two Faces of Contract Ambiguity Claims*", 100 Illinois Bar J. 264. See also Solan, who makes a distinction between the two but prefers to use the term ambiguity for both of them as courts do. SOLAN, L.M., "*Pernicious*

The problem with the term "context", in terms of international commercial contracts (and also in terms of other contracts which are not inside the scope of this research), is that it may be used for not one but a plurality of factual matrices that may coexist in the life of a contract, and its scope is very difficult to establish. In the frame of this book and for practical purposes, we will try to distinguish here different types of "contexts" which form the unique "context" of a particular international commercial contract.

For this purpose, we will first try to make a distinction between two competing "specific contexts" in which an international commercial contract is placed, namely, "international" and "commercial" context. Then, we will try to explore three different types of "general context" that may affect not only the interpretation of international commercial contracts, but also interpretation of every contract. From that point of view, it can be said that there are three different factual matrices which may have an influence on the interpretation process. First, there are elements inherent to contractual parties, such as their abilities (including linguistic) and the "context" in which each of them is situated at the time of contracting. Second, there are elements inherent to the contract itself and the "context" in which the contract itself is concluded. And finally, third, there is the "interpreter" or the "reader" who, after the occurrence of a disagreement between the parties on the meaning of contractual terms, aims to interpret the contract.

The interpreter is also situated in a "context", which is mainly constituted of his/her linguistic, cultural and legal background. Accordingly, as a user of the language, he/she has a view concerning the meanings of words used by contracting parties (that he/she can "extract" with more or less reference to the contextual matrix of the contract) as well as the purpose and the function of contract interpretation. He/she has a view on fairness and on to what extent it should be taken into account when interpreting a particular contract and so forth.

Let us try to further distinguish between these different contexts in order to better understand and apply the fully contextualist interpretation technique adopted by the CISG, PICC, PECL and DCFR.

Ambiguity in Contracts and Statutes", 79 Chicago-Kent Law Review 859 (2004), p. 859 et seq.; for an example of ambiguity of a term, see also the famous case of *Raffles v. Wichelhaus*, (1864) 2 H. & C.906.

4.2.3. *Two "Competing", "Specific" Contexts*

4.2.3.1. The "Commercial" Context

In a world where contextualist approaches continue to gain ground over formalism, neo-formalistic arguments are becoming more and more present in the context of commercial contracts.[200] It is now put forward that even in a system where "contextualist interpretation" would be the general rule to be applied in contract law, the specific context of commercial contracts may point to "formalistic rules" of interpretation as better adopted rules to govern interpretation of commercial contracts.[201] In other words, commercial context itself may necessitate a rejection of the context. In favor of formalistic rules of interpretation, Bernstein observes that in a given specific market, buyers and sellers who deal prefer to have their disputes governed by the private rules and procedures supplied by their individual trade organizations, because those rules and procedures are more formalistic and provide more certainty and protection with lower cost.[202] In the same direction, Schwartz and Scott emphasize that formalistic rules are better suited for commercial transactions and put forward that this is the choice of actual contracting parties, although this choice cannot be said to have an important impact on actual legal rules in general.[203] From that point of view, formalistic interpretation rules such as the "plain meaning rule", "four corners rule" and "parol evidence rule" increase certainty in contractual relationships and reduce transaction costs.[204] They are also better adapted to commercial contracts because they promote efficiency in contracting, given the ability of firms to maximize welfare by negotiating efficient contracts.[205]

---

200 For the term neoformalism see KATZ, A.W., "*The Economics of Form and Substance in Contract Interpretation*", 103 Columbia L. Rev. 496–538 (2004).

201 See MITCHELL, C., *Interpretation of Contracts, Current Controversies in Law*, Routledge-Cavendish, London 2007, p. 10.

202 BERNSTEIN, L., "Private Commercial Law in the Cotton Industry: Creating Cooperation Through Rules, Norms and Institutions", 99 Mich. L. Rev. 1724 (2001), pp. 1735–1744.

203 SCHWARTZ, A., SCOTT, R.E., "*Contract Interpretation Redux*", 119 Yale L.J. 926–964 (2010).

204 See DiMATTEO, L., OSTAS, D.L., "*Comparative Efficiency in International Sales Law*", 26 Am. U. Int'l. L. Rev. 371 (2011), p. 412 fn. 211, and BERNSTEIN, L., "*Private Commercial Law in the Cotton Industry: Creating Cooperation Through Rules, Norms and Institutions*", 99 Mich. L. Rev. 1724 et seq (2001).

205 SCHWARTZ, A., SCOTT, R.E., "*Contract Theory and the Limits of Contract Law*", 113 Yale L. J. 541 (2003).

Accordingly, a strong application of the parol evidence rule in commercial contracts would prevent the risks of judicial discretion (which is what commercial parties prefer)[206] and reduce litigation costs.[207]

So why did the instruments that we are examining here and especially the CISG and PICC, which only apply to commercial contracts, not opt for interpretative rules that are considered more cost effective and, thus, efficient and adopt instead a highly contextual interpretation technique? This choice, in this author's opinion, may be better understood based on the second competing context, namely, international context.

4.2.3.2. The "International" Context

As an international commercial contract cannot solely be defined by its commercial character, it is not sufficient to take only such economic criteria into consideration in deciding on the most suitable rules of interpretation to be applied. The "international character" of the contract which brings a particular factual reality into the equation needs also to be taken into account. Accordingly, in an international setting, where the same language and the same legal and cultural background information to process that language are often not shared by the parties (or the court), linguistic errors are more likely to be observed.

Indeed, while the "objectivity of the language" is already the subject of a big debate (that we are not going to explore here) in homogenous domestic contexts, the debate gains another dimension in an exceptionally heterogeneous international setting. Can (or should) a contract between a Chinese company and a Russian company, written in English, be interpreted by a French arbitrator according to the ordinary meaning of the contractual clauses as understood by a competent user of the

---

206 SCHWARTZ, A., SCOTT, R.E., "*Contract Theory and The Limits of Contract Law*", 113 Yale L.J. 541 (2003), p. 547: "Business firms, that is, commonly prefer courts to adhere as closely as possible to the ordinary meanings of words, to apply a 'hard' parol evidence rule and to honor 'merger clauses' (which) state that the parties intended their writing to be interpreted as if it were complete" and also p. 618. See also KORNET, N., *Contract Interpretation and Gap-Filling: Comparative and Theoretical Perspectives*, Intersentia Antwerpen-Oxford, 2006, p. 411: "if legal certainty, predictability and expediency of litigation are to be preferred, as in the context of the commercial transactions ... a relatively restrictive set of evidentary materials should be admitted."

207 It can indeed be supported that the more contextual elements are considered by the courts in interpreting contracts, the more the litigation process may become time and money consuming.

English language? Can we obtain "predictability" in commercial transactions with such an approach?

One can say that if the parties are very well-informed big corporations, immune to the linguistic and cultural errors,[208] who regularly enter into the same kind of transactions in the same foreign language, and if the interpreter focuses exclusively on the linguistic information in resolving the litigation and puts aside his or her own legal, linguistic and cultural background, this goal can be reached. But does this ideal picture reflect the realities of international commercial contracts?

It should first be emphasized that not all the actors in international trade are such well-informed parties. Kim points out that the increasing globalization of commerce, the internet and the improvement of transportation have enabled new economic players (who would normally lack the necessary resources to enter into this kind of transactions in the past) to participate in international commerce, and technology has made possible that even small dollar transactions can occur across international boundaries.[209] As a result of this greater diversity among contracting parties who might not share the same set of "cultural references", "vocabulary", or "business practices", the likelihood of misunderstandings in international trade has increased.[210]

Thus, while it is put forward that formalistic rules would be better choices for merchants or firms who are considered sophisticated bargainers and who understand and consent to all the terms of the contracts,[211] these above-mentioned developments in international trade

---

208 See DiMATTEO, L.A., MORANT, B.D., "*Contract in Context and Contract as Context*", 45 Wake Forest L. Rev. 549 (2010). The authors underline that formalistic rules can be adopted to the extent that firm-to-firm contracts can be considered immune from contextual influences. On this matter see also Leonhard on presumptions in U.S. contract law: "rational" and "well informed" parties will drive a hard bargain on their own behalf for their own best interests and the resulting agreement reflects the free will of the parties, and the Courts will generally refuse to look beyond the four corners of the written contract. LEONHARD, C., "*Beyond the Four Corners of a Written Contract: A Global Challenge to U.S. Contract Law*", 21 Pace Int'l L. Rev. 1 (2009).

209 See KIM, N.S., "*Evolving Business and Social Norms and Interpretation Rules: The Need for a Dynamic Approach to Contract Disputes*", 84 Neb. L. Rev. 506 (2005), pp. 531–532.

210 KIM, N.S., "*Reasonable Expectations in Sociocultural Context*", 45 Wake Forest L. Rev. 641 (2010).

211 See MILLER, M.R., "*Contract Law, Party Sophistication and New Formalism*", 75(2) Missouri L. Rev. 493–496 (2010). For a discussion on this matter, see also DiMATTEO, L.A., MORANT, B.D., "*Contract in Context and Contract as Context*", 45 Wake Forest L. Rev. 549 (2010), pp. 557–558.

invite us to question this affirmation, as smaller actors enter more and more into international commercial transactions.

Garvin rightly underlines that dichotomies – consumer versus non-consumer, merchant versus non-merchant, and, worst of all, consumer versus merchant – are false, because small businesses do not fall cleanly into any of these categories, as they most resemble consumers and non-merchants in their abilities in many ways.[212] While lack of abilities may put these firms in disadvantageous positions already in domestic settings, it may render them even more vulnerable in an international setting, as the linguistic and cultural information is more diverse, difficult and onerous to gather.

Uniform and harmonized instruments conceived in order to respond to the growing needs of international business could not and did not overlook cultural and linguistic "diversity" in the world, whose relevance grew and continues to grow with the evolution of new technologies in transportation and communication. Moreover, one important goal of these instruments is to help promote and facilitate international trade.

Adopting interpretative approaches advantageous only to most experienced parties, which may "exclude" or "scare" newcomers and less experienced actors, would certainly be at odds with such a goal. The CISG has been ratified by 89 countries so far. One can hardly imagine the linguistic and cultural diversity as well as varying levels of ability of the actors involved.

4.2.4. Three Types of "General" Context

As it is mentioned above, there are three different types of "general context" that may affect the interpretation process of not only international commercial contracts but also every contract.

Accordingly, first, there are elements inherent to contractual parties such as their abilities (including linguistic) and the "context" in which each of them is situated at the time of contracting. All four instruments that we are examining in terms of this book consider this first type

212 See GARVIN, L.T., "*Small Business and the False Dichotomies of Contract Law*", 40 Wake Forest L. Rev. 295 (2005), pp. 296–297. On bargaining power and contextual interpretation see also BARNHIZER, D.D., "*Context as Power: Defining the field of Battle for Advantage in Contractual Interactions*", 45 Wake Forest L. Rev. 607 (2010).

of context relevant by adopting first a subjective test and then by construing the reasonable person in the shoes of actual parties.[213]

Second, there are elements inherent to the contract itself and the "context" in which the contract itself is concluded. Again, all four instruments consider all relevant circumstances related to the contract during the interpretation process in both subjective and objective tests.

And finally, third, as previously noted, there is the context in which the "interpreter" or the "reader" is situated, which is mainly constituted of his/her linguistic, cultural and legal background. Accordingly, as a user of the language, he/she has a view concerning the meanings of words used by contracting parties (that he/she can "extract" with more or less reference to the contextual matrix of the contract) as well as the purpose and the function of contract interpretation. He/she has a view on fairness and on to what extent it should be taken into account when interpreting a particular contract and so forth.

While factual information on the first and the second contexts may generally be considered relevant (in varying degrees), in contextualist approaches, the third context is indeed a matter of concern.[214] Both textualists and contextualists agree on this point: the court should respect the principle of freedom of contract and not make the contract for the parties according to its own beliefs.

While there is "subjectivity" in all "interpretation" and agreement that subjective elements inherent to the interpreter's context are not desirable in the interpretation process, the solutions that are traditionally put forward in relation to the problem simply do not fit within the setting of international contracts.[215]

First, to make a distinction between the notions of "interpretation" and "understanding of a text" based on the common and ordinary speaker of the language, and to consider the problem purely a matter of grammar and dictionary in order to reach objectivity and efficiency, is of little help where the language of the contract is generally foreign to

213 See, for instance, PICC Comments on Article 4.1. On the interpreter putting himself in the shoes of the actual parties; see also CORBIN, A.L., "*The Interpretation of Words and The Parol Evidence Rule*", 50 Cornell L.Q. 161–190 (1965); and Roger J. Traynor in *Pacific Gas & Electric Co. v. Thomas Drayage etc., Co.* 69 Cal. 2d 33 (Cal. 1968).

214 See for instance CORBIN, A.L., "*The Interpretation of Words and The Parol Evidence Rule*", 50 Cornell L.Q. 161–190 (1965).

215 It is also highly debatable that these solutions help prevent "subjectivity" in domestic context but we are not going to address this issue here as our context is limited with the context of international commercial contracts.

at least one of the parties and/or the court. Second, a classical conception of the reasonable person is insufficient to cover the diversity between "the real-life reasonable parties" who enter into international commercial contracts.

DiMatteo and Morant[216] underline that freedom of contract, in its purely theoretical form, has as its foundation the reasonable person who is typified by neutrality. Accordingly, she is neither black nor white, neither lower- nor upper-class, neither male nor female, neither big nor small. Those authors stress that to ignore such contextual factors, however, does not promote neutrality, but rather prevents the court from examining the effects of biases related to those factors. This author completely agrees with these remarks.

In any case, no predictability or certainty will be obtained in commercial transactions if we try to fit this classical view of the reasonable person to this new diverse environment. In the absence of data related to the actual parties, this author believes that the interpreter will turn to his her *own* "context" to solve the dispute, which definitely is the complete opposite of the result that is aimed for. From that point of view, it can be said that the more we put the reasonable person in the shoes of the contracting parties, the more this hypothetical personality stays outside the shoes of the interpreter.[217]

It should be noted that minimizing the interference of the interpreter's context has very important aspects in the setting of international commercial contracts. In a domestic setting, the interpreter may have a *false consensus bias* as to the "meaning" of the words and falsely think that his or her categorization of the linguistic data is naturally shared by others as the predominant view.[218] This potential *linguistic* bias is also valid for international settings and may even become more problematic because of linguistic divergences and "*faux amis*" (i.e. the same term (legal or otherwise) having different meanings in different places). In addition, in an international setting, *cultural biases* also become more likely to occur because of the cultural heterogeneity. In any case, it is not easy to separate language from culture, as the former is necessarily contextual.

216 DiMATTEO, L.A, MORANT, B.D., "*Contract in Context and Contract as Context*", 45 Wake Forest L. Rev. 549 (2010).

217 See also DiMATTEO, L.A., "*Reason and Context: A Dual-Track Theory of Interpretation*", 109 Penn. State L. Rev. 397 (2004), p. 470, fn 366.

218 For False Consensus Bias, see in general SOLAN, L, ROSENBLATT, T, OSHERSON, D., "*False Consensus Bias in Contract Interpretation*", 108 Columbia Law Review 1268 (2008).

The case of *White City Shopping Center, LP v. PR Restaurants, LLC*[219] is a perfect example of both a *linguistic* and *cultural bias*. The issue was about a contract provision which provided that the landlord would not rent space in its plaza to any other business that sold sandwiches. The Massachusetts Superior Court stated that an establishment that sold burritos did not violate the tenant's exclusivity right because the plain meaning of "sandwich" did not include burritos.[220] The Court based this decision on "common sense" and on the following definition of the word "sandwich": "two thin pieces of bread, usually buttered, with a thin layer (as of meat, cheese, or savory mixture), spread between them". Florestal makes an extensive analysis of the notion of *cultural bias* based on this rather unfortunate decision.[221] We are not going deal with this notion in detail here. But it is important to emphasize that culture is an omnipresent and constantly evolving notion, which has a huge impact on individual opinions.

Is a burrito a sandwich? Maybe not a central case example, but the answer may also depend on how it is consumed in a particular place. Do people in that country eat that food in 10 minutes during a lunch break or do they eat it in a restaurant with their family in the weekends? Accordingly, a burrito can be considered a sandwich in one country but not in another, in one period of time but not in another. The best way to avoid the interference of the interpreter's personal context (linguistic or cultural), is to focus on the context related to the particular contract and contractual parties.

In the light of these arguments, it can be argued that from an economical point of view, a formalistic approach may work and save transaction costs in the setting of a domestic commercial agreement, where the language and the legal backgrounds of the parties and of the court coincide with the language and the legal background of the contract, because in such a setting the risk of linguistic discrepancy or "*faux amis*" will be small.

---

219 *White City*, 2006 WL 3292641.

220 For the latter example see the famous case of *White City Shopping Ctr. v PR Restaurants*, No. 2006196313, 2006, WL 3292641, Mass. Superior Ct. Oct, 31, 2006. For critics of this case see for instance; FLORESTAL, M., "*Is a Burrito a Sandwich? Exploring Race, Class, and Culture in Contracts*", 14(1) Michigan Journal of Race and Law 1–60 (2008) exploring the notion of cultural bias in contract interpretation, see also DiMATTEO, L.A, MORANT, B.D., "*Contract in Context and Contract as Context*", 45 Wake Forest L. Rev. 549 (2010).

221 FLORESTAL, M., "*Is a Burrito a Sandwich? Exploring Race, Class, and Culture in Contracts*", 14(1) Michigan Journal of Race and Law 1–60 (2008).

In an international setting, however, the same language and the same legal and cultural background information to process that language are often not shared by the parties (or the court). As our understanding of the words is generally conditioned by our background, an interpretation method which focuses only on the written language of the contract could create more uncertainty than certainty and increase transaction costs, as costs related to linguistic information will most likely add to the costs related to attempting to manipulate the formal text (which can be observed in any commercial setting), because parties contracting in a foreign language will have to be more careful concerning the language of their contract and will need a higher level of linguistic information.

Such an approach would, moreover, be more disadvantageous for parties which will have to contract in the language of their opposite number, which could create a fear of entering into contractual relationships and thus discourage the promotion of international trade. Although these effects would be less important for experienced firms which constantly enter into the same type of international contracts in a given language and a given country, it could be more present for newcomers and less experienced actors.

4.2.5. The Highly Contextualist Interpretation Approach of the CISG, PICC, PECL and DCFR

After reading all these arguments in favor of contextualism in international commercial contracts, one can rightly ask about the practical impacts of this method on the litigation process. Will the court gather all information about the whole factual matrix – relating to the characteristics of the parties and the contract, preliminary negotiations, subsequent conduct, practices established between the parties, usages etc. – in construing the reasonable person each time there is a dispute over the meaning of a contractual clause? Let us not forget that the list of relevant circumstances provided by the CISG, PICC, PECL and DCFR is a non-exhaustive one. Accordingly, it is possible to ask where this inquiry is going to start and where it is going to end. At the end, the litigation process needs to have some efficiency and should not waste time and money in vain.

The answer to this question is also in the notion of "context" itself. Adopting a fully contextualist approach means that the interpretation rules in a given system make all contractual data available for the court to resolve issues related to the interpretation of contracts. This does not mean, however, that there must not be any selection between all the available circumstances in a given case. The context itself provides the best criteria for the selection of the relevant context. From this point of view, it would be wrong to say that the arguments put forward by new formalism on the commercial context do not have any relevance at all once we adopt a fully contextualist approach.

In fact, characteristics related to the parties and the contract provide the best guidance for the court in order to decide on the relevant context to be taken into account. How informed are the contracting parties? What is the nature of the contract? How detailed is the contract?

It is important for the court to be able to have access to contextual information in order to be able to decide which circumstances are indeed relevant in a given case. Accordingly, the reasonable person in the shoes of a well-informed big multi-national corporation which enters into the same kind of detailed, well-negotiated contracts in a given country, in a given language may not be construed in the same manner as the reasonable Nusquamian peasant.[222]

Consequently, the court may find that it would be unreasonable for the *first* kind of reasonable person to rely on preliminary negotiations in the circumstances of the case, and may not consider preliminary negotiations as relevant context in a given case, but do the exact opposite and give them an important weight in construing the *second* kind of reasonable person in another case. In both cases, the result should also be in accordance with the principle of good faith and fair dealing, which in the present author's opinion, has a very important function in the fully contextual interpretation method adopted by uniform and harmonized instruments, as it provides the "flexibility" that "international commercial context" requires. It is, thus, crucial that the principle acquires a uniform and autonomous content determined by the "international commercial context" and not by the interpreter's own context. We will focus on the principle of good faith and fair dealing and try to establish its scope and importance in terms of our research subject below.

Finally, it is also important to emphasize that parties are invited to provide interpretation clauses[223] in their contract in order to provide

222 For this example, see, FELTHAM, J., "The United Nations Convention on Contracts for the International Sale of Goods", J. Bus. L. 349 (1981).

223 For a list of different types of interpretation clauses see DE LY, F., "*Interpretation Clauses in International Contracts, (Characterization, Definition, Entire Agreement,*

guidance to the court about their intentions. An individually negotiated merger clause, for instance, will prevent recourse to preliminary negotiations in order to contradict or supplement the writing. It will, however, not prevent the court having recourse to prior negotiations in order to interpret the contract. If parties, however, do not want prior negotiations to be used in order to interpret the contract either, they can agree on an individually negotiated clause expressly stating this intention.[224]

Headings, Language, NOM-Clauses, Non-Waiver Clauses and Severability)", 6 I.B.L.J. (2000), pp. 719–812.

224 See PECL supra n. 169, Comments on Article 5:102.

CHAPTER 2
SPECIFIC RULES OF INTERPRETATION

Besides the general rules of interpretation, the Convention on Contracts for the International Sale of Goods (CISG), Principles of European Contract Law (PECL), Principles of International Commercial Contracts (PICC) and Draft Common Frame of Reference (DCFR) also contain some specific rules which need to be examined.

1. *CONTRA PROFERENTEM* RULE

The *contra proferentem* rule is a widely recognized interpretation rule which also found its place in the PECL, the UNIDROIT Principles and the DCFR. The CISG does not contain an express article on *contra proferentem*, which created a discussion about the application of the rule to contracts governed by this instrument.

1.1. DEFINING THE RULE

The *contra proferentem* rule is an interpretation rule which holds that ambiguities in the language of a contract should be construed against the drafter of the unclear contract clause.[1] It is an interpretative maxim of *ius commune* which found its place in continental jurisdictions "under the guise of judge-made rules developed alongside the codifications".[2]

---

1 See for instance, McMEEL, G., "*Language and the Law Revisited, An Intellectual History of Contract Interpretation*", 34 Comm. L. World Rev. 256 (2005).

2 VOGENAUER, S., "*Interpretation of Contracts*" in *The Max Planck Encyclopedia of European Private Law*, Vol. 1, Basedow, J., Hopt, K.J., Zimmermann, R., Stier, A. (eds.), Oxford University Press, Oxford 2012, p. 974.

It is expressed by the ancient formula *verba cartarum fortius accipiuntur contra proferentem* in Bacon's Maxims of the Law.[3] Bacon states that "this rule, that a man's deeds and his words shall be taken strongliest against himself, though it be one of the most common grounds of the law, it is notwithstanding a rule drawn out of the depth of reason". He acknowledges that "the force of this rule is in three things, in ambiguity of words, in implication of matter, and reducing and qualifying the exposition of such grants as were against the law, if they were taken according to their words".[4]

Four grounds have been given in the literature for the application of the *contra proferentem* rule.[5] Accordingly,

1) Nobody should benefit from his own wrong and it is wrong to formulate a defective clause;
2) A party who drafted or otherwise supplied a contractual term may be responsible for its formulation and should bear the risk of the ambiguity of that particular term;
3) The ambiguity might have misled the other party and induced him to conclude the contract; and
4) The bargaining power between the parties is unequal.

It is the second rationale which is adopted in the comments of the PECL Article 5.103 and the Article 4.6 UNIDROIT Principles on *contra proferentem* rule that we will examine below.[6]

As the *contra proferentem* rule reflects a paternalistic approach aiming to protect the weaker party, its incorporation in the field of commercial contracts, where the unequal bargaining power between contracting parties is less common, can be considered rather interesting.

---

3 Bacon's Maxims III, *The Works of Francis Bacon, Baron of Verulam, Viscount St. Alban, and High Chancellor of England: Law Tracts. Maxims of the Law*, Printed for C. and J. Rivington, London 1826, pp. 21–22.

4 Bacon's Maxims III, *The Works of Francis Bacon, Baron of Verulam, Viscount St. Alban, and High Chancellor of England: Law Tracts. Maxims of the Law*, Printed for C. and J. Rivington, London 1826, pp. 21–22.

5 See CSERNE, P., "*Policy Considerations in Contract Interpretation: The contra proferentem rule from a comparative law and economics perspective*", p. 12, No. 5 Műhelytanulmányok Working Papers 2007: http://works.bepress.com/peter_cserne/28.

6 See, *Principles of European Contract Law, Parts I and II*, O. Lando, H. Beale (eds.), Kluwer Law International, The Hague 2000 p. 294 and UNIDROIT Principles of International Commercial Contracts 2016, Comments on Article 4.6.

Cserne explains the adoption of the rule in the context of commercial contracts by the fact that it constitutes a penalty default providing a remedy for asymmetric information and that it should be understood as an incentive to the drafting efforts of the drafting party as it represents a low-cost technique that may be implemented in order to prevent parties from drafting ambiguous clauses.[7]

1.2. *CONTRA PROFERENTEM* RULE IN THE PECL, THE UNIDROIT PRINCIPLES, THE DCFR AND THE CISG

Article 5:103 of the PECL on the *contra proferentem* rule states that "where there is doubt about the meaning of a contract term not individually negotiated, an interpretation of the term against the party which supplied it is to be preferred."

This article applies against the party who "supplied" the not-individually-negotiated term. It may be the drafter or the user of a pre-drafted clause, prepared by a third party, for example the professional association to which the party employing the clause belongs.[8]

In fact, the *contra proferentem* rule can only be applied when it can clearly be established which party supplied the formulation of the ambiguous clause and this generally is not the case when the deal was negotiated between the parties.[9] That is one important reason why the *contra proferentem* rule has been typically applied to standard form contracts (general conditions of business, boilerplates) in practice. The terminology on standard form contracts and the definition thereof is given below in section 1.3 below.

Article 5:103, by stating that the interpretation against the party who supplied the term is to be "preferred", does not bring a strict rule of interpretation. Thus, the judge could, "in appropriate circumstances,

---

7 CSERNE, P., "*Policy Considerations in Contract Interpretation: The contra proferentem rule from a comparative law and economics perspective*", No. 5 Műhelytanulmányok Working Papers 2007 p. 14 et seq. http://works.bepress.com/peter_cserne/28. For different functions of penalty defaults see AYRES, I., GERTNER, R., "*Majoritarian and Minoritarian Defaults*", 51 Stan. L. Rev. 1591 (1999), p. 1605.

8 *Principles of European Contract Law, Parts I and II*, O. Lando, H. Beale (eds.), Kluwer Law International, The Hague 2000 p. 294.

9 CSERNE, P., "*Policy Considerations in Contract Interpretation: The contra proferentem rule from a comparative law and economics perspective*", p. 9, http://works.bepress.com/peter_cserne/28.

interpret a clause which has not been individually negotiated, in favour of the party who proposed it".[10]

According to Article II-8:103 of the DCFR the title of which is "Interpretation against supplier of term or dominant party":

(1) Where there is doubt about the meaning of a term not individually negotiated, interpretation of the term against the party who supplied it is to be preferred.
(2) Where there is doubt about the meaning of any other term, and that term has been established under the dominant influence of one party, an interpretation of the term against that party is to be preferred.

Thus, in the DCFR, the scope of application of the *contra proferentem* rule has been broadened compared to the PECL. First, the *contra proferentem* rule applies against the "supplier" of a term not individually negotiated in the same way as in Article 5:103 PECL. Secondly, even if the term cannot be classified as a "not-individually-negotiated term", the rule applies if it is established that it has been used under the dominant influence of one of the parties. Like the PECL, the DCFR is not strict about the application of the rule. The interpretation against the supplier or the dominant party is simply "preferred". Thus, the judge may, in appropriate circumstances, ascertain the meaning favorable to the supplier or dominant party.

In terms of Article 4.6 on the *contra proferentem* rule of the UNIDROIT Principles, "If contract terms supplied by one party are unclear, an interpretation against that party is preferred."

As presented above, it is submitted in the comments on the article that the second rationale is taken into account in the formulation of the article. Accordingly, a party may be responsible for the formulation of a contractual term because it has drafted or otherwise supplied it. Such a party should bear the risk of the defect in the formulation. It is for this reason that this article states that if a contract term supplied by one party is unclear, there is a preference for its interpretation against that party.[11]

---

10 *Principles of European Contract Law, Parts I and II*, O. Lando, H. Beale (eds.), Kluwer Law International, The Hague 2000, p. 294.

11 UNIDROIT Principles of International Commercial Contracts 2016, Comments on Article 4.6. https://www.unidroit.org/instruments/commercial-contracts/unidroit-principles-2016, p. 147.

An illustration of the application of the rule to contracts governed by the UNIDROIT Principles is given by the authors of that instrument. Accordingly, a contract for the construction of an industrial plant contains a provision drafted by the contractor, and not discussed further, stating that

> the contractor shall be liable for and shall indemnify the purchaser for all losses, expenses and claims in respect of any loss of or damage to physical property (other than the works), death or personal injury caused by negligence of the contractor, its employees or agents.

If one of contractor's employees play around with other party's equipment after working hours and damages it, the contractor cannot deny liability, contending that the provision covers only damages where the employees act within the scope of their employment, as, in the absence of any indication to the contrary, the provision will be interpreted in the manner which is less favorable to the contractor, namely also covering cases where its employees are not acting within the scope of their employment.[12]

As stated above there is a discussion about the application of the *contra proferentem* rule to contracts governed by the CISG, which does not contain an explicit article on that issue.[13] There are authors who consider Article 8(2) on objective interpretation – which reads "statements made by and other conduct of a party are to be interpreted according to the understanding that a reasonable person of the same kind as the other party would have had in the same circumstances" – to be an application of the *contra proferentem* rule.

Huber underlines that unless the recipient knows the actual intent of the declaring party in terms of Article 8(1), the interpretation will always have to be made according to an objective standard from the perspective of the recipient. Thus, if the statement made by the declaring party is ambiguous, this will usually lead to the understanding that is less favorable to the declaring party.[14]

---

12 UNIDROIT Principles of International Commercial Contracts 2016, Comments on Article 4.6.

13 HUBER, P., "*Some Introductory Remarks on the CISG*", Internationales Handelsrecht (6/2006) 228–238: http://www.cisg.law.pace.edu/cisg/biblio/huber.html.

14 HUBER P., "*Some Introductory Remarks on the CISG*", Internationales Handelsrecht (6/2006) 228–238: http://www.cisg.law.pace.edu/cisg/biblio/huber.html.

Honnold writes that the provision in Article 8(2) has roots in the classic rule that doubts are to be resolved against the drafter (*contra proferentem*) and that it places the burden on person who prepares a communication or who drafts a contract to communicate clearly to a reasonable person in the same position as the other party. Accordingly, it contains

> a principle that responds to the fact that only the one who communicates has an opportunity to consider and choose among alternative modes of expression and also takes account of a drafter's opportunity to hide an unpleasant meaning through "the intellectual superiority of the legal virtuoso".

His suggestion is that ambiguity in a statement is to be resolved under Article 8(2) against the party who formulated the statement.[15]

This point of view is not unanimously accepted in the literature. Indeed, according to Farnsworth, if paragraph (1) is not applicable, paragraph (2) applies, and under that paragraph a party's conduct is to be interpreted according to the understanding that a reasonable person of the same kind as the other party would have had in the same circumstances. Thus, under this paragraph the offeror's intent will prevail if he can show that this would have been the understanding of a reasonable person of the same kind and in the same circumstances as the offeree. If the offeror's meaning does not prevail, this must mean that the offeree actually had a different intent. The offeree may then be able to invoke the rule of paragraph (2) by showing that, when s/he accepted the offer, a reasonable person of the same kind and in the same circumstances as the offeror would have had the same understanding as him/her. The offeree's meaning would then prevail. So, the effect of paragraph (2) will usually be the interpretation that is the more reasonable in the light of the kind of parties involved and their circumstances.[16]

In this author's opinion, it cannot be said that the CISG contains an express rule on *contra proferentem* by giving reference to Article 8(2). This does not mean, however, that the *contra proferentem* rule does not apply to contracts governed by that Convention.

Lookofsky writes that Article 8 – which provides us with a tool to help deal with common situations where parties attach different meanings to the same contractual language – hardly provides all the tools needed

---

15 See HONNOLD, J.O., *Uniform Law for International Sales under the 1980 United Nations Convention*, 3rd ed., Kluwer Law International, The Hague 1999, [107.1].

16 FARNSWORTH, E.A., "*Article 8*" in *Commentary on the International Sales Law*, C.M. Bianca, M.J. Bonnell (eds.), Giuffrè, Milan 1987, p. 101.

to interpret one party's standard terms, especially when two reasonable meanings, each favoring one party, may be extracted from the language.[17] He supports that in a case like this it may be "most reasonable" to interpret the standard clause "narrowly" against the drafter especially if the standard terms do not lead to a balanced result. Thus "the *contra proferentem* idea perhaps not discernable as a CISG 'general principle' is at least consistent with the letter and spirit of article 8, it is also an internationally accepted rule".[18]

As is submitted in the literature, the PECL and the UNIDROIT principles may be used in order to interpret or supplement the Article 8 CISG.[19] As the *contra proferentem* rule is explicitly accepted by these two instruments, the "gap" in CISG may be supplemented by using the terms of Articles 5:103 PECL and 4.6 UNIDROIT Principles which are consistent with Article 8.

In the light of the explanation above, it should be said that the *contra proferentem* rule should not be applied automatically in the first place in any case where there is an ambiguity in the formulation of a clause supplied unilaterally by one of the parties. Instead, the interpretation rules in Article 8 should be applied first in order to ascertain the meaning of the ambiguous term.

If there are two reasonable meanings which can be ascertained, then the meaning unfavorable to the supplier should be preferred, taking into Account the circumstances of the case, and especially if the application of Article 8(2) does not lead to a balanced result. The same remark can be made for the application of Articles 5:103 PECL, II-8:103 DCFR and 4.6 UNIDROIT Principles which, as stated above, do not give a strict rule of interpretation to be applied automatically.

---

17 LOOKOFSKY, J.M., *Understanding the CISG in the USA: a compact guide to the 1980 UN Convention on contracts for the international sale of goods*, Kluwer Law International, The Hague 2004, pp. 147–148.

18 LOOKOFSKY, J.M., *Understanding the CISG in the USA: a compact guide to the 1980 UN Convention on contracts fort he international sale of goods*, Kluwer Law International, The Hague 2004, pp. 147–148. See also, LOOKOFSKY in F. Ferrari, H. Flechtner, R. Brand, *The Draft UNCITRAL Digest and Beyond*, Sellier, European Law Publishers, Munich 2004, p. 232.

19 For the interpretation of the Article 8 in the light of these instruments see, PERILLO, J.M., "*Editorial Remarks on the Manner in which the UNIDROIT Principles may be used to Interpret or Supplement CISG Article 8*", www.cisg.law.pace.edu/cisg/principles/uni8.html and STANIVUKOVIC, M., "*Editorial Remarks on the Manner in which the PECL may be used to Interpret or Supplement CISG Article 8*", www.cisg.law.pace.edu/cisg/text/peclcomp8.html.

Thus the judge will in the first place interpret the term in question according to interpretation rules existing in these instruments by considering all the relevant circumstances of the case. The result of this inquiry will determine whether the *contra proferentem* rule should be applied to the case or not. Farnsworth stresses this "last resort rule" character of the *contra proferentem* interpretation. Accordingly, although the *contra proferentem* rule may encourage care in the drafting of contracts, it can scarcely be said to be designed to ascertain the meanings attached by the parties. It is not applicable if the language is unambiguous and it is often denigrated as a rule of "last resort".[20]

1.3. GENERAL CONDITIONS OF CONTRACT, STANDARD FORM CONTRACTS AND CONTRACTS OF ADHESION

In the literature different terminology (such as "general conditions of contract", "standard form contracts", "contracts of adhesion", "adhesion contract", "boilerplate") is used in order to describe contract terms which are by their nature unilaterally supplied by one of the contracting parties.

In the Comments on Article 5:103 PECL, it is noted that the *contra proferentem* rule "applies in particular to general conditions of contract unilaterally drawn up by one party, but it may also apply to a contract of adhesion which has been drawn up for the particular occasion but which is non-negotiable".[21] In UNIDROIT Principles the phrase "standard terms" is preferred.[22]

Theoretically, the different terms used to describe unilaterally drawn up contracts do not refer to exactly the same notions. Schmitthoff classifies standard form contracts and general conditions of business as "standard contracts" and points out that in commercial practice the term "standard contract" has two different meanings: model contract

20 FARNSWORTH, A.E., *Farnsworth on Contracts*, 3rd ed., Aspen Publishers, New York 2004, pp. 302–303; see also the definition given in an American case *United States v. Seckinger*, 397 US 203 (1970): "In case of ambiguity when all other rules of construction fail, the doubt is removed by construing the document adversely against the writer". http://supreme.justia.com/us/397/203/case.html.

21 *Principles of European Contract Law, Parts I and II*, O. Lando, H. Beale (eds.), Kluwer Law International, The Hague 2000, p. 294.

22 The term is used throughout the UNIDROIT Principles of International Commercial Contracts 2016, See in particular Comments on Article 4.6.

forms and contracts of adhesion, only the latter being proposed by one party on a take-it-or-leave-it basis.[23]

Farnsworth also makes a distinction between standard form contracts according to their adhesive and non-adhesive character. Indeed, he points out that interpretation *contra proferentem* is much favored in the context of standard form contracts, "particularly if adhesive", where it often favors a party that is at a distinct disadvantage in bargaining.[24]

Bolgar uses the terms "adhesion contracts", "standardized contracts" and "standardized terms" interchangeably "even though there is a difference in the meaning". She stresses that standard contracts, in their technical term, denote model contract forms used by businessmen and are frequently amended in the course of negotiations. They do not display the adhesion contract's outstanding features: imposition on, and inalterability by the signing party, and the inequality of the parties' bargaining positions. However, since standard contract terms are frequently incorporated in adhesion contracts, the difference does not seem to be of importance in the present terms of reference.[25]

Other writers, in practice also use the terms "standard form contracts", "general conditions of contract"[26] and "adhesion contracts" interchangeably.[27] In this respect, a standard form contact (or contract of adhesion or boilerplate) is a document prepared by one party (usually by the supplier of goods and services) and routinely used by that party

---

23 SCHMITTHOFF, C.M., "*The Unification or Harmonisation of Law by Means of Standard Contracts and General Conditions*", 17 I.C.L.Q. 551 (1968).

24 FARNSWORTH, A.E., *Farnsworth on Contracts*, Aspen Publishers, 3rd ed., New York 2004, p. 302.

25 BOLGAR, V., "*The Contract of Adhesion, A Comparison of Theory and Practices*", 20 Am. J. Comp. L. 53 (1972). Compare with the definition in Merriam-Webster's Dictionary of Law, 1996: an adhesion contract is a contract that is not negotiated by the parties and that is usually embodied in a standardized form prepared by the dominant party. See also BONELL, M.J., *An International Restatement of Contract Law, The Unidroit Principles of International Commercial Contracts*, 3rd ed., Transnational Publishers Inc., New York 2005 p. 157: This rule, which formally applies in general to all contract terms supplied by one party, will in practice become particularly relevant with respect to standard terms which by their very nature are supplied by one of the parties and are not subject of further negotiations between the parties.

26 See DiMATTEO, L., *Law of International Contracting*, 2nd ed., Wolters Kluwer Law & Business, 2009, p. 169.

27 See for instance PATERSON, J., ROBERTSON, A., HEFFEY, P., *Principles of Contract Law*, LawBook Co., 2005, p. 248. See also, DiMATTEO, L., *Law of International Contracting*, 2nd ed., Wolters Kluwer Law & Business, 2009, p. 26.

in transactions of a similar kind.[28] Usually written in fine print, standard forms often pass unread by the other contracting party.[29]

These forms are a result of mass production and, as they are supplied by one of the parties and generally on a take-it-or-leave-it basis, they are by their nature against the principle of freedom of contract.[30] They are extensively used in contracts between individuals and business, which makes them an important issue in consumer protection. However, as consumer contracts are not dealt with in this book, we will not discuss these issues here. Instead we will deal with standard forms which are used between businesses, be it between traders in grain or between factories and suppliers of parts or materials.[31]

In the Comments on Article 4.6 of the UNIDROIT Principles a gradual approach is adopted in order to establish the degree of the "adhesive character" of a contract clause. In this respect, the extent to which the rule applies depends on the circumstances of the case; "the less the contract term in question was the subject of further negotiations between the parties, the greater the justification for interpreting it against the party who included it in the contract".[32]

The main justification for a "narrow or *contra proferentem* interpretation" of standard form contracts is the fact that they are susceptible to containing apparently unfair terms, in particular exclusion (exemption) or limitation clauses, against the adherent party. Such clauses exclude some rights that the adherent party would otherwise have had under the applicable law, or reduce remedies available to him.[33] From a law and economics perspective, "combined with asymmetric information and certain characteristics of the market, standard form can

---

28 PATERSON, J., ROBERTSON, A., HEFFEY, P., *Principles of Contract Law*, LawBook Co., Sydney 2005, p. 248.

29 See DiMATTEO, L., *Law of International Contracting*, 2nd ed., Wolters Kluwer Law & Business, Alphen aan den Rijn 2009, p. 26.

30 For the relationship between adhesion contracts and the principle of freedom of contracts see in general WILSON, N.S., "*Freedom of Contract and Adhesion Contracts*", 14 Intl. Comp. L.Q. 172 (1965).

31 Standard forms are also used extensively between businesses, See PATERSON, J., ROBERTSON, A., HEFFEY, P., *Principles of Contract Law*, LawBook Co., Sydney 2005, p. 248.

32 UNIDROIT Principles of International Commercial Contracts 2016, Comments on Article 4.6.

33 BEALE, H.G., BISHOP, W.D., FURMSTON, M.P., *Contract Cases and Materials*, 5th ed., Oxford University Press, Oxford 2008, p. 975.

harm non-drafting parties (both businesses and consumers) by being both inefficient and unfair".[34]

1.4. CASE LAW

There is a considerable number of cases on CISG Article 8, where standard form contracts are dealt with.[35] They are mostly related to questions on efficient incorporation of standard terms and conditions into the contract. Among these cases the ones presented below give indications as to the interpretation of standard terms used.

In the German case of District Court of 13 September 2000,[36] the seller opposed to the application of the CISG, referring to his General Sales Conditions which stated that German Law was applicable. The Court held in the first place that the general conditions, which were not in English (the language of business dealings), were not properly incorporated into the contract and noted that even if they were effectively incorporated, they would not waive the application of the CISG which must be considered as part of the German legal system. The Court did not interpret the applicable law clause within the general conditions in the light of Article 8, which would normally apply.[37] In the circumstances of the case, if standard terms were effectively incorporated within the contract and if the application of Article 8(2) led to two reasonable meanings being ascertained, the *contra proferentem* rule could be applied as a last resort rule and would lead to the same result.

In another German case,[38] the buyer asserted that a choice of law leading to German Law has been made implicitly by the parties, as its

---

34 CSERNE, P., "*Policy Considerations in Contract Interpretation: The contra proferentem rule from a comparative law and economics perspective*", No. 5 Műhelytanulmányok Working Papers 2007, p. 13. http://works.bepress.com/peter_cserne/28.

35 See computer list of annotated cases on Article 8 in the database of www.cisg.law.pace.edu.

36 Germany, 13 September 2000, Landgericht Memmingen, 2H O 382/99, (*Plastic filter plate case*), http://cisgw3.law.pace.edu/cases/000913g1.html. Jan Henning Berg (trans.), Veit Konrad (ed.).

37 LOOKOFSKY, J.M., "Article 6 Freedom of Contract: Convention as Supplementary Regime" in *The 1980 United Nations Convention on Contracts for the International Sale of Goods*, published in J. Herbots (ed.), R. Blanpain (general ed.), *International Encyclopaedia of Laws – Contracts*, Suppl. 29 (December 2000) 1–192, Kluwer law International, paragraph 71, fn 2: http://www.cisg.law.pace.edu/cisg/biblio/loo6.html.

38 Germany, 25 July 2003, Appellate Court (*Oberlandesgericht*) Düsseldorf [I-17 U 22/03]), *Rubber sealing parts case*, Mariel Dimsey (trans.), http://cisgw3.law.pace.edu/cases/030725g1.html.

standard terms of purchase (which became part of the contract through a reference in its deliveries) expressly referred to the fact that the place of performance and jurisdiction was in Germany. The Court held that although it was true that an express agreement on a uniform place of jurisdiction and a uniform place of performance could be an indication of a choice of law, it was doubtful whether this approach would also be applied if the agreements on the place of jurisdiction and place of performance were not based upon the agreement of the parties in a classical sense, but were merely part of standard terms provided unilaterally by one contracting party, as in the present case.

In the China International Economic and Trade Arbitration Commission CIETAC (PRC) Arbitration Award Australian Barley Case of March 2006,[39] the arbitrators held that the key dispute was how to interpret the term "financial settlement" in Article 17(B) of INCOGRAIN 12 (the standard contract terms issued by Syndicat de Paris du Commerce et des Industries de Grain (Paris Trade Association of Commerce and Grain Industries)) which stipulated "where a financial settlement is involved, there is no time limit for lodging a claim." Although the CISG was the applicable law in the case, Article 8 was not mentioned by the arbitrators. The *contra proferentem* rule was applied based on the Article 41 of the Contract Law of China.

An Australian case[40] involved the supply of wine bottles from an Italian manufacturer to an Australian company. The bottles allegedly broke repeatedly during bottling processes. The seller claimed the price and damages for breach in an Italian court. The buyer sought damages for contractual breach on the basis that the bottles were not fit for purpose and did not match the sample in an Australian court. The main issue was interpretation of clause 11 of the General Sales Conditions of the defendant. The Australian Court did not apply the CISG although it was applicable and applied Australian law instead. However, the result that was reached would be the same if the court would apply the CISG.[41]

---

39 Jingyuan Sun (trans.), http://cisgw3.law.pace.edu/cases/060300c1.html.

40 *Vetreria Etrusca Srl v. Kingston Estate Wines Pty Ltd* [2008] SASC 75. See the full text available at http://www.austlii.edu.au/cgi-bin/sinodisp/au/cases/sa/SADC/2007/102.html?query=kingston%20estate.

41 See SPAGNOLO, L., "The Last Outpost: Automatic CISG Opt Outs, Misapplications and the Costs of Ignoring the Vienna Sales Convention For Australian Lawyers", (2009) 10(1) Melb. J. Int'l Law 141, http://www.austlii.edu.au/cgi-bin/sinodisp/au/journals/MelbJlIntLaw/2009/10.html.

An important case on *contra proferentem* is the Chinese Arbitral Award of 7 January 2000[42] where both parties' interpretations of the clause of the contract "made sense to a certain extent". The tribunal could not locate any guidance from the CISG and noted that the clause in question was from the standard contract drafted by the seller. The "basic principle of *contra proferentem*" according to which "if a contract term supplied by one party is unclear, an interpretation against that party should be adopted" was applied. Thus, the arbitrators ruled that the *contra proferentem* rule was not embodied in the CISG, but applied it to a contract governed by this Convention as a basic principle of contractual interpretation. They did not make any reference to the UNIDROIT Principles or to the PECL.

In another German case,[43] the Court ruled that the *contra proferentem* rule applied to both the CISG and the BGB but did not mention the reasoning leading to this conclusion.

There are also cases on *contra proferentem* where the PICC are applied.

In a French case,[44] the dispute concerned the faulty packaging of machinery transported from Michigan to France via the port of Antwerp. A standard term supplied by the carrier contained an arbitration clause which designated the "International Arbitration Court of The Hague (Netherlands)"[45] as the authority to nominate the arbitrators. The clause needed to be interpreted due to the fact that there was not a court of this name in The Hague. The drafter insisted that the court to which it referred in the standard term was "The Permanent Court of Arbitration of the Hague" in accordance with the CNUDCI regulation which was used as a model for the formulation of the term. The court held that the defective clause did not mention anything about CNUDCI and conferred a direct power of designation to a non-existent authority. An interpretation unfavorable to the supplier of the term was adopted.

In another arbitral award,[46] there was a reference to the interpretation rules of the UNIDROIT Principles as a whole, including Article 4.6.

---

42 China International Economic & Trade Arbitration Commission (CIETAC) Arbitration proceeding (*Cysteine case*), http://cisgw3.law.pace.edu/cases/000107c1.html.

43 Germany, 31 March 2008, Appellate Court (*Oberlandesgericht*) Stuttgart (*Automobile case*), http://cisgw3.law.pace.edu/cases/080331g1.html. Daniel Nagel (trans.).

44 Cour d'appel de Grenoble 24.01.1996, *Société Harper Robinson v. Société Internationale de Maintenance et de Réalisation Industrielle*, http://www.unilex.info/case.cfm?id=633.

45 Specifically: "La cour internationale d'arbitrage de La Haye (Pays Bas)" Author's translation.

46 ICC International Court of Arbitration, Milan, No. 8908, 09. 1998.

The arbitrators stressed that the rules relating to interpretation and good faith contained in the UNIDROIT Principles (in particular, Articles 1.7 and 4.1–4.8), were in all events a useful reference framework for applying and judging a contract of an international nature. In two other decisions, Article 4.6 UNIDROIT Principles has been applied.[47]

2. REFERENCE TO CONTRACT OR STATEMENT AS A WHOLE

According to Article 4.4. PICC, "Terms and expressions are to be interpreted in the light of the whole contract or statement in which they appear." Article 5:105 PECL contains a similar clause. Accordingly, "terms are to be interpreted in the light of the whole contract in which they appear".

Similarly Article II.-8:105 DCFR states that "terms and expressions are to be interpreted in the light of the whole contract in which they appear".

Both in the Comments on the PECL and the DCFR it is emphasized that it is reasonable to assume that the parties expressed themselves coherently. It is thus necessary to interpret contracts as a whole and not to isolate clauses from each other and read them out of context. The contract must be interpreted in a way that gives it basic coherence so that the clauses do not contradict each other.[48]

An illustration is given in the Comments on Article 4.4. PICC: Accordingly, a licensee hears that, despite a provision in their contract granting him an exclusive license, the other party has concluded a similar contract with one of his competitors. He sends a letter to his contractor complaining of the breach and ending with the words, "your behavior has clearly demonstrated that it was a mistake on our part to rely on your professional correctness. We hereby avoid the contract we have with you". Despite the use of the word "avoid", his letter should be understood as a notice of termination in the light of the whole text.[49]

---

47 ICC International Court of Arbitration, Paris, No. 8261, 27.09.1996; Ad Hoc Arbitration, Buenos Aires, 10.12.1997: Full Text not available.

48 See *Principles of the European Contract Law: Parts I and II*, Prepared by The Commission on European Contract Law, O. Lando, H. Beale (eds.), Kluwer Law International, The Hague 2000, p. 296 and Official Comments on DCFR.

49 See UNIDROIT Principles of International Commercial Contracts 2016, Comments on Article 4.4.

In terms of the three international instruments, in principle, there is no hierarchy between different contract terms if no such hierarchy is provided by the parties themselves, except that a clause of specific character would prevail over a term of general character. In the comments on the PECL and DCFR it is, however, underlined that definitions clauses and terms that are incorporated in the preamble should be given special emphasis, and in the comments on the PICC it is stated that declarations of intent made in the preamble may or may not be of relevance for the interpretation of the operative clauses of the contract.[50]

Although CISG does not contain a specific clause on this matter, there are CISG cases where this logical hermeneutical rule was applied by the courts.

Indeed, in a Russian arbitration award of 27 May 2005,[51] the arbitrators applied the interpretation rule which holds that terms are to be interpreted by taking the contract into account as a whole, in the light of Article 8 CISG, holding that

> considering the provisions of art. 8 CISG, the meaning of the contractual term is determined by comparison of the content of that term with that of the other contractual terms and the tenor of the contract as a whole with due regard to the subsequent conduct of the parties.

Similarly, in the Swiss case of 12 December 2006,[52] it was pointed out that "The Convention requires that the interpretation take account of the contract as a whole. Individual clauses must be considered as an integral part of the contract and are to be interpreted in their context rather than in isolation".

---

50 See *Principles of the European Contract Law, Parts I and II*, Prepared by The Commission on European Contract Law, O. Lando, H. Beale (eds.), Kluwer Law International, The Hague 2000, p. 296, Comments on DCFR and UNIDROIT Principles of International Commercial Contracts 2010, p. 142.

51 Tribunal of International Commercial Arbitration (Russian Federation Chamber of Commerce and Industry), Russia, 27 May 2005, Arbitration proceeding 95/2004, http://cisgw3.law.pace.edu/cases/050527r1.html. Gayane Nuridzhanyan (trans.), Alexander Morari (ed.).

52 Switzerland, 12 December 2006, Canton Appellate Court Thurgau (*Building materials case*), http://cisgw3.law.pace.edu/cases/061212s1.html. Veit Konrad, (trans.), Jan Henning Berg (ed.). See also Netherlands, 14 October 2008, Appellate Court (*Gerechtshof*) Arnhem (*Hoogenboom BVBA v. Nijmidon B.V.*), http://cisgw3.law.pace.edu/cases/081014n1.html. Abstract by Sonja Krusinga.

Finally, it should be noted that if a group of contracts is in question the frame-work (master) contract and various contracts that are concluded under it can be considered as a whole.[53]

3. ALL TERMS TO BE GIVEN EFFECT

According to Article 4.5 PICC, "Contract terms shall be interpreted so as to give effect to all the terms rather than to deprive some of them of effect". Article 5:106 PECL also states that "An interpretation which renders the terms of the contract lawful or effective is to be preferred to one which would not". Similarly Article II–8:106 DCFR provides that "An interpretation which renders the terms of the contract lawful, or effective, is to be preferred to one which would not".

These provisions contain two important hermeneutical principles: namely, *ut res magis valeat quam pereat*, meaning that the thing may rather have effect than be destroyed,[54] which "considers parties as sensible persons who intended that their contract should be effective"; and *favor negotii*, which provides that if a clause has two meanings without distortion of the language (ambiguity) and that one meaning renders the clause valid while the other would make it invalid, the former should prevail.[55] As a last resort rule, the rule applies only if ambiguity persists after the application of general rules of interpretation.[56]

An illustration can be found in the Comments on the PICC. Accordingly, a commercial television network enters into an agreement with a film distributor, for the periodic supply of a certain number of films to be transmitted on the network in the afternoon, when only those films that are admissible for all viewers may be transmitted. According to the contract, films submitted "must have passed the admissibility test" of the competent censorship commission. A dispute arises concerning the meaning of the term. The distributor maintains that it implies

53 See *Principles of the European Contract Law, Parts I and II*, Prepared by The Commission on European Contract Law, O. Lando, H. Beale (eds.), Kluwer Law International, The Hague 2000, p. 296.

54 See http://legal-dictionary.thefreedictionary.com/Ut+res+magis+valeat+quam+pereat.

55 See *Principles of the European Contract Law, Parts I and II*, Prepared by The Commission on European Contract Law, O. Lando, H. Beale (eds.), Kluwer Law International, The Hague 2000, p. 296.

56 See VOGENAUER, S., in *Commentary on the UNIDROIT Principles on International Commercial Contracts*, Stefan Vogenauer (ed.), Oxford University Press, Oxford 2015, on Article 4.5 PICC, p. 602.

only that the films have to have been released for circulation, even if they are X-rated, while the network insists that they have to have been classified as admissible for everybody. If it is not possible to establish the meaning of the term by applying general rules of interpretation, this latter understanding prevails since the former deprives the provision of any effect.[57]

Both in the Comments on the PECL and the DCFR it is also submitted that if one of two possible interpretations would lead to an absurd result, the other must be taken.[58]

Muthorst suggests that this latter point, despite being a perfectly reasonable assumption, remains outside the scope of the *favor negotii* rule and that interpretation rules should be cautiously formulated in a binding form.[59]

4. LINGUISTIC DISCREPANCIES

Article 4.7 PICC provides that

> Where a contract is drawn up in two or more language versions which are equally authoritative there is, in case of discrepancy between the versions, a preference for the interpretation according to a version in which the contract was originally drawn up.

The problem is also addressed by PECL and DCFR which provide that

> Where a contract is drawn up in two or more language versions none of which is stated to be authoritative, there is, in case of discrepancy between the versions, a preference for the interpretation according to the version in which the contract was originally drawn up.[60]

---

57 See UNIDROIT Principles of International Commercial Contracts 2016, Comments on Article 4.5.

58 See *Principles of the European Contract Law, Parts I and II*, Prepared by The Commission on European Contract Law, O. Lando, H. Beale (eds.), Kluwer Law International, The Hague 2000, p. 296 and Comments on DCFR.

59 MUTHORST, O., "*Contract Interpretation under the German BGB and under the DCFR*" in *Interpretation in Polish, German and European Private Law*, Bettine Heiderhoff, Grzegorz Zmij (eds.), Sellier European Law Publishers, Munich 2011, p. 56.

60 Article 5:107 PECL, Article II.-8:107 DCFR. Vogenauer stresses the "innovative" character of these rules: VOGENAUER, S., "*Interpretation of Contracts*" in *The Max Planck Encyclopedia of European Private Law*, Vol. 1, Basedow, J., Hopt, K.J., Zimmermann, R., Stier, A. (eds.), Oxford University Press, Oxford 2012, p. 977.

It should be noted that there is a difference between the formulations of the two provisions which differentiates their scopes. Indeed, while the PICC article only covers the cases where the different language versions are stated to be equally authoritative, the PECL and DCFR articles apply in cases where none of the versions are stated to be authoritative.[61] Thus the PECL and DCFR articles do not apply if different versions are stated to be authoritative, as in that case general interpretation rules should be addressed in order to establish which wording corresponds better to the intention of the parties.[62]

The solutions provided by these articles may vary in specific cases where, for instance, the *contra proferentem* rule could apply if the original version was drawn up by one party or where the contract refers to instruments such as Incoterms and that despite being the original one, another version would be much clearer concerning the issue in question.[63]

5. PREFERENCE FOR NEGOTIATED TERMS

According to Article 5:104 PECL and Article II.-8:104 DCFR, "terms which have been individually negotiated take preference over those which have not".

When a standard form contract contains a negotiated term, this raises a rebuttable presumption that the clause reflects the common intention of the parties. Thus, modifications made to a standard form contract in any form, even orally are preferred to standard clauses.[64] This rule is consistent with the *contra proferentem* rule.

---

61 See Notes on Article 5:107 PECL, *Principles of the European Contract Law, Parts I and II*, Prepared by The Commission on European Contract Law, O. Lando, H. Beale (eds.), Kluwer Law International, The Hague 2000, p. 298.

62 *Principles of the European Contract Law, Parts I and II*, Prepared by The Commission on European Contract Law, O. Lando, H. Beale (eds.), Kluwer Law International, The Hague 2000, p. 298.

63 See UNIDROIT Principles of International Commercial Contracts 2016, Comments on Article 4.7; *Principles of the European Contract Law, Parts I and II*, Prepared by The Commission on European Contract Law, O. Lando, H. Beale (eds.), Kluwer Law International, The Hague 2000, p. 298.

64 See *Principles of the European Contract Law, Parts I and II*, Prepared by The Commission on European Contract Law, O. Lando, H. Beale (eds.), Kluwer Law International, The Hague 2000, p. 298. It should also be noted that from a law and economics point of view, this rule can be defined as a penalty default.

CHAPTER 3

GOOD FAITH AND FAIR DEALING AND CONTRACT INTERPRETATION

1. PARTY AUTONOMY AS AN UNDERLYING PRINCIPLE OF CISG, PECL, PICC AND DCFR

The principle of freedom of contract, which applies as a general rule in all European legal systems, is also expressed in the CISG, PECL, PICC and DCFR. Article 1:102 PECL provides that:

> Parties are free to enter into a contract and to determine its contents, subject to the requirements of good faith and fair dealing, and the mandatory rules established by these Principles (§1). The parties may exclude the application of any of the Principles or derogate from or vary their effects, except as otherwise provided by these Principles (§2).

In the DCFR also freedom of contract is the starting point. It is submitted in the section on underlying principles that as a rule, natural and legal persons should be free to decide whether or not to contract and with whom to contract, to agree on the terms of their contract and to agree at any time to modify the terms of their contract or to put an end to their relationship. This freedom is of course subject to the application of mandatory rules.[1]

The UNIDROIT Principles on International Commercial Contracts contain a similar rule in the Article 1.1. According to this article,

---

1 See Principles in DCFR; See also Article II.–1:102, which states that "(1) Parties are free to make a contract or other juridical act and to determine its contents, subject to any applicable mandatory rules. (2) Parties may exclude the application of any of the following rules relating to contracts or other juridical acts, or the rights and obligations arising from them, or derogate from or vary their effects, except as otherwise provided."

"The parties are free to enter into a contract and to determine its content." Moreover, in Article 1.5, the PICC provide that "The parties may exclude the application of these Principles or derogate from or vary the effect of any of their provisions, except as otherwise provided in the Principles". In the comments on the PICC Article 1.1., it is emphasized that the principle of freedom of contract is of paramount importance in the context of international trade:

> The right of business people to decide with whom they will offer their goods or services and by whom they wish to be supplied, as well as the possibility for them freely to agree on the terms of individual transactions are the cornerstones of an open, market-oriented and competitive international economic order.[2]

Similarly, Article 6 of the UN Convention on Contracts for the International Sale of Goods (CISG), states that the parties may exclude the application of this Convention or, subject to Article 12, derogate from or vary the effect of any of its provisions.

2. LIMITING PARTY AUTONOMY

Early in the nineteenth century, as a result of the rise of the market economy and decline of the belief in value objectivity, the principle of freedom of contract emerged as a "powerful symbol of individual autonomy and community well-being".[3] Early in the twentieth century however, the power given to the principle during the nineteenth century started to be questioned,[4] and it was emphasized that unlimited freedom of contract, like unlimited freedom in other directions, does not necessarily lead to public or individual welfare.[5] We will now try to examine limitations to this principle existing in the CISG, PICC, PECL and DCFR.

---

2 See, Official Comments on Art. 1.1. PICC.

3 LU, S., "*Gap Filling and Freedom of Contract*", https://digitalcommons.law.uga.edu/cgi/viewcontent.cgi?referer=https://www.google.com/&httpsredir=1&article=1029&context=stu_llm, pp. 3–4; see also ATIYAH, P.S., *The Rise and Fall of Freedom of Contract*, Oxford University Press, Oxford 1979, pp. 660–779.

4 LU, S., "*Gap Filling and Freedom of Contract*", https://digitalcommons.law.uga.edu/cgi/viewcontent.cgi?referer=https://www.google.com/&httpsredir=1&article=1029&context=stu_llm, pp. 3–4.

5 WILLISTON, S., "*Freedom of Contract*", VI(4) Cornell L.Q. 365 (May 1921), p. 374.

3. LIMITATIONS EXISTING IN CISG, PICC, PECL AND DCFR

In terms of Article 1:102 PECL, party autonomy is limited by the requirements of good faith and fair dealing and the mandatory rules existing in the PECL ((1)). Parties can exclude the application of the Principles or derogate from or vary the effect of any of their provisions, except as otherwise provided in the PECL ((2)).[6]

The authors of the PECL, in the Comments on Article 1:102 explain that there are three types of restriction to freedom of contract in terms of PECL. First, the parties' freedom to decide the terms of the contract is subject to principles of good faith and fair dealing. Thus, "a party cannot enforce an agreed contract or contract term which is unconscionable towards the other party". Second, the freedom is restricted by the mandatory rules of the PECL and, third, both the freedom to decide the terms of the contract and to decide with whom to contract may be limited by the mandatory rules of national law applicable to the contract.[7]

In Article 1:103(2), effect is given to mandatory rules of national, international or supranational character, which are applicable according to the relevant rules of private international law, irrespective of the national law governing the contract.

In the Comments on the DCFR Article II.-1:102 it is also provided that party autonomy is not absolute. As the DCFR is not a legislative instrument, it does not have the power to restrict party autonomy. Thus, the mandatory character of the related DCFR provisions is only an indication that if a legislator would adopt the rules "it might be expected" to make them mandatory or limit derogations from them. Accordingly, a provision where a party would reserve the right to ignore any duty to act in accordance with good faith would be ineffective because of Article III-1:103 on good faith and fair dealing, designed as a mandatory provision.[8]

The limitation clause existing in Article 1.5 PICC is exactly the same as in Article 1:102(2) PECL. Although Article 1.1. PICC does not contain an

6 See p. 97 above.

7 *Principles of the European Contract Law, Parts I and II*, Prepared by The Commission on European Contract Law, O. Lando, H. Beale (eds.), Kluwer Law International, 2000, p. 99.

8 See Official Comments on Article II.-1:102.

express limitation concerning the good faith and fair-dealing principles, Article 1.7 §2 PICC provides that parties may not exclude or limit the duty to act in accordance with good faith and fair dealing. Thus, the good faith principle exists as a limitation to the freedom of contract in both instruments.

In the Comments on Article 1.1., it is emphasized that there are possible limitations to the principle of freedom of contract, and in the context of the limitation of the parties' freedom to decide with whom to contract, the economic sectors which states may decide, in the public interest, to exclude from open competition should be taken into account. Moreover, the PICC contain provisions from which the parties may not derogate and there are both public and private rules of a mandatory character enacted by states, which may prevail over the rules contained in the PICC. In order to be more precise, the Comments on Article 1.5 should also be taken into account. According to these, the reason for the mandatory character of some provisions of the PICC is their importance in the system of the Principles. It is also underlined that the standards of behavior and rules provided by these articles are also of a mandatory character under domestic laws. The principles of good faith and fair dealing are of this character, with some other provisions, like, for instance, the provisions of Chapter 3 PICC on substantive validity.[9]

The position taken by the CISG in this matter is different from the positions taken by the PECL and PICC. In fact, as stated above, Article 6 CISG provides that the parties may exclude the application of this Convention or, subject to Article 12, derogate from or vary the effect of "any" of its provisions. Article 12 of the Convention deals with the possibility of the contracting states to make a declaration in order to derogate from Articles 11, 29 or Part II of the Convention, which allow a contract of sale – or its modification or termination by agreement or any offer, acceptance, or other indication of intention – to be made in any form other than in writing.

The parties may not derogate from or vary the effect of this article, which makes this rule the only mandatory rule of the CISG. Consequently, where at least one of the parties has its place of business in a state which has made a declaration, courts must apply the conflict rules of the forum in order to determine which law governs requirements as to form. Thus, the rules of the CISG providing freedom of form do not apply.

9 See, Official Comments on Arts. 1.1. and 1.5. PICC.

However, this does not mean that the rules as to form of the reservation state will always prevail because if it did, the rules of this state would exclude the private international law rules of other contracting states.[10]

Honnold explains that the degree of freedom provided in Article 6 CISG was made possible by excluding certain transactions and issues from the Convention. In this respect, the Convention does not apply to consumer contracts (Article 2 (a)), to liability for death or personal injury (Article 5) or to questions related to the validity of the contract.[11]

Although, in legal doctrine, there are writers who have suggested that other provisions of the CISG – such as Articles 4, 7, 28, 89 et seq. – are also mandatory, it is generally submitted that none of these articles brings a limitation on freedom of contract.[12] Bonell's suggestion to give a mandatory character to the Article 7, being related to the discussions concerning the interpretation of the contracts according to CISG, will however be examined in more detail below.

Concerning the applicability of national, supranational or international mandatory rules, there is an important difference between the Convention and the two sets of principles (the PECL and PICC) because of its different legal nature.

In fact, CISG in its contracting states, forms part of the substantive law that the courts have to apply (*lex fori*). So the contracting states have accepted under public international law to apply the Convention instead of any other legal rule whenever the Convention provides uniform rules.

Accordingly, the national, supranational and international mandatory rules are irrelevant concerning the matters covered by the CISG and they only become relevant when the Convention is applied solely because of the parties' choice.[13] Moreover, the Convention contains neither a restriction according to good faith and fair dealing principles, nor an express general clause of good faith such as Article 1.7 PICC or

---

10 See, SCHLECHTRIEM, P., *Commentary on the UN Convention on The International Sale of Goods (CISG)*, Oxford University Press, Oxford 1998, pp. 91–92.

11 HONNOLD, J.O., *Uniform Law for International Sales*, 3rd ed., Kluwer Law International, The Hague 1999, p. 77.

12 In this respect, see SCHROETER, U.G., "*Freedom of Contract: Comparison between Provisions of the CISG (Art. 6) and Counterpart Provisions of the Principles of European Contract Law*": July 2002, http://www.cisg.law.pace.edu/cisg/text/peclcomp6.html.

13 SCHROETER, U.G., "*Freedom of Contract: Comparison between Provisions of the CISG (Art. 6) and Counterpart Provisions of the Principles of European Contract Law*", July 2002, http://www.cisg.law.pace.edu/cisg/text/peclcomp6.html.

Article 1:201 PECL (and its implication is very controversial in legal doctrine). These issues will be examined below.

3.1. GOOD FAITH AND FAIR DEALING

3.1.1. In General

The concept of objective good faith can be described as a norm related to the conduct of contracting parties, generally associated with moral standards. The principle is sometimes said to be a legal-ethical principle, meaning honesty, and loyalty etc., and sometimes it is seen as a gateway through which moral values enter the law.[14] The reference to moral standards in the determination of the content of good faith, however, is said to be causing problems of uncertainty, given that there is not any clear moral reference point.[15] Storme points out that in the tradition of Latin countries (in Europe) there is often a tendency to restrict good faith to an ethical concept, "expressing a moral rule, more specifically an altruist morality, to the extent that the formal rules of law permit it". He adds that

> the contents of good faith may be colored more subjectively, as in a traditional French view reducing good faith to the absence of bad faith in a subjective sense; they may be colored more objectively, as in Demogue's theory of the contract as a microcosm.[16]

The content of good faith is sometimes defined by the Aristotelian concept of equity and it is said that good faith plays a role in cases where the strict application of the abstract rules may lead to an unjust result, in

---

14 HESSELINK, M.W., "*The Concept of Good Faith*" in *Towards a European Civil Code*, 4th ed., Kluwer Law International, Alphen aan den Rijn 2011, p. 621.

15 BARNES, N.J., "*Good Faith under the UNIDROIT Principles of International Commercial Contracts: A Struggle for Meaning*", http://www.dundee.ac.uk/cepmlp/car/html/CAR9_ARTICLE14.pdf, p. 73.

16 See STORME, M.E., "*Good Faith and the Contents of Contracts in European Private Law*", http://www.ejcl.org/71/art71-1.pdf. According to Demogue, a contract is like a little partnership where each party must work for a common purpose which is the sum (or more) of individual purposes pursued by each. See DEMOGUE, R., *Traité des Obligations en Général*, vol. VI, Librairie Arthur Rousseau, Paris 1931, p. 9. For different connotations of the good faith principle, see also CREMADES, B.M., "*Good Faith in International Arbitration*", 27 Am. U. Int'l L. Rev. 761 (2012), pp. 765–766.

such a way that its application may provide the basis for an exception in the concrete circumstances of the case.[17]

Another conception of good faith is described as a gateway for constitutional values to enter law. In Germany, for instance, the most important set of values used to explain further the notion of good faith, is found in the German Constitution. In this respect, the general clause of good faith in the German Civil Code (BGB §242) is seen as a means for applying these values (such as human personality) to private dealings and contracts.[18]

Finally, a classical definition of good faith in contract law refers to the need to take into account the legitimate interests of the other party.[19] The concretization of the concept, however, seems strictly related to the functions and roles given to it in a legal system.

3.1.2. Functions of Good Faith

The notion of good faith (*bona fides*) has its origins in Roman law. During the Middle Ages and the early modern period, the notion was absorbed into the broader notion of *aequitas* and *bona fides* and/or *aequitas* became a fundamental principle of medieval and early modern *lex mercatoria*.[20] Accordingly, *Caseragis* described good faith as "the prime mover and life-giving spirit of commerce" and *Baldus de Ubaldis* stated that "good faith is much required of those, who trade most".[21]

In Germany, the notion of good faith (*Treu und Glauben*) found its way into the German Civil Code of 1900 (BGB) §242 (on the performance

---

17 HESSELINK, M.W., "*The Concept of Good Faith*" in *Towards a European Civil Code*, Hartkamp et al (eds.), 4th ed., Kluwer Law International, Alphen aan den Rijn 2011, p. 621.

18 SCHLECHTRIEM, P., "*Good Faith in German Law and in International Uniform Laws*", Centro di studi e ricerche di diritto comparato e straniero diretto da M.J. Bonell, Saggi, Conferenze e Seminari 24, Rome 1997: https://www.cisg.law.pace.edu/cisg/biblio/schlechtriem16.html.

19 Storme points out that such a definition does indeed cover the field of good faith, STORME, M.E., "*Good Faith and the Contents of Contracts in European Private Law*", http://www.ejcl.org/71/art71-1.pdf.

20 WHITTAKER, S., ZIMMERMANN, R., "*Good faith in European Contract Law: surveying the legal landscape*" in *Good Faith in European Contract Law*, R. Zimmermann, S. Whittaker (eds.), Cambridge University Press, Cambridge 2000, p. 17.

21 Expressions taken from WHITTAKER, S., ZIMMERMANN, R., "*Good faith in European Contract Law: surveying the legal landscape*" in *Good Faith in European Contract Law*, R. Zimmermann, S. Whittaker (eds.), Cambridge University Press, Cambridge 2000, pp. 17–18.

of the debtor) and §157 (on the determination of the content of the contract). Although the notion of good faith referred to in the BGB seems to have a restricted field of operation, the applications of the notion in practice made of the §242 BGB "a legal principle of such persuasive influence that it is sometimes claimed the codified provisions could be dispensed with; the whole system of private law".[22]

As this persuasive influence of good faith in German practice led scholars to concretize the notion, Siebert, followed by other scholars, distinguished three functions of §242 BGB, which are: supplementation of duties, limitation of rights and *Wegfall der Geschäftsgrundlage*.[23] This third function, enabling courts to adjust terms of contracts to changed circumstances, is considered a rough equivalent of the common law doctrine of *frustration of purpose*.[24] The notion of changed circumstances will be examined further in detail.

In addition, there is the good faith interpretation based on §157. It is said that this trichotomy is based on Wieacker's assimilation of the functions of good faith to those which *Papinian* had attributed to the *praetorian* law: "*Ius praetorium est, quod praetores introduxerunt adiuvandi vel supplendi vel corrigendi iuris civilis gratia propter utilitatem publicam*."[25]

Although Wieacker considers *iuvare* as supplementation of duties, whereas under Roman law it is *supplere*, and the abuse of rights as (*exceptio doli*) *supplere*, whereas under Roman law it is seen as *corrigere*, this choice is explained by the fact that he was stating the functions of §242 BGB and not the functions of good faith. *Iuvare*, which is interpretation/concretization, is provided in §157 BGB, which made all the categories move down one place and created space for a fourth function.[26]

Hesselink points out that in most European legal systems good faith has three functions, which correspond to the functions that *Papinian*

---

22 SCHLECHTRIEM, P., "*Good Faith in German Law and in International Uniform Laws*", Centro di studi e ricerche di diritto comparato e straniero diretto da M.J. Bonell, Saggi, Conferenze e Seminari 24, Rome 1997, https://www.cisg.law.pace.edu/cisg/biblio/schlechtriem16.html.

23 HESSELINK, M.W., "*The Concept of Good Faith*" in *Towards a European Civil Code*, 4th ed., Kluwer Law International, The Hague 2011, pp. 624–625.

24 AUER, M., "*Good Faith: A Semiotic Approach*", 10(2) European Review of Contract Law 279 (2002), p. 286.

25 Digest. 1.1.7.1.

26 HESSELINK, M.W., "*The Concept of Good Faith*" in *Towards a European Civil Code*, 4th ed., Kluwer Law International, The Hague 2011, p. 627.

attributed to *praetorian* law: 1) concretization/interpretation (*adiuvare*); 2) supplementation (*supplere*); and 3) correction/limitation (*corrigere*). Sometimes a distinction is made between correction/limitation because of the improper behavior of a party and correction/limitation because of the changing circumstances, which creates a fourth function of good faith.[27]

The question now is: What are the roles that the principle can play within the framework of these different functions?

Beale extracts different possible roles that the principle may play (in terms of the PECL). Accordingly good faith may be seen as:

- a "*general principle*" that may either underline various norms of contract law without having any independent force and/or be used as a foundation for new legal developments;
- an "*interpretative device*" to interpret legal instruments or contract clauses in order to exclude any result that is contrary to good faith;
- a "*source of rules*" that go beyond interpretation of the express words either to exclude any result that seems contrary to good faith or to impose positive obligations;
- a "*general control mechanism*", either over the way the contract was made or over the substance of the contract.[28]

3.2. GOOD FAITH AND FAIR DEALING IN CISG, PICC, PECL AND DCFR

3.2.1. Related Articles

In terms of Article 1:201 PECL:

> (1) Each party must act in accordance with good faith and fair dealing.
> (2) The parties may not exclude or limit this duty.

---

27 HESSELINK, M.W., "*The Concept of Good Faith*" in *Towards a European Civil Code*, 3rd ed., Kluwer Law International, The Hague 2004, p. 627.

28 See, BEALE, H., "*General Clauses and Specific Rules in the Principles of European Contract Law: The 'Good Faith' Clause*" in *General Clauses and Standards in European Contract Law, Comparative Law, EC Law and Contract Law Codification*, Stefan Grundmann, Denis Mazeaud (eds.), Kluwer Law International, The Hague 2006, pp. 216–217.

Similarly, Article 1.7 PICC provides that:

(1) Each party must act in accordance with good faith and fair dealing in international trade.
(2) The parties may not exclude or limit this duty.

According to DCFR Article III.–1:103 (paragraphs (1) and (2)):

(1) A person has a duty to act in accordance with good faith and fair dealing in performing an obligation, in exercising a right to performance, in pursuing or defending a remedy for non-performance, or in exercising a right to terminate an obligation or contractual relationship.
(2) The duty may not be excluded or limited by contract or other juridical act.

It is, thus, important to say that all three instruments contain a restriction to freedom of contract on the basis of good faith and an express duty of good faith, which do not exist in the CISG. In fact, a proposal during the 1980 Vienna Conference to add a sentence to the wording of Article 6 CISG, stating that "the obligations of good faith, diligence and reasonable care prescribed by this Convention may not be excluded by agreement", was rejected by a substantial majority.[29]

However, as we will examine below, there are scholars who submit that a duty to act in accordance with good faith can be extracted from either Article 7(1) or Article 7(2) CISG;[30] Article 7 providing that:

(1) In the interpretation of this Convention, regard is to be had to its international character and to the need to promote uniformity in its application and the observance of good faith in international trade.
(2) Questions concerning matters governed by this Convention which are not expressly settled in it are to be settled in conformity with the general principles on which it is based or, in the absence of such principles, in conformity with the law applicable by virtue of the rules of private international law.

---

29 SCHROETER, U.G., "*Freedom of Contract: Comparison between Provisions of the CISG (Art. 6) and Counterpart Provisions of the Principles of European Contract Law*", July 2002: http://www.cisg.law.pace.edu/cisg/text/peclcomp6.html.

30 For an overview of different suggestions on this matter, see for instance, FARNSWORTH, E.A., "*Duties of Good Faith and Fair Dealing under the Unidroit Principles, Relevant International Conventions, and National Laws*", 3 Tulane Journal of International and Comparative Law 47–64 (1995); GOODE, R., KRONKE, H., MCKENDRICK, E., *Transnational Commercial Law, Text, Cases and Materials*, Oxford University Press, Oxford 2007, p. 233 et seq.

3.2.2. *PECL*

In the Comments on Article 1:201 PECL, it is stated that this article "sets forth a basic principle running through the Principles" and imposes upon each party "a duty to observe reasonable standards of fair dealing and to show due regard for the interests of the other party".

Good faith is required in the formation, performance and enforcement of the parties' duties and in the exercise of the parties' rights under a contract. Its content, however, to some extent, depends upon the content of parties' agreement. Although there are many special applications of the good faith and fair dealing principles throughout the PECL (as for instance in Article 6:102, providing that good faith and fair dealing is a factor which should be taken into account in the determination of the implied terms of a contract), the general good faith clause in Article 1:201 is broader than any of these applications.[31]

It should be emphasized that these specific rules requiring the exercise of good faith must always be read in conjunction with Article 1:201, for this is a mandatory rule, whereas the specific rules are not so designated and derive their mandatory force solely from Article 1:201.[32]

The concepts of "good faith" and "fair dealing" are used together in both PECL Article 1:201 and PICC Article 1.7. The authors of the PECL made a distinction between the two concepts in the comments on Article 1:201 PECL. Accordingly, while good faith refers to the subjective concepts of honesty and fairness in mind (a person should, for instance, not be entitled to exercise a remedy if his only purpose is to harm the other party), fair dealing is more related to the objective test of observance of fairness in fact.[33] It is also underlined by the authors of the PECL that in the French language both these concepts are covered by the expression "bonne foi" and in German by "Treu und Glauben".[34]

---

31 *Principles of the European Contract Law, Parts I and II*, Prepared by The Commission on European Contract Law, O. Lando and H. Beale (eds.), Kluwer Law International, The Hague 2000, p. 113.

32 GOODE, R., KRONKE, H., MCKENDRICK, E., *Transnational Commercial Law, Text, Cases and Materials*, Oxford University Press, Oxford 2007, p. 531.

33 *Principles of the European Contract Law, Parts I and II*, Prepared by The Commission on European Contract Law, O. Lando, H. Beale (eds.), Kluwer Law International, 2000, pp. 115–116.

34 *Principles of the European Contract Law, Parts I and II*, Prepared by The Commission on European Contract Law, O. Lando, H. Beale (eds.), Kluwer Law International, 2000, p. 116.

Another important matter is the relation between the terms "good faith and fair dealing" and "reasonableness". In the comments on the PECL, it is emphasized that the purpose of the concept of good faith and fair dealing is "to enforce community standards of decency, fairness and reasonableness in commercial transactions".[35] Article 1:302 states that, reasonableness is to be judged under the PECL, by "what persons acting in good faith and in the same situation as the parties would consider to be reasonable". Thus, the good faith principle also plays an important role in the determination of what should be considered reasonable in terms of the PECL. However, Beale criticizes the interchangeable use of two concepts in the PECL stating that "Having two provisions 'good faith and fair dealing' and 'reasonableness' suggests a difference between them; but often there seems to be none".[36]

As was submitted before, the recourse to the notions of reasonableness and reasonable expectations of the parties of a contract is especially used in English law, which does not recognize a general duty of good faith. The notion has long been used to provide piecemeal solutions in response to demonstrated problems of unfairness in the issues of interpretation and gap-filling, and the results that it leads to are dealt with in other legal systems by a general requirement of good faith.[37] Accordingly, Lord Steyn submitted that "There is not a world of a difference between the objective requirement of good faith and the reasonable expectations of the parties".[38]

As stated above, in the system of the PECL, however, the notion of reasonableness is used together with the notions of good faith and fair dealing, the latter being a factor to determine the content of the former. One of the important applications of the reasonableness test in the

---

35 *Principles of the European Contract Law, Parts I and II*, Prepared by The Commission on European Contract Law, O. Lando, H. Beale (eds.), Kluwer Law International, The Hague 2000, p. 113.

36 Beale gives the example of Art. 9:201 where the comments refer to the principles of good faith and fair dealing when the test is one of reasonableness. See, BEALE, H., "*General Clauses and Specific Rules in the Principles of European Contract Law: The 'Good Faith' Clause*" in *General Clauses and Standards in European Contract Law, Comparative Law, EC Law and Contract Law Codification*, Stefan Grundmann, Denis Mazeaud (eds.), Kluwer Law International, The Hague 2006, pp. 216–217.

37 See, WHITTAKER, S., ZIMMERMANN, R., "*Good faith in European Contract Law: surveying the legal landscape*" in *Good Faith in European Contract Law*, R. Zimmermann, S. Whittaker (eds.), Cambridge University Press, Cambridge 2000, pp. 45–46.

38 STEYN, J., "*Contract Law: Fulfilling the Reasonable Expectations of Honest Men*", 113 L.Q.R. 433 (1997), pp. 446–450.

context of this book is Article 5:101, which can be considered a special application of good faith, where the reasonable person criterion is used to determine the intentions of the parties by the application of the objective method of interpretation.

If we take an overview based on the system of the PECL concerning the relevance of the concepts of good faith and fair dealing principle in the context of this book, we can say that they apply both in interpretation and gap-filling processes. Concerning the interpretation process, the notions play an important role first in determination of the parties' intention by using the objective method (via the reasonableness test as stated above),[39] second in the recourse to the relevant circumstances in interpreting a contract (Article 5:102) and third they underlie certain rules of interpretation such as the *contra proferentem* rule, which aims to prevent unfair clauses in contracts.[40]

Concerning the gap-filling process, Article 6:102 provides that the good faith and fair dealing principle is one of the criteria to determine the implied terms of a contract.

Moreover, the notion of reasonableness is used on several occasions in the gap-fillers existing in the PECL, especially in the determination of price. Furthermore, if we use the term "determination of the content of a contract" in a broader sense, meaning not only the techniques of determination of the content of a contract – namely the processes of interpretation and gap-filling – but also the special applications existing in the PECL, the field of application of the good faith principle in this context will be more than it is submitted here.

A last point concerning the role of the good faith principle in the interpretation and gap-filling processes is that the requirements of good faith and fair dealing should also be taken into account in the interpretation of the provisions of the PECL on interpretation and gap-filling. Indeed, Article 1:106(1) states that, "These Principles should be interpreted and developed in accordance with their purposes. In particular, regard should be had to the need to promote good faith and fair dealing, certainty in contractual relationships and uniformity of application".

---

39 Cf. DiMATTEO, L.A., DHOOGE, L.J., GREENE, S., MAURER, V.G., PAGNATTARO, M.A., *International Sales Law A Critical Analysis of CISG Jurisprudence*, Cambridge University Press, Cambridge 2005, p. 28: "Reasonable person is seen as always acting in good faith."

40 The *Contra proferentem* rule is examined above in specific rules of interpretation.

3.2.3. DCFR

The field of application of the principle of good faith and fair dealing in the DCFR in terms of this book is quite similar to that of the PECL. Besides the general provision of Article III.–1:103, recognizing a duty to act in good faith, the DCFR contain several special applications of the principle in the process of determination of the content of the contract.

Like in the PECL, in the DCFR good faith is also a relevant factor to be taken into account in both subjective and objective interpretation tests (Article II.-8:102). Moreover, good faith and fair dealing is a criterion to be used in the implication of an additional term into the contract (Article II.-9:101(2)). The principle is also an underlying principle of some specific rules of interpretation such as the *contra proferentem rule* and the *preference to negotiated terms* provision, which complements the former rule.

The DCFR defines good faith and fair dealing as referring to a standard of conduct characterized by honesty, openness and consideration for the interests of the other party to the transaction or relationship in question.[41] Unlike the PECL, the DCFR article on the definition of reasonableness does not refer to good faith and fair dealing. Instead it provides that reasonableness is to be objectively ascertained, having regard to the nature and purpose of what is being done, to the circumstances of the case, and to any relevant usages and practices.[42]

Finally, good faith and fair dealing is an underlying principle to be taken into account in the interpretation and development of the DCFR and thus applies also to the interpretation of the interpretation rules contained in this instrument.[43]

3.2.4. PICC

In the Comments on Article 1.7 stated above of the UNIDROIT Principles, "good faith and fair dealing are presented as a fundamental idea underlying the Principles" and it is submitted that even in the absence of special provisions, the parties' behaviors throughout the life of a contract must conform with good faith and fair dealing.[44]

---

41 Article I.-1.103(1).
42 Article I.-1:104.
43 Article I.-1:102(3).
44 Official Comments on Articles of the UNIDROIT Principles 2016, Article 1.7.

It is also put forward by the authors of the PICC that as the Principles are essentially conceived to be applied to international commercial contracts, reference is made to "good faith and fair dealing in international trade" so that the concepts should not be construed based on the standards of a particular national law which are not accepted among various legal systems. Instead, the principle should be construed taking into account both the special context of international trade and the special context of the contract such as the sizes and skill levels of the parties.[45]

Schlechtriem suggests that this restriction and directive of the PICC for the search for the standards of good faith and fair dealing in so far as they must exist in international trade, render most national judgments based on national convictions of what constitutes good faith and fair dealing almost useless even if, despite the warnings of the commentary on Article 1.7, courts and arbitrators will continue to some extent to inject convictions based on their national law and tradition into what they consider good faith and fair dealing in international trade.[46]

According to Schlechtriem, the absence of such a limitation concerning the determination of the content of good faith and fair dealing in the PECL might render the PECL prone to being interpreted in the light of particular national convictions.[47] But it is also submitted that the concept of "good faith and fair dealing in international trade", which is not defined in the PICC, is no more precise than existing national notions of good faith.[48]

However, as Magnus underlines, first, there might be business branches with long-standing tradition where an international standard of good faith already exists. Secondly, such standards can be developed by business circles, arbitrators and courts especially for fresh and modern

45 Official Comments on Articles of the UNIDROIT Principles 2016, Article 1.7.

46 SCHLECHTRIEM, P., "*Good Faith in German Law and in International Uniform Laws*", Centro di studi e ricerche di diritto comparato e straniero diretto da M.J. Bonell, Saggi, Conferenze e Seminari 24, Rome 1997, https://www.cisg.law.pace.edu/cisg/biblio/schlechtriem16.html.

47 SCHLECHTRIEM, P., "*Good Faith in German Law and in International Uniform Laws*", Centro di studi e ricerche di diritto comparato e straniero diretto da M.J. Bonell, Saggi, Conferenze e Seminari 24, Rome 1997, https://www.cisg.law.pace.edu/cisg/biblio/schlechtriem16.html.

48 See BARNES, N.J., "*Good Faith under the UNIDROIT Principles of International Commercial Contracts: A Struggle for Meaning*", http://www.dundee.ac.uk/cepmlp/car/html/CAR9_ARTICLE14.pdf.

trade branches.[49] Indeed, the arbitral awards giving judgment in a multitude of situations and in a variety of trade can be guidance in interpreting this concept,[50] and the help of neutral experts, like the International Chamber of Commerce in the case of usages, may be required.[51]

Although, the PICC refer to the reasonableness test on several occasions, the meaning of this term is not defined in the text of the PICC. However, it should be understood from the text that, like the PECL, the PICC also refer to "reasonableness" and to "good faith and fair dealing" as two different concepts (may be partly overlapping but different) because, as we will examine below, in Article 4.8 on supplementation of an omitted term, reasonableness and good faith are shown as two different factors to be taken into account.

For the PICC also, "good faith and fair dealing" plays an important role in the fields of interpretation and gap-filling. First, the objective method of interpretation is also prescribed in the PICC for the interpretation of both the contract and the statements or other conduct of a party (Articles 4.1 and 4.2).

Although, unlike the PECL, good faith and fair dealing are not stated as factors to be taken into account in having recourse to the relevant circumstances in the interpretation of the contracts (Article 4.3), some of the applications of Article 4.3 show that the concepts could also play a role in this matter via the reference by Article 4.3 to the conduct of the parties as one of the relevant factors to be taken into account in the interpretation process.

Other than these applications of good faith in the interpretation process, the PICC refer both to "good faith and fair dealing" and the "reasonableness" test in the supplementation of an omitted term (Article 4.8) and the determination of an implied obligation. Good faith and fair dealing also play an important role in the interpretation of the gap-fillers existing in the PICC especially via the reasonableness test

---

49 MAGNUS, U., "*Guide to Article 7, Comparison with UNIDROIT Principles of International Commercial Contracts*", Editorial Remarks, http://www.cisg.law.pace.edu/cisg/principles/uni7.html.

50 See VAN HOUTTE, H., "*The UNIDROIT Principles of International Commercial Contracts*", 2 Int'l Trade & Bus L. Ann. 1 (1996), p. 12.

51 SCHLECHTRIEM, P., "*Good Faith in German Law and in International Uniform Laws*", Centro di studi e ricerche di diritto comparato e straniero diretto da M.J. Bonell, Saggi, Conferenze e Seminari 24, Rome 1997, https://www.cisg.law.pace.edu/cisg/biblio/schlechtriem16.html.

(e.g. Article 5.1.6 on the determination of the quality of performance, Article 5.1.7. on the determination of the price etc.) and as an underlying principle of some interpretation rules such as the *contra proferentem* rule.

Apart from these, the concepts can be used in the interpretation of the provisions on interpretation and gap-filling, even if there is not any express reference to them in Article 1.6 on the Interpretation and the Supplementation of the Principles. Indeed, in Article 1.6(2), it is provided that, "Issues within the scope of these Principles but not expressly settled by them are so far as possible to be settled in accordance with their underlying general principles" and in the Comments on Article 1.7 stated above, "good faith and fair dealing" is classified as an underlying principle of the PICC.

3.2.5. CISG

The CISG contains no express provision that imposes a duty of good faith on the parties. As stated above, a proposal to include a duty of good faith in the Article 6 was rejected by a substantial majority during the Vienna Conference.

Three main reasons for this rejection are shown: First, at the time of the CISG, common lawyers (especially English lawyers) were more hostile to the recognition of the duty of good faith than they are now, secondly the CISG (unlike the PICC and PECL) would have a binding character and be part of the legal systems and thirdly, there was the desire to ensure that as many states as possible ratified the Convention.[52] But the good faith principle was not rejected as a whole, and found its place in Article 7(1), referring to good faith in international trade as a maxim in the interpretation of the CISG. This reference by the Article 7(1) to good faith is seen as a result of the compromise between civil lawyers, who wished to see good faith as a positive obligation directed to the parties' behavior, and common lawyers (especially English lawyers), who thought that such a duty would lead to uncertainty in the determination of the rights and obligations of the contracting parties.[53]

52 GOODE, R., KRONKE, H., MCKENDRICK, E., *Transnational Commercial Law, Text, Cases and Materials*, Oxford University Press, 2007, p. 528.

53 GOODE, R., KRONKE, H., MCKENDRICK, E., *Transnational Commercial Law, Text, Cases and Materials*, Oxford University Press, 2015, p. 233; Klein describes the negotiations concerning Article 7 as "hotly contested", see KLEIN, J., "*Good Faith in International Transactions*", 15 Liverpool Law Rev. 115 (1993), p. 121; Farnsworth describes the provision as a "hard-won compromise" that the "troubled history" of

As to the Article 7(2) CISG, it refers to the "general principles" on which the Convention is based for supplementation purposes. However, the questions concerning the recognition of a duty of good faith by the CISG seem not to have been settled after the adoption of the CISG as it is.

The main issue that remains to be decided is whether CISG should, despite its drafting history, be interpreted dynamically in order to extract such a duty. If adopted, a dynamic interpretation should allow articles 7 and 8 to combine into a general duty of good faith.[54] The question whether the CISG imposes a duty of good faith on the parties is answered mainly in three different ways in legal literature:[55]

First, there are scholars who claim that the history of the Convention (the rejection of the proposal) and the content of Article 7 exclude the possibility to extract such a duty from the terms of the Convention. This view, based upon the literal reading of the Convention, sees good faith as a criterion to be applied by judges and arbitrators only in the interpretation of the CISG. In favor of this solution, Farnsworth submitted that a result which will impose a duty of good faith on the parties of contracts governed by the CISG would let "a general principle of good faith in by the back door".[56] Honnold, who suggests that the good faith principle (which is a "common core" of meaning) should be promoted by a liberal interpretation of some provisions of the CISG (on formation, performance or remedies), rejects a general duty of good faith, but gives important content to the good faith principle as an interpretative device.[57]

Felemegas, also in favor of this first solution, supports that when the legislative history of the Convention is taken into account it can be deduced that the principle finds a limited field of application in terms of

---

the Convention demonstrates. See FARNSWORTH, E.A., "*Duties of Good Faith and Fair Dealing under the Unidroit Principles, Relevant International Conventions*, and National Laws", 3 Tulane Journal of International and Comparative Law 47 (1995), p. 56.

54 See ANDERSEN BAASCH, C., "*Good Faith? Good Grief!*" 17 Int'l Trade and Bus. L. Rev. 310 (2014), pp. 317–318.

55 See FARNSWORTH, E.A., "*Duties of Good Faith and Fair Dealing under the Unidroit Principles, Relevant International Conventions, and National Laws*", 3 Tulane Journal of International and Comparative Law 47–64 (1995); GOODE, R., KRONKE, H., MCKENDRICK, E., *Transnational Commercial Law, Text, Cases and Materials*, Oxford University Press, Oxford 2015, p. 233, §8.37.

56 See FARNSWORTH, E.A., "*Duties of Good Faith and Fair Dealing under the Unidroit Principles, Relevant International Conventions, and National Laws*", 3 Tulane Journal of International and Comparative Law 47–64 (1995).

57 HONNOLD, J.O., *Uniform Law for International Sales*, 3rd ed., Kluwer Law International, The Hague 1999, pp. 100–101.

covering cases that involve interpretation of the CISG to promote good faith in international trade. Although he acknowledges that the "highest degree of confusion is generated by the legitimate recognition of good faith as a 'general principle' of the CISG" for *praeter legem* gap-filling purposes, he strongly rejects any recognition of a positive duty to act in good faith.[58]

According to a second view, Article 7(1) CISG imposes a positive duty of good faith. According to this point of view, "interpretation does not exist in the abstract; it inevitably impacts on the rights and duties".[59]

In favor of this solution, Bonell points out that "the need to promote … the observance of good faith in international trade" stated in Article 7(1) is also necessarily directed to the parties to each individual contract of sale.[60]

Eörsi also suggests that interpretation of the contract and the Convention cannot be separated "since the Convention is necessarily interpreted by the parties also; after all, the Convention constitutes the law of the parties insofar as they do not make use of the Article 6 on freedom of contract."[61] Accordingly, a distinction between good faith interpretation of the Convention and the obligation of the parties to act in good faith seems likely to be "more apparent than real".[62]

Besides, as Koneru rightly stresses, if good faith in international trade were to be promoted, how else can this goal be reached other than by requiring the parties to behave in good faith? Accordingly, "good faith

58 FELEMEGAS, J., *The United Nations Convention on Contracts for the International sale of Goods: Article 7 and Uniform Interpretation*, Kluwer Law International, The Hague 2000–01. See also Baasch Andersen who states that "The drafting history of the CISG makes it clear that they rejected the notion of good faith", ANDERSEN BAASCH, C., "*Good Faith? Good Grief!*", 17 Int'l Trade & Bus. L. Rev. 310 (2014), p. 318. See also ICC Arbitration Case No: 8611/1997: http://www.unilex.info/case.cfm?id=229: The arbitrators stated that Article 7(1) concerns only the interpretation of the Convention.

59 GOODE, R., KRONKE, H., MCKENDRICK, E., *Transnational Commercial Law, Text, Cases and Materials*, Oxford University Press, Oxford 2015, p. 235.

60 BONELL, M.J., "*Interpretation of Convention*" in *The Commentary on the International Sales Law*, C.M. Bianca, M.J. Bonell (eds.), Giuffrè, Milan 1987, pp. 84–85. See for instance Munich Court of Appeal, 8 February 1995, No. 7 U 1720/94, http://cisgw3.law.pace.edu/cases/950208g1.html where the court directly imposed a duty of good faith to the parties where CISG applied.

61 EORSI, G., "*General Provisions*" in *The UN Convention on Contracts for the International Sale of Goods*, N.M. Galston and H. Smit (eds.), Matthew Bender, New York 1984, [2.03].

62 HERBOTS, J.H., "*What Precisely is Interpretation?*" in *Elgar Encyclopedia of Comparative Law*, 2nd ed., Jan M. Smits (ed.), Edward Elgar, Cheltenham 2012, p. 444.

cannot exist in a vacuum and does not remain in practice as a rule unless the actors are required to participate."[63]

In favor of a solution according to which a positive duty of good faith under the CISG would be recognized, DiMatteo also suggests that interpretation of the CISG to promote "the observance of good faith in international trade" can be read to imply a good faith obligation. Moreover, the author emphasizes that other provisions of the CISG can also be read in this direction in order to extract a positive duty of good faith, in a similar manner to the authors adopting the third approach, which will be presented below. Accordingly, he refers to the "reasonable person criterion" set forth by the above-mentioned general rules of interpretation, stating that "a reasonable person is generally taken to act and react in a good faith manner" and to Article 9(2) which imply "trade usage and custom" into every contract of sale, supporting that good faith is a universal trade usage or custom. He finally puts forward that the recognition of a duty of good faith is consistent with the goals of the Convention and may also be implied through positive reading of its express articles. For this purpose he gives the example of Article 77, which expressly adopts the duty to mitigate as "the nonbreaching party's duty to mitigate is the counterpart to the breaching party's duty of good faith performance".[64]

Another controversy arises in the literature in relation with the mandatory character of Article 7 CISG. According to Bonell, Article 7 CISG should be considered a mandatory rule. In favor of this

---

63 KONERU, P., "*The International Interpretation of the UN Convention on Contracts for the International Sale of Goods: An Approach Based on General Principles*", 6 Minnesota Journal of Global Trade 105 (1997), pp. 138–141.

64 DiMATTEO, L.A., "*The CISG and the Presumption of Enforceability: Unintended Contractual Liability in International Business Dealings*", 22 Yale Journal of International Law 111 (1997), pp. 145–146. Other authors also held that it is necessary to accept a general duty of good faith addressed to the parties in terms of the CISG. See for instance, Klein, stating that "while the CISG's only explicit reference to good faith is directed at those charged with the interpretation of the Convention, many of the provisions directed at parties to CISG contracts would be rendered meaningless without recognizing a general good faith obligation": KLEIN, J., "*Good Faith in International Transactions*", 15 Liverpool Law Rev. 115 (1993), p. 124; see also Keily who stresses that the Convention "must be regarded as an autonomous system, capable of generating new rules. If good faith truly is a principle recognised internationally, then the CISG should be allowed to reflect this development to its full extent. To suggest otherwise is to confine the CISG to its historical vacuum." KEILY, T., "*Good Faith and the Vienna Convention on Contracts for the International Sale of Goods (CISG)*", 3(1) Vinodoba Journal of International Commercial Law and Arbitration 15 (1999), p. 40.

approach, he says that any legislation has to be interpreted in accordance with the criteria specifically laid down in it or generally adopted within the legal system it emanates. Thus, the parties to an international sales contract are free to choose between the application of the Convention and the application of a particular domestic law. Once they have accepted that their contract be governed by the Convention, the Convention must be applied in accordance with the interpretation established in Article 7. Thus to permit the parties to derogate from Article 7 by agreeing on rules of interpretation used with respect to ordinary domestic legislation would be inconsistent with the international character of the Convention and jeopardize the Convention's ultimate aim.[65]

Schroeter points out that parties may always use Article 6 on freedom of contract of the Convention to derogate from *any* of its provisions, including Article 7. In that respect, he suggests that parties may agree upon the application of the CISG "as interpreted by German Courts" or "as construed according to the principles of English law".[66] In my opinion, such contractual clauses do not have any concrete content. First, this is because there is no such thing as "the CISG interpreted by German Courts". The aim of the CISG is to be interpreted uniformly and this exactly the rationale behind the existence of the Convention. Secondly, it would be a useless effort to "construe the CISG according to the principles of English Law" because it is an autonomous international set of rules and these characteristics should necessarily be taken into account in its interpretation.

Third, it is suggested to consider good faith as a general principle on which the Convention is based and apply Article 7(2) in order to impose a duty of good faith on the parties. It should be emphasized that although the term good faith is not directly referred to in the various articles of the Convention, the term reasonableness *is*. Zeller points out 37 provisions in the CISG (the most important of which being Article 8(2)) where reference to the term "reasonable" is made.[67]

---

65 BONELL, M.J., "*Interpretation of Convention*" in *The Commentary on the International Sales Law*, C.M. Bianca, M.J. Bonell (eds.), Giuffrè, Milan 1987, pp. 93–94.

66 SCHROETER, U.G., "*Freedom of Contract: Comparaison between Provisions of the CISG (Art. 6) and Counterpart Provisions of the Principles of European Contract Law*", July 2002, http://www.cisg.law.pace.edu/cisg/text/peclcomp6.html.

67 ZELLER, B., "*Four-Corners – The Methodology for Interpretation and Application of the UN Convention on Contracts for the International Sale of Goods*", May 2003, PhD Thesis at the University of Melbourne, http://www.cisg.law.pace.edu/cisg/biblio/4corners.html, fn 451.

Schlechtriem, in favor of this third solution, puts forward that although the rejection of a good faith rule may be regretted, its function can probably be fulfilled by the rule that the parties must conduct themselves according to the standard of the "reasonable person" as it is expressly described in a number of provisions, and therefore must be regarded as a general principle of the Convention by virtue of Article 7(2).[68]

According to Sim, such a proposition cannot be accepted because of the lack of coherent content of the principle of good faith in the Convention. She submits that Article 7(1) is not in itself sufficient to extract a general principle of good faith and the consistency of the articles of the Convention with ideas of fairness and reasonableness is no surprise because most of the rules are consistent with these ideas, but the individual consistency of these rules is not sufficient to extract a general principle. Furthermore, "imposition of substantive obligations of good faith on contracting parties would undermine the objective of the CISG to promote certainty and predictability in international trade."[69]

If we turn to the provisions of the CISG on the interpretation of "contracts",[70] namely to Article 8, we observe that no reference is made to a good faith principle. The reasonable person criterion, however, is used concerning the objective method of interpretation.

Although the Convention does not give any definition of reasonableness or the reasonable person, it is submitted that the definition of the concept in the PECL also fits the manner in which this concept is used in the CISG and that this definition can help researchers apply reasonableness to the

68 SCHLECHTRIEM, P., *Uniform Sales Law – The UN Convention on Contracts for the International Sale of Goods*, Manz, Vienna 1986, p. 39. See also Weiszberg, who considers reasonableness as an inductive general principle of the CISG and although not explicitly stated as a general principle, an essential preoccupation of the authors, WEISZBERG, G., "*Le raisonnable en Droit du Commerce International*", http://www.cisg.law.pace.edu/cisg/biblio/Reasonableness.html, §258. For special applications of the principle of good faith throughout the CISG see for instance, KASTELY, A.H., "*Unification and Community: A Rhetorical Analysis of the United Nations Sales Convention*", Symposium: Reflections on the International Unification of Sales Law, 8 Nw. J. Int'l. L. & Bus. 574 (1988), pp. 596–597; KLEIN, J., "*Good Faith in International Transactions*", 15 Liverpool L. Rev. 115 (1993), p. 124 et seq.

69 SIM, D., "*The Scope and Application of Good Faith in the Vienna Convention on Contracts for the International Sale of Goods*", http://www.cisg.law.pace.edu/cisg/biblio/sim1.html.

70 In its Article 8, CISG do not use the term contract but statements and other conduct of the parties.

CISG provisions in which it is specifically mentioned and as a general principle of the Convention.[71]

As the PECL make an interchangeable and thus a rather confusing use of the concepts of reasonableness and good faith and fair dealing, in this author's opinion the above-mentioned definition of reasonableness provided by the DCFR should be preferred, as it also could serve better in the development of an autonomous content of reasonableness in time on a case-by-case basis in terms of the CISG.

The development of an autonomous content of the principle of good faith seems, however, to be quite difficult. Indeed, the principle of good faith is a very fundamental and yet very broad concept which has different applications in national laws. It is not surprising to observe that judges may follow the homeward trend and transfer their understanding of the principle based on national laws without generally further discussing the autonomous content of the principle in the context of international commercial contracts governed by the CISG.[72]

German courts, for instance, will generally be susceptible to referring to good faith and fair dealing more extensively than other courts. Thus, uniformity of application will always be an issue whether the first, the second or the third approach is followed. This, however, should not mean that all three approaches are equal in terms of uniform application of the rules provided by the Convention.

If the first approach is accepted, the answer would be sought in the rules of private international law and domestic laws would apply to problems of fairness.[73] I think that such a solution would undermine certainty and predictability in international transactions even more than

---

71 See "*Reasonableness, Overview Comments*", KRITZER, A.H., (ed.), http://www.cisg.law.pace.edu/cisg/text/reason.html.

72 On this matter see for instance, ANDERSEN BAASCH, C., "*Good Faith? Good Grief!*", 17 Int'l Trade and Bus. L. Rev. 310–321 (2014), claiming that good faith in the context of international commercial law is a source of homeward trends and "*faux amis*", which ceased to be useful and must be either clarified or abolished. According to Sim, "while some semblance of an international doctrine may finally emerge, this would be extremely long time in coming and would undermine the certainty, predictability and stability in international transactions in the meantime": SIM, D., "*The Scope and Application of Good Faith in the Vienna Convention on Contracts for the International Sale of Goods*", 2001, http://www.cisg.law.pace.edu/cisg/biblio/sim1.html. In the same direction see SHEEHY, B., "*Good Faith in the CISG: The Interpretation Problems of Article 7*": https://papers.ssrn.com/sol3/papers.cfm?abstract_id=777105, especially at pp. 45 et seq.

73 See FARNSWORTH, E.A., "*Duties of Good Faith and Fair Dealing under the Unidroit Principles, Relevant International Conventions, and National Laws*", 3 Tulane Journal of International and Comparative Law 47 (1995), p. 57.

any difficulties that we might have in determining a uniform content of the principle in terms of the CISG. If we consider the broadness of the field of application of the principle,[74] it is clear that such a solution would make an autonomous and uniform application of CISG rules even more impossible and would not be consistent with the interpretation objectives put forward in Article 7. This, in my opinion, cannot be the goal of the authors of the Convention. Besides, interpretation does indeed not exist in the abstract and it inevitably impacts on the rights and duties.[75]

It should also be noted that the recognition of a general duty of good faith in terms of CISG would pave the way for the use of other harmonized instruments which recognize such a duty (especially of the PICC which has the most closest scope of application to the CISG) in order to interpret and supplement CISG Article 8 and could help in the development of an autonomous international content to be applied to international commercial contracts. On this matter Magnus writes that both the CISG and the Principles acknowledge that good faith plays an important role for international contracts. He further explains that both texts do not exclusively rely on one abstract and general rule of good faith but try to specify the concept by more specific rules that elaborate on the principle in some detail. Accordingly, "combining the CISG and the Principles one gets a good impression of what good faith in international commercial relations should and could mean".[76]

If such a duty is rejected, in my opinion, recourse to non-binding instruments such as the PICC or PECL in order to interpret or supplement CISG rules on interpretation and gap-filling would lose both its foundation (in cases where the parties did not expressly referred to these instruments) and its practicality, as the general duty to act in good faith is an omnipresent principle in all aspects of interpretation and gap-filling in the system of these instruments.

These points gain even greater importance if one considers the fact that when it comes to the determination of the content of the contract,

---

74 On this matter see also CREMADES, B.M., "*Good Faith in International Arbitration*", 27(4) Am. U. Int'l L. Rev. 761 (2012), p. 787: "The fact that principle of good faith appears in one form or another in the majority of arbitral awards is clear evidence of its importance in international arbitration".

75 See p. 115 above.

76 See MAGNUS, U., "*Die allegemeinen Grundsatze im UN-Kaufrecht*" (General principles under the UN Sales Convention (English Translation), 3 International Trade and Business Law Annual vol. III, Australian Institute of Foreign and Comparative Law, 1997, §25.

rules provided by Articles 8 and 9 CISG fall quite short in covering all the aspects of the issue, as they are not as detailed as the provisions contained in other harmonized instruments, including the PICC. The acceptance of a general duty of good faith could at least lead to a "relative uniformity" even if an absolute uniformity of application is unrealistic.[77]

It should be noted that rejecting the first view does not eliminate all the problems related with the use of the PICC or PECL in interpreting and supplementing Article 8 CISG.

Indeed, the third view, suggested by Schlechtriem, considers reasonableness as a synonym of good faith more or less in the line with the PECL. This is, however, rather confusing because the two concepts may or may not have the same content.[78] Even the PECL, which use these concepts interchangeably, refer to both concepts distinctly, which suggests that there is a difference between the two.

The PICC do not define reasonableness but, as will be seen in the first chapter, they show reasonableness and good faith as two different sources of supplementation of the contract and thus make a distinction between them. Thus, in my opinion, the best solution to be adopted is the second solution, which does not refer to reasonableness in accepting a general duty to act in good faith in terms of the CISG.

4. CASE LAW

Examples of decisions where courts refer to Article 8 together with the good faith principle will be examined below in order to see how the principle plays a role in cases where Article 8 is applied.

---

77 For this concept, see DiMATTEO, L.A., DHOOGE, L.J., GREENE, S., MAURER, V.G., PAGNATTARO, M.A., *International Sales Law A Critical Analysis of CISG Jurisprudence*, Cambridge University Press, Cambridge 2005, p. 10.

78 For different meanings of "good faith" see BEALE, H., "*General Clauses and Specific Rules in the Principles of European Contract Law: The 'Good Faith' Clause*" in *General Clauses and Standards in European Contract Law, Comparative Law, EC Law and Contract Law Codification*, Stefan Grundmann, Denis Mazeaud (eds.), Kluwer law Interational, 2006, p. 208. Accordingly, good faith can mean "merely not in bad faith", "must take the other party's interests before his own", "must not do something against the other party's interests that no reasonable person would do" or "must act reasonably". For the difference between the last two meanings see *Paragon Finance plc. v. Nash* [2001] EWCA Civ. 1466, [2001] 1 WLR 685 (pet. dis. [2002] 1 WLR 2263) cited by Beale.

In a German case,[79] the court rejected the buyer's view that the contractual exclusion in question violated the principle of good faith after underlining that "although that principle is relevant in general in the application of the CISG, the circumstances of this case gave no reason to rely on this principle in favor of the defendant". Therefore, according to this decision, for matters covered by the CISG, the principle of good faith also applies to interpretation of contractual terms under Article 8.

In a Chinese Arbitration Award,[80] it was pointed out that the general provisions of the CISG stipulated the principle of good faith in international trade. Arbitrators read Article 8 in the light of the good faith principle and concluded that the buyer's allegation was not consistent with this principle, so not established according to the laws.

Similarly, in the Swiss decision of 12 December 2006,[81] it is held that the good faith principle is an important guideline for contractual interpretation in the light of Article 8 CISG and that "Even if not expressly mentioned, the principle of good faith always applies in any event".

The Brazilian decision of 20 May 2009 followed the same approach. Indeed, in this case, the Appellate Court held that the buyer did not act as a reasonable businessman in the same circumstances with reference to Article 8(3) of the CISG and reinforced the doctrine that the confidence and expectations generated between the parties are guided by the contractual principle of good faith. The Court held that the principle of good faith provides a basis for the expectation that contractual duties will be duly performed and that it requires a model of conduct socially accepted by the parties at the time of the conclusion of the contract. In this respect, "it imposes a code of behavior on both parties, calling on each to consider the interests of the other contracting party. These codes represent a collaborative component within the contractual relationship".[82]

---

79 Germany, 5 October 1998 Appellate Court Hamburg (*Circuit boards case*): http://cisgw3.law.pace.edu/cases/981005g1.html. Translation by Ruth M. Janal.

80 http://cisgw3.law.pace.edu/cases/000331c1.html. China, 31 March 2000, CIETAC Arbitration proceeding (*Methyl methacrylate monomer case*), translation by Zheng Xie; Meihua Xu (ed.).

81 Switzerland, 12 December 2006, Canton Appellate Court Thurgau (*Building materials case*): http://cisgw3.law.pace.edu/cases/061212s1.html. Translation by Veit Konrad, Jan Henning Berg (ed.).

82 Brazil, 20 May 2009 Tribunal de Justiça Rio Grande do Sul [Appellate Court] (*Electro-erosion machine case*) translation by Luiz Gustavo Meira Moser: http://cisgw3.law.pace.edu/cases/090520b5.html.

In the same line, in the German case of 12 November 2001,[83] the court considered the good faith principle embodied in Article 7 on the interpretation of the Convention as implying an obligation on the parties of the contract in question to act according to good faith. Thus, the conduct of the parties was interpreted in accordance with the observation of good faith.[84]

Similarly, in a Russian Arbitration case,[85] it was ruled that even if the supplement in question was concluded in unclear circumstances, the seller's subsequent conduct proved the existence of its obligation to deliver the goods as performance under this supplement. The Court held that this reasoning corresponds to the provisions of Article 8 CISG and the principle of good faith in international trade on which the CISG is based.

In a Dutch case,[86] a similar approach has been adopted and the court held that, in accordance with the principle of good faith to be upheld in international trade (Article 7 CISG), the seller should have informed the buyer if it did not have the intention to apply an international standard of quality to the goods.

In a French case[87] the court stated that in interpreting the elements of the evidence that were put before the court "with respect to the principles set out in Article 8 CISG, and namely the principle which states that the contracts must be interpreted in good faith", the Court of Appeal was able to deduce that the agreement contained reciprocal obligations to deliver and purchase determined goods, at an agreed price such that it constituted a sale, which was subject to the Vienna Convention of 11 April 1980.

---

83 Appellate Court Hamm (*Memory module case*): http://cisgw3.law.pace.edu/cases/011112g1.html.

84 See also Serbia, 28 January 2008 Foreign Trade Court attached to the Serbian Chamber of Commerce (*Siemens Telephone Booths case*): http://cisgw3.law.pace.edu/cases/080128sb.html. Translation by Marija Marosan, Milena Djordjevich and Marco Jovanovic (eds.): The buyer could have refused the delivery. Even his complete indifference could have been considered as a refusal and could be explained by the fact that he did not know that the place of delivery was changed (although, only the opposite can be concluded from the witness statements). In such a case, he would not have to act. However, he did not remain passive.

85 Russia, 13 April 2006 Arbitration proceeding 105/2005: http://cisgw3.law.pace.edu/cases/060413r1.html. Translation by Alexandre Morari.

86 Netherlands, 23 April 2003, Appellate Court's-Gravenhage (*Rynpoort Trading v. Meneba Meel*): http://cisgw3.law.pace.edu/cases/030423n1.html. Translation by Patrick Bout.

87 France, 30 June 2004, Supreme Court (*Société Romay AG v. SARL Behr France*): http://cisgw3.law.pace.edu/cases/040630f1.html. Translation by Julia Hoffmann.

Similarly in a Russian Arbitration Award[88] it is held that the claimant failed to act in accordance with one of the basic principles of international trade, i.e. the principle of good faith as laid down in general terms in Article 1.7 of the UNIDROIT Principles and Articles 7 and 8 of the CISG. This, according to Article 5.1.2 of the UNIDROIT Principles, is an implied obligation which – as stated in Comments 1 to 3 to Article 1.7 of the UNIDROIT Principles – the parties have to observe throughout the life of the contract.

In a German decision,[89] it was also held that

> According to Article 8 CISG in conjunction with the principle of good faith, it has to be considered in this respect, whether the clause differs from the expectation of the contractual partner to such an extent that the latter cannot reasonably be expected to have anticipated that such a clause might be included.

In the Swiss case of 26 November 2008[90] the court also read Article 8 in conjunction with the principle of good faith, stating that in cases where an actual concurrence of intent remains unproven in court, Article 8(2) provides that a presumptive intent may be determined. The court further commented that, for this purpose, the declarations of the parties must be interpreted according to their reasonable meaning in the light of wording, context and the principle of good faith, underlining also that such an interpretation according to the principle of good faith seeks to determine the normative consensus, while the crucial factor will be an interpretation from the perspective of the recipient.

In a Finnish case, however,[91] the District Court and the Court of Appeal applied the principle of loyalty which "has been widely recognized in scholarly writings" by stressing that "According to this principle, the parties to a contract have to act in favor of the common goal; they have to reasonably consider the interests of the other party".

---

88 Russia, 8 February 2008, Arbitration proceeding 18/2007 (*Natural gas case*). See the abstract in http://www.unilex.info/case.cfm?pid=1&do=case&id=1497&step=Abstract.

89 Germany, 12 June 2008, District Court Landshut (*Metalic slabs case*): http://cisgw3.law.pace.edu/cases/080612g2.html. Translation by Daniel Nagel.

90 Switzerland, 26 November 2008, *Handelsgericht* [Commercial Court] Aargau (*Fruit and vegetables case*): http://cisgw3.law.pace.edu/cases/081126s1.html. Translation by Jan Henning Berg.

91 Finland, 26 October 2000, Helsinki Court of Appeals (*Plastic carpets case*): http://cisgw3.law.pace.edu/cases/001026f5.html.

In the editorial remarks on the case, Kuoppala[92] points out that by this decision the status of good faith as a general principle of the Convention regulating the parties' behavior is not, at least according to the literal meaning of the Convention, confirmed. Thus, in its reasoning, the Court referred to the principle of loyalty, which is recognized in scholarly writings as one of the general principles on which the Convention is based. She states that in essence, the principle of loyalty embodies the principle of good faith, which rationally includes the requirement to act reasonably. Moreover, this principle of loyalty is supported in this case by the fact that an applicable international usage embodies the principle.[93]

In a Russian Arbitration award, the arbitrators interpreted the contract according to Article 8 CISG and "the general principle of reasonableness on which the Vienna Convention of 1980 is based".[94]

In a Spanish case,[95] the court referred to the concept of reasonableness as provided in Articles 8 and 9 and stated that the return of the defective goods cannot either be classified as "reasonable" to be borne by the seller according to Articles 8 and 9 of the CISG. Being goods that cannot be sold, there is no cause that would oblige their transport, nor the impossibility or the higher cost of destroying or rejecting the goods in the place where they were sitting.

In an Austrian case,[96] the Supreme Court overruled the decision of the Appellate Court which stated that the contracts were concluded between the plaintiff and the defendant and that, according to the principle of good faith (Article 7(1) CISG), and considering the type of business, the plaintiff was entitled to assume that the orders and confirmations came from the defendant. Supreme Court held that the provisions of Articles 7 and 8 CISG could not be utilized to decide

---

92 KUOPPALA, S., "*The Application and Interpretation of the CISG in Finnish Case Law 1997–2005*" (April 2009).

93 KUOPPALA, S., "*The Application and Interpretation of the CISG in Finnish Case Law 1997–2005*" (April 2009).

94 Russia, 13 January 2006, Arbitration proceeding 137/2004 http://cisgw3.law.pace.edu/cases/060113r1.html. Translation by Gayane Nuridzhanyan.

95 Spain, 10 March 2009, Appellate Court Madrid (*Wine case*): http://www.cisgspanish.com/wp-content/uploads/2013/03/SAPMadrid10.03.2009englishtranslation.pdf, Translation by Iñigo Basurto.

96 Austria, 22 October 2001, Supreme Court [1 Ob 49/01i] (*Agricultural products case*): http://cisgw3.law.pace.edu/cases/011022a4.html. Translation by Ruth M. Janal, Jan Henning Berg (ed.).

whether one party was liable for giving the other party the impression of a legal position, and this could already be deduced from the wording of these two articles.

In conclusion, by taking into account the cases on Article 8 CISG, it can be said that the status of good faith as a general principle of the Convention regulating parties' behavior is generally accepted in case law. Accordingly, it would not be wrong to suggest, with the words of Farnsworth, that the "principle entered in by the back door" which I think seems to be inevitable.

Court decisions from countries such as Germany and Switzerland, where the principle plays an important role in the framework of national law, refer more extensively to the principle. This shows that decisions are influenced by national laws. This does not mean, however, that the courts do not take into account the relevant circumstances of each case and construe the reasonable person accordingly. Nevertheless, it would not be wrong to say that the good faith principle is always there in order to eliminate doubts or to justify the solution reached.

Although the good faith principle inevitably applies to contracts governed by the CISG, as the observance of good faith while interpreting the Convention cannot be reached in abstract, I think that a systematic use in decisions of the good faith principle in a way influenced by the national laws would not help develop the autonomous content of the good faith principle and the reasonable person criterion in relation to Article 8 CISG (a reasonable person who enters into international commercial relationships, in a foreign language etc.).

In the following cases the principle of good faith is used to interpret Article 8 CISG.

In a Swiss case,[97] the ambiguity in a contract was resolved by reference to subsequent conduct of the parties, which "according to good faith principle", became relevant for the ascertainment of the content of the contract. It was thus held by the Court that when the content of the contract cannot be determined by the application of the interpretation rules existing in Article 8 CISG, according to the good faith principle, the conduct of the parties should determine the content.

Although the reference to the good faith principle might seem to be superfluous, this approach of the Court could be considered as an

---

97 Switzerland, 5 July 2005, Obergericht [Canton Appellate Court] Zug (*Diesel oil case*) http://cisgw3.law.pace.edu/cases/050705s1.html. Translation by Jacob Heidbrink, Maril Dimsey (ed.).

interpretation of Article 8 CISG in the light of the good faith principle, unlike the decisions where the good faith principle is used in order to interpret the statement or conduct itself and not the provisions of Article 8.

Another interpretation of Article 8 in accordance with the good faith principle may be seen concerning the question of the incorporation of standard terms into the contract. As the CISG does not provide a specific rule on that issue, the Article 8 is applied in order to determine whether these terms are effectively incorporated into the contract or not.[98]

The courts, following an interpretation of the Article 8 in the light of the good faith principle, pointed out on different occasions that it cannot be reasonably expected that a contracting party will inquire about the content of the general contractual conditions of the other party. Although in their reasoning, the courts have also referred to "the duty to act in good faith" or "the duty to cooperate" (thus to the second role of the good faith principle), the wording of Article 7, which requires that its international character and the observance of good faith in international trade (points which are also developed in decisions) should be taken into account in the interpretation of the Convention, would be sufficient in order to interpret the "reasonable person" in Article 8 in the same direction.

On this matter, a German case of 31 October 2001[99] can be cited. According to this decision, whether the standard terms had become

---

98 See for instance, Belgium, 19 September 1995, District Court Nivelles (*Gantry v. Research Consulting Marketing*): http://cisgw3.law.pace.edu/cases/950919b1.html; Austria, 14 January 2002, Supreme Court (*Cooling system case*): http://cisgw3.law.pace.edu/cases/020114a3.html; Austria, 1 February 2005, Appellate Court Innsbruck (*Powdered tantulum case*): http://cisgw3.law.pace.edu/cases/050201a3.html; The Netherlands, 10 February 2005, Netherlands Arbitration Institute (*interim award*): http://cisgw3.law.pace.edu/cases/050210n1.html; Austria, 23 March 2005, Oberlandesgericht [Appellate Court] Linz (*Conveyor band case*): http://cisgw3.law.pace.edu/cases/050323a3.html; Austria, 8 August 2005, Appellate Court Linz (*Spacers for insulation glass case*): http://cisgw3.law.pace.edu/cases/050808a3.html; Germany, 12 December 2006, District Court Coburg (*Plants case*): http://cisgw3.law.pace.edu/cases/061212g1.html.

99 Germany, 31 October 2001, Supreme Court (*Machinery case*): http://cisgw3.law.pace.edu/cases/011031g1.html. Translation edited by William M. Barron, Birgit Kurtz. Compare with The Netherlands, 25 February 2009, District Court Rotterdam (*Fresh-Life International B.V. v. Cobana Fruchtring GmbH & Co., KG*): http://cisgw3.law.pace.edu/cases/090225n1.html: "To that extent, under non-uniform German law, in commercial relations and in transactions between businesses, the standard terms referred to become part of the contract even if the client does not know them but

part of the offer is to be determined in accordance with Article 8 and the recipient must be given a reasonable chance of considering the standard conditions, if these conditions are to become part of the offer.

If the recipient, on the other hand, had to inquire about the standard terms, this would contravene good faith in international trade, as embodied in Article 7(1) CISG, as well as the parties' duty to cooperate.

In the editorial remarks on the case, DiMatteo points out that according to the Court the burden of providing the terms was on the party wishing to insert such clauses. Accordingly, the court emphasized that parties to an international contract should not be expected to know the particular terms and conditions that might be familiar to parties that share the same national legal system and business customs. For this purpose, according to the court, requiring one party to make general terms and conditions available to the other party would promote the CISG's goals of good faith and uniformity.[100]

5. CONCLUSION

In conclusion, it should be said that while the PICC, PECL and DCFR, which recognize a general duty of good faith, give an important content to the principle of good faith and fair dealing in the field of interpretation of contracts, there have been important differences of opinion in legal literature on the position of the CISG on this matter. I think that court decisions from all over the world have "clarified" the question by systematically referring to the good faith principle in cases on the

had the opportunity to reasonably get to know them, for example, by requesting them from the other party. However, this does not apply in international commerce because due to the duty to act in good faith, a duty to inquire cannot be placed on the other party)." Compare also with Germany, 24 July 2009, Appellate Court Celle (*Broadcasters case*): http://cisgw3.law.pace.edu/cases/090724g1.html: "Considering the significant differences among the particular domestic standard terms regulations, as well as the missing differentiation between commercial and other traders within the scope of the Convention (Art. 1(3) CISG), it would violate the principle of good faith in international trade as stated under Art. 7(1) CISG and the parties' general duties of cooperation and information, if the recipient of standard terms and conditions was obliged to enquire about the content of the standard terms and conditions which had not been transmitted, thus laying upon him the risk and disadvantage of unknown standard terms being introduced by the other side".

100 DiMATTEO, L.A., et al., "The Interpretive Turn in International Sales Law: An Analysis of Fifteen Years of CISG Jurisprudence", 34 Northwestern Journal of International Law & Business 299 (Winter 2004), pp. 346–349.

interpretation of the contracts governed by the CISG. Accordingly, it can be said that the prediction made by Winship who stated that the recognition of a general duty of good faith was winning the academic debate and that eventually such an obligation was more likely to be accepted became a reality.[101]

Reference to principles such as "the principle of loyalty" by courts may be supported because of the legislative history of the Convention with regard to the recognition of a general duty of good faith. However, such a principle does not have an autonomous international content either and is often defined with reference to the notion of "good faith" itself.[102]

I think that recognizing a general duty of good faith in terms of the CISG is also in accordance with the interpretation of the Convention according to the goals set forth in Article 7(1), namely, promoting uniformity of application and observance of good faith in "international trade". First, because, as good faith principle has a very broad field of application and national laws attribute divergent contents to this principle, application of the national laws to questions of fairness in relation with international contracts governed by the CISG would jeopardize the uniformity of application of the Convention. Second, the Convention aims the observance of good faith in "international trade". Such a goal can only be reached by the establishment of an autonomous concept of good faith applied to international transactions. Accordingly, like the rest of the Convention, the Article 7 should itself be interpreted by taking these points into account.

Moreover, the recognition of a positive duty of good faith also means that other harmonized instruments, (especially the PICC which have the closest scope of application) may be used in order to interpret or supplement CISG rules on interpretation and gap filling. Indeed, the PICC which contain more detailed provisions than the CISG can have

---

101 WINSHIP, P., "International Sales Contracts under the 1980 Vienna Convention", 17 UCC L.J. 55 (1984), p. 67 fn. 40.

102 See for instance, SUND-NORRGARD, P., KOLEHMAINEN, A., SUHONEN, O.A., "*The Principle of Loyalty and Flexibility of Contracts*", 2 Lapland Law Rev. 190 (2015): https://www.ulapland.fi/loader.aspx?id=ec90abd9-ff6d-49cd-bf4c-c5a80d363ba4, p. 190, stating that "The principle of loyalty, the Nordic equivalent to the principle of good faith in the civil law countries of Continental Europe, requires that the parties to a contract have due regard to the other party's interests during the contract negotiations and performance, but also after the contract has been executed." In the light of this citation, one can ask if such references in court decisions where CISG applies are not the result of a homeward trend themselves.

an important impact on the applications of this latter instrument and help give an international autonomous content in accordance with the needs of the international trade to the rules contained by the CISG. Indeed, one can observe the growing importance of the PICC as an autonomous international legal instrument Accordingly, it is not a surprise to see court decisions referring to the PICC even when they are not the applicable law either for evaluating the result obtained by the application of a national law[103] or in order to interpret and supplement the rules contained in the CISG.[104]

It should, however, not be understood that recourse to the PICC should be systematic in all cases involving interpretation of contracts. In this respect, a solution should first be sought inside the CISG and if necessary directions of the article 7(2) should be followed and reference to underlying principles of the Convention should be made in order to supplement the Convention.[105]

After examining the scope of application of the good faith and fair dealing principle in interpreting international commercial contracts governed by the CISG, PICC, PECL and DCFR, it can be said that the subject of interpretation of international commercial contracts cannot be fully grasped by referring solely to the notions of "meaning" and "intent" and that interpretation process serves also to regulate the market activity by protecting the weaker party. Although the idea of protecting weaker party by restoring fairness in contractual relationships is not a new idea, this pillar of contractual interpretation continues to have its place in the core of the legal debate because of the current need for autonomous content for notions such as "fairness in contractual relationship" or "weaker party" according to the needs of the international trade. Indeed, international commercial contracts have their own context to be taken into account and the highly contextualist approach of interpretation will certainly help for this purpose.

---

103 See ICC award No. 8908.

104 See *Scafom* decision which will be examined in detail in the next chapter.

105 In the *Scafom* case the Court directly applied PICC as underlying principles of the CISG. See also Koch who is in favour of applying PICC as an interpretative tool under article 7(1) because of its "international character and shared purpose" and a gap-filler under Article 7(2) as general principles underlying the Convention in relation to Article 25 CISG; KOCH, R., "*Commentary on Whether the UNIDROIT Principles of International Commercial Contracts May Be Used to Interpret and Supplement Article 25 CISG*": http://www.cisg.law.pace.edu/cisg/biblio/koch1.html.

CHAPTER 4

GAP FILLING IN THE PICC, CISG, PECL AND DCFR

1. SUPPLEMENTATION OF TERMS IN CONTRACTS

1.1. TERMINOLOGICAL ISSUES

While interpretation is the process used in order to discover the meaning of contractual terms, gap filling can be described as the process of completing a contract where the parties have not provided some clause which is necessary for its working.[1] In other words, it is used when the contract contains a gap.

Kornet states that, in a broader sense "contracts can leave gaps in varying degrees, ranging from ambiguity in the terms of a contract due to missing detail to a total failure to deal with a particular situation".[2] However, in a narrower sense, a gap in the contract exists because contracting parties do not provide any term for a particular contingency and thus completely fail to deal with it in terms of a contract. This is a "true gap", in a sense that the terms do not address a particular contingency at all.[3]

Generally, the terms of the contract do not address the particular contingency because of a lack of foresight at the time of contracting.[4]

---

1 See *Principles of the European Contract Law, Parts I and II*, Prepared by The Commission on European Contract Law, O. Lando, H. Beale (eds.), Kluwer Law International, The Hague 2000, p. 302.

2 KORNET, N., *Contract Interpretation and Gap-Filling: Comparative and Theoretical Perspectives*, Intersentia, Antwerpen-Oxford 2006, p. 4.

3 KORNET, N., *Contract Interpretation and Gap-Filling: Comparative and Theoretical Perspectives*, Intersentia Antwerpen-Oxford 2006, p. 4.

4 See COOTER, R.D., ULEN, T., *Law and Economics*, Pearson Series in Economics, 6th ed., Pearson Education, Harlow 2012, pp. 291–292: in a perfect contract "Every contingency is anticipated; every risk is internalized; all relevant information is communicated; no gaps remain for courts to fill; no one needs the court's protection from deceit or abuse; nothing can go wrong. Perfect contracts pose no conundrums

The following example may be given:[5] The parties to a construction contract agree on a special interest rate to be paid by the purchaser in the event of delay in payment of the price. Before the beginning of the work, the parties decide to terminate the contract. When the constructor delays restitution of the advance payment, the question of the applicable interest rate arises.

In another example, *First National Bank v. Methodist Home*,[6] an elderly lady enters a home for the aged, paying a significant sum, to be returned to her "if it should be found advisable to discontinue her stay" during a two-month probation period. Must the home return the money if she dies within this period? In this example, maybe the parties foresaw the problem and preferred not to deal with it.[7]

In practice, however, the distinction between interpretation and gap filling may sometimes be difficult to make for both policy and technical reasons, as the difference between the two concepts may vary according to one's conception of the degree of freedom which should be used by courts while ascertaining the meaning and the effects of an agreement, and it is not always easy to distinguish between a vague clause[8] needing

---

of interpretation." In real life, it is impossible to address all the issues in the contract, a fact which is even more obvious for complex and long-term contracts. For construction contracts see, for instance, ILIFF, A., HALLS, P., TEDJESKE, J., "*The Shifting Sands of Contract Drafting, Interpretation and Application*", 32 The Construction Lawyer 31 (2012), p. 32. In real life, incompleteness in contracts can be explained mainly with economic concepts of "bounded rationality" and "transaction costs". See RILEY, C.A, "*Designing Default Rules in Contract Law, Consent, Conventionalism and Efficiency*", 20(3) Oxford Journal of Legal Studies 367–390 (2000), especially p. 370. For an economic analysis on incompleteness in contracts see for instance: COHEN, G.M., "*Implied Terms and Interpretation in Contract Law*" in *Encyclopedia of Law and Economics*, Bouckaert, B., De Geest, G. (eds.), Edward Elgar, Cheltenham 2000, pp. 78–98; AYRES, L., "*Default Rules for Incomplete Contracts*" in *The New Palgrave Dictionary of Economics and the Law*, Peter Newman (ed.), Palgrave Macmillan, London 2002, pp. 585–590. DiMATTEO, L., OSTAS, D.L., "*Comparative Efficiency in International Sales Law*", 26 Am. U. Int'l L. Rev. 371 (2011).

5 See the Comments of UNIDROIT Principles of International Commercial Contracts 2016 Article 4.8.

6 *First National Bank of Lawrence, Kansas v. Methodist Home for the Aged*, 181 Kan 100, 309 P. 2d 389 (1957).

7 Maybe one or both parties have foreseen the problem but did not want to bring it up in order not to lose the bargain, FARNSWORTH, E.A., "'*Meaning' in the Law of Contract*", 76 Yale L.J. 939 (1967), pp. 956–957.

8 For the notion of vagueness see for instance: McMEEL, G., *The Construction of Contracts*, 3rd ed., Oxford University Press, Oxford 2017, p. 63; FARNSWORTH, E.A., "'*Meaning' in the Law of Contract*", 76 Yale L.J. 939 (1967), p. 953. See also CHRISTIE, G.C., "*Vagueness and Legal Language*", 48 Minn. L. Rev. 885, (1963–1964); QUINE, W., *Word and Object*, MIT Press, Cambridge MA 1964, para 17; SOLAN, L.,

interpretation and a gap, as the more a clause vague is, the more creative and closer to gap filling the process of determination of its content is.[9]

Nevertheless, the difference between the two may be established as follows: if a contract contains a "best efforts" clause, determining the requirements of the existing clause is a question of interpretation even if it contains vague terms, but if the contract contains no such clause, the court may have to decide whether to fill the gap by implying a best efforts obligation and may determine the content of that obligation.[10]

Accordingly, if the parties to a contract have foreseen the problem but chose to deal with it only in general terms, there is not a gap in the contract which needs to be filled but there is a vague clause which needs to be interpreted.

Although gap filling, like interpretation, serves to establish the content of the contract, this difference between interpretation and implication of terms in a contract has led scholars and legal practitioners to question whether implication may be seen as part of the interpretative process.[11]

In *National Commercial Bank Jamaica Ltd. v. Guyana Refrigerator Ltd.*, Lord Steyn clearly distinguished the two processes, stating that "The process of construction and implication of terms are closely linked, but as a matter of legal analysis they need to be kept separate."[12] Mason J., however, took a different position in *Codelfa Construction Pty. Ltd. v. State Rail Authority of New South Wales*, stating that when we say that the implication of a term raises an issue as to the meaning and effect of the contract we do not intend by that statement to convey that the court is embarking upon an orthodox exercise of interpretation of the language of the contract; that is, assigning a meaning to a particular provision. He stressed that nonetheless, the implication of a term is an exercise in interpretation, though not an orthodox instance.[13] Lord Hoffman also acknowledged that implication of terms in a contract is also an

ROSENBLATT, T., OSHERSON, D., "*False Consensus Bias in Contract Interpretation*", 108 Columbia Law Review 1268 (2008), pp. 1268–1270. See also SOLAN, L., "*Pernicious Ambiguity in Contracts and Statutes*", 79 Chicago-Kent Law Review 859 (2004).

9 Compare also, FARNSWORTH, E.A., "*'Meaning' in the Law of Contract*", 76 Yale L.J. 939 (1967), pp. 956–957.

10 See COHEN, G.M., "*Implied Terms and Interpretation in Contract Law*" in Bouckaert, B., De Geest, G. (eds.), *Encyclopedia of Law and Economics*, Edward Elgar, Cheltenham 2000, p. 79.

11 LEWISON, K., *The Interpretation of Contracts*, Sweet & Maxwell, London 2004, p. 196.

12 (1998) 53 W.I.R. 229.

13 (1982) 149 C.L.R. 337.

exercise of interpretation, with the difference that in implying terms it is necessary to interpret the meaning of the whole contract.[14]

At the end it can be said that, the more related to the ascertainment of parties' intent the inquiry for implied terms in a specific case is, the more a part of the interpretation process, if not a central case example, it can be considered.

In legal doctrine different terms are used in relation to the gap-filling process. The concepts of completive interpretation and implication are generally used as synonyms of gap filling. As to constructive interpretation and supplementation, it is important to emphasize that they are often considered two sub-categories within the concept of gap filling. The concept of constructive interpretation refers generally to terms implied in fact – in other words, to terms "that are read into a contract on a contract-by-contract basis from the often very detailed contextual scene of the particular contract"[15] – and supplementation refers to terms implied on the basis of sources external to the parties' agreements, such as legislation, custom and trade usage, open-ended norms and policy considerations.[16]

Thus, if we take this terminological distinction, we can say that while constructive interpretation is closer to ordinary interpretation, supplementation is a rather different process. Either way, it seems to be useful not to make sharp distinctions because the interpretative method chosen in a legal system affects also implication rules.[17]

---

14 See Lord HOFFMANN, "*The Intolerable Wrestle with Words and Meanings*", 114 S. African L.J. 656 (1997); see also *Belize v. Belize Telecom Ltd.*, [2009] UKPC 10, [2009] 1 W.L.R. 1988. On this matter, see also, ROBERTSON, A., "*The Limits of Interpretation in the Law of Contract*", 47 Victoria U. Wellington L. Rev. 191 (2016), pp. 194–196.

15 KORNET, N., *Contract Interpretation and GapFilling: Comparative and Theoretical Perspectives*, Intersentia, Antwerpen-Oxford 2006, p. 181.

16 See KORNET, N., *Contract Interpretation and GapFilling: Comparative and Theoretical Perspectives*, Intersentia, Antwerpen-Oxford 2006, pp. 231–232. Peden emphasizes that the policy factors influencing courts to imply terms by law reveal a desire to ensure that parties cooperate with each other and with society's standards: See PEDEN, E., "*Policy Concerns Behind Implication of Terms in Law*", 117 L.Q.R. 459–476 (2001). Although the distinction between these two different types of implication, namely in fact and by law, is also relevant in terms of the CISG, PICC, PECL and DCFR, as will be seen below, this terminological distinction between constructive interpretation and supplementation is not followed in the wording of these legal instruments.

17 English law which adopts the objective method of interpretation, and until recently a textualist approach, is more reluctant to fill gaps in cases of implication in fact. For the business efficacy and officious bystander tests of English Law, see PHANG, A., "*Implied terms, Business Efficacy and Officious Bystander, A modern History*", [1998] J.B.L. 1–34.

Moreover, it may not always be easy to determine when one of these processes (interpretation, constructive interpretation and supplementation) finishes and the other starts. Finally, all these processes are closely linked with each other because they determine together the content of a contract.[18]

1.2. SOURCES OF IMPLIED TERMS

Let us consider different sources of implication in the light of the distinction between constructive interpretation and supplementation.

Accordingly, possible sources of implication may be "internal" or "external" to the contract. They are internal when the particular textual and contextual circumstances of the case are decisive in order to decide on the term to be implied (terms implied in fact). Then, the term implied is an *ad hoc* gap filler tailored for the needs of the particular circumstances of the case (constructive interpretation). In other words, it is the individualized term which parties would have agreed if they had considered the problem at the time of contracting.

Kramer calls this process "the process of pragmatic inference" and explains the need for such a process by the fact that conveying all the intended meaning by including all in the linguistic meaning of the words used, is unnecessarily (and probably impossibly) time consuming. Thus, the process of pragmatic inference allows information to be conveyed impliedly without encoding it within the linguistic meaning of an utterance:

> By assuming normality on the part of the communicator, and assuming optimal design (that the communicator designed the utterance correctly in the light of the surrounding circumstances, his apparent purpose and the usual process of pragmatic inference), the communicator can convey information without needing to encode it all.[19]

---

18 See STORME, M.E., "*The Binding Character of Contracts – Cause and Consideration*" in *Towards a European Civil Code*, A.S. Hartkamp, M.W. Hesselink, E.H. Hondius (eds.), 2nd revised and expanded ed., Kluwer/Ars aequi, 1998, pp. 239–254: "This is the question of the relationship between the various elements which are traditionally accepted as determining the contents of a contract, i.e. clauses, implied intentions, custom and practice, statutory provisions, and reasonableness and/or equitableness. Whether we apply a broad or a narrow view of what constitutes interpretation, the contents of a contract are invariably determined by combining, or 'integrating', these different sources, usually on the basis of a certain hierarchy between them."

19 KRAMER, A., "*Implication in fact as an instance of Contract Interpretation*", 63(2) C.L.J. 384 (2004).

The source of implication may also be an objective source external to the specific contract, such as a trade usage, legislation, reasonableness or the objective standard of good faith and fair dealing (supplementation or terms implied by law).

While the first type of gap-filling rules concentrates on the construction of the hypothetical intent of the parties of a specific contract, the second type of implied terms is more based on objective legal requirements than the ascertainment of the parties' intent.

It should be noted that one of the main challenges in contract interpretation is to avoid an extensive use of objective standards, leading to court-made contracts, and to protect the contracts' autonomous content against arbitrariness. In this respect, Ramberg points out that making a distinction between the "real" or "true" content of the contract in its entirety and the supplementation process is of great value, but emphasizes that it can be queried whether it is suitable or even possible to apply in practice.[20]

But it would be wrong to suggest that objective sources are always entirely external to the contextual setting of the contract and never refer to it. In this respect, let us consider the reasonableness standard, which plays an important role on the implication of terms by law. This standard puts forward an objective criterion for implication but its content can generally be understood in a given case with reference to the contextual setting.

Although the distinction between the two types of implied terms may be seen as a clear one, in practice it may be controversial whether a particular case may be properly classified as a term implied by law or as one in fact. Lewison points out that courts do not always adhere to any rigid division between different types of implied terms and that rather they treat them as shades of a "continuous spectrum".[21] For this reason, as is suggested above, sharp distinctions between different processes should be avoided. That is probably why the CISG, PECL, PICC and DCFR did not follow such a terminological distinction.

---

20 RAMBERG, J., "*Autonomy of Contract and Non-Mandatory Law*", 37 Scandinavian Stud. L. 141 (1993), p. 147.

21 LEWISON, K., *The Interpretation of Contracts*, Sweet & Maxwell, London 2004, p. 195. See also KORNET, N., *Contract Interpretation and Gap Filling: Comparative and Theoretical Perspectives*, Intersentia, Antwerpen-Oxford 2006, p. 232. See also McMEEL, G., *The Construction of Contracts*, 3rd ed., Oxford University Press, Oxford 2017, p. 330 and *Liverpool City Council v. Irwin* [1977] A.C. 239.

1.3. IMPLIED TERMS AND THE CISG, PICC, PECL AND DCFR

Before examining gap filling in terms of the CISG, PICC, PECL and DCFR it should also be noted that in case of a gap, "stop-gap rules" or "suppletive" rules of general character existing in these instruments apply (by law) first in order to fill it. These rules may be default gap fillers on specific issues such as determination of the price or quality of performance etc., general rules implying obligations on parties (e.g. Article 5.1.2 PICC) and rules making usages impliedly applicable.[22] If these rules are not applicable because of the specific circumstances of the case, then a suitable *ad hoc* gap filler is aimed to be designed (in fact).

Consequently, we will first examine some default gap fillers on specific issues existing in these instruments on a comparative basis. Our aim here is not to give a complete review of these rules, which would be outside the scope of this book, but to give some examples to see how these rules may be applied to fill the gap in order to be able to make some general remarks.

1.3.1. Examples of Default Gap Fillers on Some Specific Issues

1.3.1.1. Determination of the Price CISG, PICC, PECL and DCFR

According to Article 55 CISG,

> Where a contract has been validly concluded but does not expressly or implicitly fix or make provision for determining the price, the parties are considered, in the absence of any indication to the contrary, to have impliedly made reference to the price generally charged at the time of the conclusion of the contract for such goods sold under comparable circumstances in the trade concerned.

This provision of the CISG on open price contracts is very controversial in the light of Article 14, which states that determination of the price is necessary for the offer to be sufficiently definite. Farnsworth and Honnold proposed two different interpretations on the existing contradiction between these articles.

---

22 For instance for UNIDROIT Principles.

According to Farnsworth, Article 55 is applicable to the extent that the contract is validly concluded. As the contract cannot be validly concluded in terms of Article 14 if price is not determined, then Article 55 cannot have any effect in cases where Article 14 applies. Article 55 may thus only be operative if the contract is validly concluded by the applicable law, which may be the law of a state which did not ratify the second part of the Convention, including Article 14.[23]

Honnold suggests that Articles 14 and 55 of the CISG deal with different issues. Thus, Article 14 deals only with the question on whether a communication should be construed as an offer when it fails to state the price and not with the validity of an open price contract already executed, while Article 55 deals with the regulation of contracts that have been validly concluded but does not make express or implied provisions for determining the price.[24] This second solution which renders Article 55 effective seems to have more supporters between writers than the first suggestion.[25]

When Article 55 is applicable, the parties are considered, in the absence of any indication to the contrary, to have impliedly made reference to the price "generally charged at the time of the conclusion of the contract for such goods sold under comparable circumstances in the trade concerned".

The PICC are not subject to a similar controversy on the validity of open price contracts. Article 5.1.7 PICC, inspired by CISG Article 55, contains in the first place a similar default rule for these contracts with the exception that the word "goods" is replaced by the word "performance" because the Principles do not only apply to sale contracts.

In the Comments, it is emphasized that the article is based on the presumed intention of the parties. Article 5.1.7 makes a further distinction

---

23 FARNSWORTH A., *International Sales: The United Nations Convention on Contracts for the International Sale of Goods*, Matthew Bender, New York 1984, Ch. 3, pp. 3-1 to 3-18.

24 HONNOLD, J., *Uniform Law for International Sales under the 1980 United Nations Convention*, 3rd ed., Kluwer Law International, The Hague 1999, pp. 353–357.

25 In favour of an interpretation making Article 55 effective see also TALLON D., *International Sales: The United Nations Convention on Contracts for the International Sale of Goods*, Matthew Bender, New York 1984, Ch. 7, pp. 7-1 to 7-20. See also ENDERLEIN, F., MASCOW, D., *International Sales Law*, Oceana Publications, New York 1992, at pp. 209–210, suggesting that validity of open price contracts shall be determined solely under national law. According to Lookofsky, it cannot be said that all open price contracts are valid under Article 55 or invalid under Article 14. Court should discern the true intention of the parties by applying Article 8. LOOKOFSKY, J., *International Encyclopaedia of Laws - Contracts*, Suppl. 29 (December 2000) 1–192.

for contracts relating to operations which are unique or at least very specific. When such a contract is in question, because the price normally charged in comparable circumstances at the time of the conclusion of the contract in the trade concerned is not available, the parties are presumed to have made reference to a reasonable price.[26]

PECL Article 6:104 states that if the parties did not fix the price or the method of its determination, they are to be treated as having agreed to a reasonable price. This article is applied if there is no doubt that the parties intended to be bound and its aim is to empower the court to save the contract.[27] It puts forward a more general standard on the determination of the price than its previous counterparts.

DCFR Article II.–9:104 does not follow the exclusive reasonable price standard provided by the PECL, but follows the criteria provided by the PICC instead with the difference that it does not refer to the trade concerned. This can be explained by the fact that the DCFR is applicable not only to commercial contracts but governs consumer contracts as well.

1.3.1.2. Determination of the Quality of Performance

According to Article 35(2) CISG:

> Except where the parties have agreed otherwise, the goods do not conform with the contract unless they:
>
> (a) are fit for the purposes for which goods of the same description would ordinarily be used;
> (b) are fit for any particular purpose expressly or impliedly made known to the seller at the time of the conclusion of the contract, except where the circumstances show that the buyer did not rely, or that it was unreasonable for him to rely, on the seller's skill and judgement;
> (c) possess the qualities of goods which the seller has held out to the buyer as a sample or model;
> (d) are contained or packaged in the manner usual for such goods or, where there is no such manner, in a manner adequate to preserve and protect the goods.

---

26 UNIDROIT Principles of International Commercial Contracts, Article 5.1.7. For presumed intention of the parties see also Secretariat Commentaries on 1978 Draft 51 counterpart of CISG Article 55.

27 *Principles of European Contract Law, Parts I and II*, O. Lando, H. Beale (eds.), Kluwer Law International, The Hague 2000, p. 105.

Although all these criteria may be relevant in the establishment of the content of the contract in relation to the quality of the goods, sub-paragraphs (a) and (d) are especially related to gap filling because they do not refer to the interpretation of an express or implicit communication between the parties.

The other criteria may be considered superfluous because they can be deducted from the application of Article 8 but "in view of the fact that the Convention addresses laymen, the express rule of article 35(2) makes sense even if it merely reiterates the result already reached by applying the general provisions".[28]

As the PICC are applicable for all types of international commercial contracts, the rule provided by this instrument is more standard-like. In this respect, as is submitted in the comments, where the quality of performance is neither fixed by, nor determinable from the contract, a party is bound to render performance of a quality that is reasonable and not less than average in the circumstances.[29]

The illustrations given in the comments distinguish the scope of this stop-gap rule from rules on interpretation of contracts.[30] In this respect, if a party undertakes to build a hotel next to a railway station and the contract provides for "adequate sound isolation", general interpretation rules are applicable because the contract made a reference to the quality and the contract elements make the quality determinable.

The vague clause provided by the contract should be understood as "high standards of sound isolation" by the application of general interpretation rules because the hotel is next to the railway station.

Only in the absence of any terms in the contract does Article 5.1.6, which provides a combination of two criteria, apply. First, if there is not any specificity related to the case, the performance should be of average quality. The average quality is determined "according to the circumstances which normally means that which is available on the relevant market at the time of performance (there may for example have been a recent technological advance)."[31]

---

28 See SCHLECHTRIEM, P., "*The Seller's Obligations Under the United Nations Convention on Contracts on the International Sale of Goods*" in *The United Nations Convention on Contracts for the International Sale of Goods*, Matthew Bender, New York 1984, Ch. 6, pp. 6-1 to 6-35.

29 Article 5.1.6.

30 UNIDROIT Principles, Official Comments on Article 5.1.6.

31 UNIDROIT Principles, Official Comments on Article 5.1.6.

This first indicator could especially work for contracts dealing with the sale of generic goods or the performance of services which are provided on a regular basis such as car rental.[32] But it may be insufficient in more complicated cases.

Let us take the illustration on the construction of a hotel next to the railway station and suppose that the contract does not contain any clause in relation to sound isolation issues. If the average quality criterion applied to the case, it would be possible to say that the isolation material to be used would be of average quality available on the market in the time of performance. But this criterion falls short in the circumstances of the case because the hotel is next to the railway station and an average quality is unreasonable. In this case, another reason leading to a similar solution can also be shown. The contract in question deals with building a hotel and not with sale of isolation materials. The hotel has to be of average quality in the given setting but this fact does not mean that the isolation material should also be of average quality. Instead, the right materials and right isolation methods have to be used.

In determining the reasonable character of the performance, factors such as the specific qualifications for which the performing party was chosen or the price may be most relevant. If a company based in country *x* organizes a banquet and orders meals from a renowned restaurant in Paris because the cuisine in country *x* is mediocre, then the average standards of the market in country *x* will not suffice to determine the quality of the performance in the specific case.[33]

The PECL adopt a similar but a differently formulated rule on this matter which, like Article 5.1.6, equally applies to goods and services. According to Article 6:108 PECL, "If the contract does not specify the quality, a party must tender performance of at least average quality". Although the wording of the rule does not refer to the reasonableness criterion, Article 1:302 on reasonableness is taken into account in the determination of the degree of quality required and factors such as whether or not the debtor is acting in the course of business[34] and the price fixed for the performance are considered.[35]

---

32 See also Comments on related article of PECL, infra note 35.

33 See UNIDROIT Principles, Official Comments on Article 5.1.6.

34 This criterion plays an important role in PECL which do not only apply to consumer contracts.

35 See *Principles of European Contract Law, Parts I and II*, O. Lando, H. Beale (eds.), Kluwer Law International, The Hague 2000 p. 302.

DCFR has adopted a rule of more general character for the quality of performance. According to Article II.–9:108:

> Where the quality of anything to be supplied or provided under the contract cannot be determined from the terms agreed by the parties, from any other applicable rule of law or from usages and practices, the quality required is the quality which the recipient could reasonably expect in the circumstances.

As can be seen, the DCFR does not provide for at least average quality of performance but refers instead to the reasonable expectations of the recipient in a given case. Thus, if the DCFR applied in a specific case, the inquiry of the quality would be made on a case-by-case basis without any (unless indicated to the contrary) automatically applicable criterion to serve as a benchmark in the determination of the quality of performance. But it can be said that in the absence of any specificities of the case, the quality of the performance that a party can reasonably expect would generally be average quality, especially if the contract deals with issues such as sale of generic goods.

1.3.1.3. Remarks – Rules vs. Standards

There are many other default gap fillers in the CISG, PECL, PICC and DCFR (on place of delivery, time of delivery etc.) and their complete examination is beyond the scope of this book. But some general remarks can be made based on these two examples below.

First, it can be said that where possible, these gap fillers try to put forward as concrete and easy to apply rules as possible, with reference for instance to the market price or average quality of goods in a given market etc. These rules "respond to specific factual issues and can be applied without recourse to underlying principles or policies".[36]

It may be relatively easier to formulate such rules when the scope of the legal instrument is narrower, and more difficult when the instrument applies to a wider range of contracts. If we take for instance the CISG, which only applies to international commercial sale contracts, we can see that the default provisions are more specific, such as "the price generally charged at the time of conclusion of the contract for such goods sold under comparable circumstances in the trade concerned" or "fit for the

---

36 For Rules and Standards, See DiMATTEO, L., "*False Dichotomies in Commercial Contract Interpretation*", 11(1) J. Int'l Trade L. & Policy 27–43 (2012).

purposes for which goods are sold under comparable circumstances in the trade concerned".

But even if the instrument applies, like the CISG, to only one type of contract, the circumstances of specific cases may differ considerably from each other and a rule may fall short to bring an answer to all contingencies. Indeed, it can be said, for instance, that although it might rarely happen, an international sale contract can deal with a unique operation where no market price can be established. Then, the standard of reasonableness provided by Article 5.1.7 may be used to supplement Article 35(2) CISG to the extent that "reasonableness" can be extracted as a principle which underlines the Convention.[37] Moreover, the type of the gap may also make the formulation of concrete rules more difficult. Indeed, it can be easier to provide a rule on determination of the price and more difficult to do this with respect to time of delivery when the CISG also provides for the standard of reasonable time (Article 33(c)).[38]

When the scope of the legal instrument is broader, standards such as reasonableness start to play a more important role in filling gaps because of their flexibility in application. That is why in filling gaps, the PICC, PECL and DCFR refer to this standard more often than the CISG. But an exclusive reference to the reasonableness standard such as the 'reasonable price' of Article 6:104 PECL can make the application of the gap filler much less straightforward. That may be why the exclusive criterion on "reasonable price" of the PECL is not followed by the DCFR, which adopted the solution provided by the PICC. Conversely, the DCFR has only referred to a standard – in contrast to other instruments – on the determination of quality by putting forward only the "reasonable expectation of the parties" criterion.

1.3.2. Usages which are Impliedly Applicable

As was explained above, parties may be bound by usages upon which they did not agree. As we have already examined usages in general and the necessary conditions for a usage to be impliedly applicable in terms of the CISG, PECL, PICC and DCFR in particular, we will not examine these issues here. We will only note that if there is a trade usage, for instance on

37 This issue is developed in a detailed way in the previous chapter of this book.

38 This reasonable time will be decided in taking into account an as concrete as possible criterion which is "acceptable commercial conduct in the circumstances of the case". See Secretariat's Commentary on Article 33, http://cisgw3.law.pace.edu/cisg/text/secomm/secomm-33.html.

the determination of the quality of the goods to be delivered, impliedly applicable in the circumstances of the case, this usage will be decisive on that issue and default gap fillers examined above will not apply.[39]

1.3.3. Rules on Gap Filling Provided by the CISG, PICC, PECL and DCFR

As opposed to the PICC, PECL and DCFR, the CISG does not provide for how to deal with gaps in cases where the above-mentioned stop-gap rules do not provide a solution because of the particularities of the case. In this respect, the CISG contains a gap which should be filled and it is submitted that the related article of the PICC may be used in order to fill this gap.[40] We will first examine this article of the PICC and then discuss its possible role in filling the gap existing in the CISG.

According to Article 4.8 PICC, entitled "supplying an omitted term",

> (1) Where the parties to a contract have not agreed with respect to a term which is important for a determination of their rights and duties, a term which is appropriate in the circumstances shall be supplied.
> (2) In determining what is an appropriate term regard shall be had, among other factors, to
> (a) the intention of the parties;
> (b) the nature and purpose of the contract;
> (c) good faith and fair dealing;
> (d) reasonableness.

In the Comments on the article, it is submitted that the terms to be supplied must be appropriate to the circumstances of the case. In order to determine what is appropriate, regard is had first of all to the intention of the parties which can be inferred from, among other factors, the terms expressly stated in the contract, prior negotiations or any conduct subsequent to the conclusion of the contract.[41]

The first criterion focuses on the hypothetical intent of the parties and thus on implication in fact. This hypothetical intent may be ascertained

---

39 For cases on this issue see Switzerland, 27 May 2005, Appellate Court Valais/Wallis (*Welding devices case*), http://cisgw3.law.pace.edu/cases/050527s1.html and also Switzerland, 28 January 2009, *Tribunal cantonal* [Higher Cantonal Court] Valais (*Fiberglass composite materials case*), http://cisgw3.law.pace.edu/cases/090128s1.html.

40 See PERILLO, J.M., "*Editorial remarks on the manner in which the UNIDROIT Principles may be used to interpret or supplement CISG Article 8*", http://www.cisg.law.pace.edu/cisg/principles/uni8.html.

41 UNIDROIT Principles of International Commercial Contracts 2016, Comments on Article 4.8.

by the text, the context or both.[42] If the parties' intention cannot be ascertained by construing the hypothetical intent, then more objective criteria such as the nature and the purpose of the contract, good faith and fair dealing and reasonableness apply (implication by law).

The reference to the nature and purpose of the contract generally refers to some particular type of clauses which are generally used in contracts of the same type.[43] Lewison writes in respect of English Law that the rules of law arise because of the nature of the contract into which parties have entered. Accordingly, by virtue of parties' express intention to enter into a relationship of employer and employee, buyer and seller etc., the law imputes to them a certain intention.[44]

In the case of *Liverpool City Council v. Irwin*, Lord Cross of Chelsea stated that when it implies a term in a contract the court is sometimes laying down a general rule for all contracts of a certain type – sale of goods, landlord and tenant and so on – and thereby some provision is to be implied unless the parties have expressly excluded it.[45]

This conception of imputed intention may also be considered true for the application of the objective criterion of "nature and purpose of contract" laid down in Article 4.8, which applies in cases where the hypothetical intent of the parties cannot be ascertained. In this respect, a further distinction made by the PICC between supplementation of omitted terms (Article 4.8) and implication of obligations (Article 5.1.2) should be noted.

In terms of the PICC, implied obligations are to be determined by taking into consideration the objective criteria, which are the nature and the purpose of the contract, practices established between the parties, good faith and fair dealing and reasonableness. Implied obligations stemming from the application of Article 5.1.2 are not considered by the PICC as a matter of gap filling but are treated as already part of the contract even if they have not been expressly stated.

If for instance a party rents a full computer network to another party and the contract says nothing as to a possible obligation to give at least some basic information concerning the operation of the system, this may be considered an implied obligation, since it is obvious and necessary for

---

42 Cf. LEWISON, K., *The Interpretation of Contracts*, Sweet & Maxwell, London 2004, p.195.

43 Concerning the implication by nature of the contract see PEDEN, E., "*Policy Concerns behind Implication of Terms in Law*", 117 L.Q.R. 459–476 (2001).

44 LEWISON, K., *The Interpretation of Contracts*, Sweet & Maxwell, London 2004, p. 195.

45 [1977] A.C. 239.

the accomplishment of the "purpose of such contract" that the provider of sophisticated goods should supply the other party with a minimum of information.[46] The solution reached is not a result of the application of Article 4.8 on gap filling but that of the application of Article 5.1.2.

Particularities of long-term contracts should also be dealt with here. In this type of contract it may happen that parties leave a term which will be relevant at a later stage of the contract open (they may, for instance, fix the price only for the first year of the contract and leave it open for subsequent years). It is submitted in the Comments on the PICC that in those cases, if the stop-gap rules that are examined above do not provide an appropriate solution in the light of the circumstances of the case, a term would be supplied by Article 4.8 or Article 5.1.2.[47]

Finally, if we come back to criteria laid down by Article 4.8, it can be said that the criteria of reasonableness and good faith and fair dealing may play a role, as independent criteria of implication in cases where the implication of a term with reference to other criteria does not give a solution, or may be coupled with the criterion of "the nature and the purpose of the contract" where, for instance, implication of a clause generally used in a certain type of contract may not be reasonable given the circumstances of the case. As is noted above, these two criteria are also used to determine implied obligations which are considered not a matter of gap filling but already a part of the contract in accordance with Article 5.1.2.

In the light of the explanations given in accordance with Article 4.8, we will now try to examine the question whether Article 4.8 PICC may be used, as suggested by Perillo, to fill the existing gap in the CISG in relation to supplementation of omitted terms. As explained before in the Chapter 3, however, the answer to this question would vary according to the position taken on the question of the scope of application of the principle of good faith and fair dealing in the CISG if parties did not provide a clause for the issue.

As was explained before, if we accept the literalist approach that rejects a general duty of good faith adopted by the CISG, we cannot use Article 4.8 to supplement the Convention and avoid normally applicable national laws because the PICC recognize a duty to act in good faith and refer to the principle of good faith for supplementation purposes.

---

46 UNIDROIT Principles of International Commercial Contracts 2016, Comments on Article 5.1.2.

47 PICC 2016, Comments on Articles 2.1.14 and 4.8.

If we adopt the second approach, however, it would be possible to use Article 4.8 in supplementing the Convention. If we accept the third approach, we should consider reasonableness as an underlying principle of the CISG and assume that reasonableness and good faith are synonymous. But Article 4.8 PICC does not see good faith as synonymous with reasonableness because it adopts these two criteria in distinct ways. Thus, if we consider that reasonableness (and not good faith) is an underlying principle of the CISG, recourse to Article 4.8 in order to fill the gap in the Convention would rather be confusing.

In conclusion, as we have also explained above, accepting the second view will also be the best solution in order to be able to have recourse to the PICC in cases where an omitted term should be filled. If we do not accept recourse to the PICC, then the solution should be found inside the Convention. In this case, for questions on good faith and fair dealing, answers must be sought in the rules of national law applicable via private international law, as suggested by Farnsworth.[48] But, as mentioned earlier, the court decisions cited above strongly indicate that a general duty of good faith is also accepted in terms of the CISG.

Article 6:102 PECL states that

> In addition to the express terms, a contract may contain implied terms which stem from
>
> (a) the intention of the parties,
> (b) the nature and purpose of the contract, and
> (c) good faith and fair dealing.

As can be seen, the formulation of this article is quite similar to that of Article 4.8 PICC. Accordingly, the first indicator "refers to the presumed intention of the parties; the court should consider what parties, acting in accordance with good faith and fair dealing, would reasonably have agreed if they had discussed the question."[49]

Accordingly, an additional reference to good faith is made by the PECL on the construction of parties' hypothetical intent. The second indicator allows the court to refer to terms usually contained in similar contracts or laid down in International Conventions dealing with

---

48 FARNSWORTH A., "*Duties of Good Faith and Fair Dealing Under the Unidroit Principles, Relevant International Conventions and National Laws*", 3 Tulane Journal of International and Comparative Law 47–64 (1995).

49 See *Principles of European Contract Law, Parts I and II*, O. Lando, H. Beale (eds.), Kluwer Law International, The Hague 2000 p. 303.

analogous contracts and the third indicator requires looking in an objective fashion.[50] The PECL does not contain a separate article on implied obligations like Article 5.1.2 PICC. Instead, the principle of good faith and fair dealing provides a solution for such cases.

The illustration given in the comment explains this point. Accordingly, a shipowner contracts to unload the ship alongside a wharf in Thames, where at low tide the ship will rest on the river-bed. The state of the river-bed is unknown to shipowner and the existence of a ridge of rock across it damages the ship. The wharfinger is under implied obligation to warn the shipowner of any such danger.[51]

According to DCFR Article II.–9:101(2),

> Where it is necessary to provide for a matter which the parties have not foreseen or provided for, a court may imply an additional term, having regard in particular to:
>
> (a) the nature and purpose of the contract;
> (b) the circumstances in which the contract was concluded; and
> (c) the requirements of good faith and fair dealing.

Paragraph (3) submits that a term implied by the application of paragraph (2) should, where possible, be such as to give effect to what the parties, had they provided for the matter, would probably have agreed.

Thus, it can be said that the DCFR provides a similar solution even if the formulation is different. The most significant difference is that DCFR contains the expression of "when it is necessary", which suggests a deliberate restriction compared to PECL.

Again, the hypothetical intent of the contracting parties is first to be determined. But if it cannot be established, then the objective criterion of the "nature and purpose of the contract" applies. Third, as in PECL Article 6:102, the objective requirement of good faith and fair dealing applies where a term is needed to be implied in order to give protection to a party.[52]

---

50 See *Principles of European Contract Law, Parts I and II*, O. Lando, H. Beale (eds.), Kluwer Law International, The Hague 2000, p. 303.

51 See *Principles of European Contract Law, Parts I and II*, O. Lando, H. Beale (eds.), Kluwer Law International, The Hague 2000, p. 303.

52 See *Principles of European Contract Law, Parts I and II*, O. Lando, H. Beale (eds.), Kluwer Law International, The Hague 2000, p. 303.

1.4. CONCLUSION

In this section we first tried to examine gap-filling rules existing in the CISG, PICC, PECL and DCFR. While the CISG contains a gap on the issue, the position of the PICC, PECL and DCFR showed us that rules on gap filling provided by these instruments are consistent with the methodology that they follow for interpretations of contracts. Accordingly, the PICC, PECL and DCFR give priority to the ascertainment of the subjective intent, to the extent that it can be extracted in the circumstances of the case. In cases where such intent cannot be (hypothetically) construed, more objective criteria apply. As these rules give an important content to the principle of good faith and fair dealing for the purposes of gap filling, again, it should be noted that they can only be useful in order to fill the gap contained in the CISG if we accept that the position of the Convention on this matter coincides with that of the PICC.

We can observe finally, that although the distinction between these two different types of implication, namely in fact and by law, is also relevant in terms of the PICC, PECL and DCFR, this terminological distinction between constructive interpretation and supplementation is not followed in the wording of these legal instruments.[53]

2. *FORCE MAJEURE* AND HARDSHIP IN THE CISG, PICC, PECL AND DCFR

2.1. LACK OF FORESIGHT IN DRAFTING CONTRACTS AND ITS CONSEQUENCES

Contracts are unavoidably incomplete in real life for the two main reasons of bounded rationality and transaction costs.[54] Parties to a contract, thus,

---

53 The instruments seem to draw, however, a distinction between interpretation and implication processes. Vogenauer suggests that as they refer, for the purposes of establishing the implied obligation, to the same circumstances to be taken into account in the interpretation process, the attempt to distinguish between interpretation and implication processes proves to be illusory: see VOGENAUER, S., "*Interpretation of Contracts*" in *The Max Planck Encyclopedia of European Private Law*, Vol. 1, Basedow, J., Hopt, K.J., Zimmermann, R., Stier, A. (eds.), Oxford University Press, Oxford 2012, p. 977.

54 See RILEY, C.A., "*Designing Default Rules in Contract Law, Consent, Conventionalism and Efficiency*", 20(3) Oxford Journal of Legal Studies 367–390, and especially p. 370.

cannot possibly foresee all possible contingencies and provide for them. Generally, such a lack of foresight by the contracting parties leads to the process of gap filling, and the gap in question is filled by the court either by a default rule or by an *ad hoc* gap filler in order to make the contract work.

Sometimes, however, an event unforeseen at the time of contracting can render the contract impossible to perform, may leave it without purpose, or may completely change the contractual equilibrium.

In the first group of cases, an external unpredictable and unavoidable event such as a natural disaster renders the performance of the contract "impossible" for one of the parties (*force majeure*). In the second group of cases, the performance is possible but the reason or the purpose of the contract for one party, known also by the other, is undermined or frustrated by an unforeseen external contingency (*frustration of purpose*).

The famous coronation cases: *Chandler v. Webster*,[55] *Hobson v. Pattenden & Co.*,[56] and *Krell v. Henry*,[57] all relating to the rent of accommodations having a view in order to watch the coronation procession of King Edward VII, are important examples of such a possibility. The coronation was postponed because of Edward VII's illness and the contracts in question were ruled void on the basis of frustration of purpose. In *Herne Bay Steamboat & Co. v. Hutton*[58] the contract involved the hiring of a steamboat in order both to watch the coronation from the sea and to undertake a cruise round the fleet. As the second purpose was not frustrated, the parties were held to the contract. In two other coronation cases: *Griffith v. Brymer*[59] and *Clark v. Lindsay*,[60] the contracts in question were made after the unforeseen external event (cancellation of the coronation procession) occurred. The parties, however, were not aware of this because the decision had not yet been publicly announced. The contracts were also ruled void, not on the ground of frustration of purpose but on the ground of mistake.

In the third group of cases, the unforeseen event neither makes the contract impossible to perform nor leaves it without purpose but fundamentally alters the equilibrium of the contract, either because the

---

55 [1904] 1 K.B. 493.

56 (1903) 19 T.L.R. 186.

57 [1903] 2 K.B. 740.

58 [1903] 2 K.B. 683.

59 (1903) 19 T.L.R. 434.

60 (1903) 19 T.L.R. 202.

cost of a party's performance is increased or because the value of the performance a party receives is diminished (hardship).[61]

It should be noted that the doctrine of frustration of purpose which covers the second group of cases was developed in English Law as an extension of impossibility of performance[62] and is generally considered as a subcategory of hardship[63] as it affects contractual equilibrium. Indeed, if we consider the coronation cases mentioned above, we can see that the value of the performance that the tenants receive is diminished as a result of the unforeseen event. However, I think that the doctrine of frustration of purpose should be distinguished from hardship, at least for theoretical reasons, as the main issue here is not the change in the value of the performance but the frustration of the reason why parties entered into the contractual relationship in the first place.

We will see, however, that the doctrine did not find a place of its own in the legal instruments that we examine in this book and is generally considered as a type of hardship. In accordance with the terminology of these instruments, the terms *force majeure* and *hardship* will be used here in order to cover cases of changed circumstances not foreseen by the parties at the time of contracting.

2.2. THE PRINCIPLE OF *PACTA SUNT SERVANDA* AND ITS EXCEPTIONS

2.2.1. *The Rule:* Pacta Sunt Servanda

Pacta sunt servanda or the sanctity of contracts is a universally accepted principle of contract law[64] which means that contracts should *prima facie* be enforced according to their terms.[65] The principle is considered as the basis of the contractual relationship, as it provides legal certainty

---

61 See Article 6.2.2. UNIDROIT Principles.

62 See for instance, BLUM, B.A., *Contracts, Examples& Explanations*, 4th ed., Aspen Publishers, New York 2007, p. 498.

63 See BRUNNER, C., *Force Majeure and Hardship under General Contract Principles, Exemption for Non-Performance in International Arbitration*, Kluwer Law International, The Hague 2009, p. 407 et seq.

64 LIU, C., "*Changed Contract Circumstances*", April 2005, http://www.cisg.law.pace.edu/cisg/biblio/liu5.html.

65 See BRUNNER, C., *Force Majeure and Hardship under General Contract Principles, Exemption for Non-Performance in International Arbitration*, Kluwer Law International, The Hague 2009, p. 1.

and stability[66] and is in line with concepts of natural justice and economic efficiency because it protects the reliance of the promisee.[67]

The principle has found an important scope of application in the context of international commercial contracts both as a fundamental principle of all legal systems,[68] generally with reference to national laws,[69] and as a transnational principle of private contract law[70] and the "cornerstone of *lex mercatoria*".[71]

The principle of *pacta sunt servanda* is not expressly mentioned in the CISG. It is, however, the underlying principle of numerous CISG articles dealing with parties obligations, such as Article 30, providing that the seller must deliver goods, hand over any documents relating to them and transfer the property in the goods, "as required by the contract" (and the Convention) and Article 53 (which is the mirror-image of Article 30), stating that the buyer must pay the price for the goods and take delivery of them "as required by the contract" (and the Convention).[72] It should also be added that *pacta sunt servanda* underlies the system of the Convention which adopts specific performance as a remedy.[73]

The UNIDROIT Principles expressly mention the principle of *pacta sunt servanda* in Article 1.3 entitled "binding character of contract",

---

66 See PUELINCKX, A.C., "*Frustration, Hardship, Force Majeure, Imprévision, Wegfall der Geschäftsgrundlage, Unmöglichkeit, Changed Circumstances*", (1986) 3(2) Journal of International Arbitration 47.

67 MASKOW, D., "*Hardship and Force Majeure*", (1992) 40 Am. J. of Comp. L. 657–669.

68 See *Liamco v. Libya*, April 12, 1977, Yb. Comm. Arb. 89 (1981), p. 101.

69 See for instance: I.C.C. award No. 3493 (1983), Yb. Comm. Arb. 111 (1984), p. 117; I.C.C. award No. 5485 (1987), Yb. Comm. Arb. 156 (1989), p. 168.

70 See for instance I.C.C. award No. 3383 (1979), Yb. Comm. Arb. 119 (1982), p. 129; see also *Sappire v. National Iranian Oil Company*, 15 March 1963, 35 International Law Review 136 (1967), p. 181.

71 See VAN HOUTTE, H., "*Changed Circumstances and Pacta Sunt Servanda*" in *Transnational Rules in International Commercial Arbitration*, E. Gaillard (ed.), (ICC Publ. Nr. 480/4), Paris 1993, pp. 105 et seq., p. 109; see also PIROZZI, R., "*Developments in the Change of Economic Circumstances Debate?*", 16 Vindobona Journal of International Commercial Arbitration 95–108 (2012), esp. p. 98; LIU, C., "*Changed Contract Circumstances*", April 2005, http://www.cisg.law.pace.edu/cisg/biblio/liu5.html.

72 See MAGNUS, U., "*General Principles of UN-Sales Law*", Lisa Haberfellner (trans.), Max Planck Institute for foreign and international Private Law, 59 Rabels Zeitschrift for foreign and international Private Law (1995) Issue 3–4, Hein Kotz in honor of his 60th birthday, Part I, cisg.law.pace.edu.

73 See Articles 46, 62 and 28. See, VANTO, J., "*Remarks on the manner in which the Principles of European Contract Law may be used to interpret or supplement article 46 of the CISG*", cisg.law.pace.edu; LIU, C., "*Changed Contract Circumstances*", April 2005, http://www.cisg.law.pace.edu/cisg/biblio/liu5.html.

stating that a contract validly entered into is binding upon the parties. Such a contract can only by modified or terminated in accordance with its terms or by agreement or as otherwise provided in the PICC.

Pacta sunt servanda is also a fundamental principle of the PECL.[74] In Article 6:111(1) PECL, which states that "A party is bound to fulfill its obligations even if performance has become more onerous, whether because the cost of performance has increased or because the value of performance it receives as diminished", *pacta sunt servanda* is strongly emphasized as the "rule".[75]

The rule set forth by Article 6:111(1) PECL has been implemented in DCFR Article III.–1:110(1), which also provides that "An obligation must be performed even if performance has become more onerous, whether because the cost of performance has increased or because the value of what is to be received in return has diminished". Both articles are designed to remind courts that the exemptions of *pacta sunt servanda* should be used carefully and should not undermine the principle.[76] These exceptions will be examined below.

2.2.2. *Exceptions to the Rule*

Like many other rules and principles which exist in legal systems, the principle of *pacta sunt servanda* can only be better understood by its exceptions.[77] Although these exceptions are named differently in different legal systems (such as frustration of contract, frustration of purpose, impossibility, *force majeure*, hardship, impractibility, *imprévision* etc.) and have different contents, there is a common cause to these exceptions, which is an external event affecting the contractual relationship by making the performance either impossible (*force majeure*) or substantially burdensome (*hardship*).

---

74 See for instance BUSCH, D., "*The Principles of European Contract Law and Dutch Law: A Commentary*", Preface written by Ole Lando, p. 7.

75 See FLAMBOURAS, D.P., "*The Doctrines of Impossibility of Performance and clausula rebus sic stantibus in the 1980 Vienna Convention on Contracts for the International Sale of Goods and the Principles of European Contract Law: A Comparative Analysis*", 13 Pace Int'l L. Rev. 261–293 (Fall 2001), p. 286.

76 See UNBERATH, H., "*Long-term Contracts and the DCFR, Interpretation and Adjustment*" in *The Common Frame of Reference: A View from Law & Economics*, Wagner, G. (ed.), Sellier, Munich 2009, p. 147.

77 See BRUNNER, C., *Force Majeure and Hardship under General Contract Principles, Exemption for Non-Performance in International Arbitration*, Kluwer Law International, The Hague 2009, p. 1.

The effects of these external events may vary but one interpretation rule can be seen as universally accepted: the exceptions to the principle of *pacta sunt servanda* should be interpreted strictly and narrowly and not in a way to undermine the sanctity of contracts and jeopardize economic requirements.[78]

It should also be emphasized that this issue has a special meaning in the setting of international commercial contracts, as the risk of unforeseen events affecting the performance of the contract is much higher in this type of contract than in the case of domestic contracts where parties are subject to the same legal and economic system – both because there are risks which only apply in international context and because the framework of these contracts is less stable compared to domestic transactions.[79] In this setting, contracts which are most affected by this kind of external event are long-term contracts, primarily because it is more difficult to foresee the farther future, and circumstances may sometimes change substantially during the life of the contract.[80] Indeed, as long-term contracts are known for both their complexity and duration, both *force majeure* and *hardship*, although not exclusively, are typically relevant in their context.[81]

Accordingly, like the principle of *pacta sunt servanda*, the doctrine of *rebus sic stantibus* – under which the validity of the contract depends on the continuance of the surrounding circumstances[82] – has been considered a principle of international law[83] and of *lex mercatoria*.[84]

---

78 PIROZZI, R., "*Developments in the Change of Economic Circumstances Debate?*", 16 Vindobona Journal of International Commercial Arbitration 95–108 (2012), p.101.

79 BRUNNER, C., *Force Majeure and Hardship under General Contract Principles, Exemption for Non-Performance in International Arbitration*, Kluwer Law International, The Hague 2009, p. 1.

80 In cases of hardship, for instance, the goods to be delivered may lose utility because of a change of technology; certain markets may be inaccessible because of political reasons, or because some new regulations may prohibit their use, etc. See FONTAINE, M., DE LY, F., *Drafting International Contracts, An Analysis of Contract Clauses*, Transnational Publishers Inc., Ardsley NY 2006, p. 453.

81 See Comment 5 PICC on Article 6.2.2 and Comment 5 PICC on Article 7.1.7. For the definition of a long-term contract see also Article 1.11 PICC and its Comment 3.

82 See FLAMBOURAS, D.P., "*The Doctrines of Impossibility of Performance and clausula rebus sic stantibus in the 1980 Vienna Convention on Contracts for the International Sale of Goods and the Principles of European Contract Law: A Comparative Analysis*", 13 Pace Int'l L. Rev. 261–293 (Fall 2001), p. 266 p. 278.

83 See *Questech* decision, 9 *Iran – US C.T.R.*, 122–123.

84 See VAN HOUTTE, H., "*Changed Circumstances and Pacta Sunt Servanda*" in *Transnational Rules in International Commercial Arbitration*, E. Gaillard (ed.), (ICC Publ. Nr. 480/4), Paris 1993, pp. 105 et seq., p. 115.

In this context, the harmonization of contract law is of paramount importance in order to give an international content to *pacta sunt servanda* and its exceptions, not only because rules in harmonized instruments are designed specifically according to the needs of international commerce but also because legal insecurity caused by divergences between national laws can only be overcome with a uniform set of rules.

2.2.2.1. *Force Majeure*

CISG

According to Article 79 CISG,

> (1) A party is not liable for a failure to perform any of his obligations if he proves that the failure was due to an impediment beyond his control and that he could not reasonably be expected to have taken the impediment into account at the time of the conclusion of the contract or to have avoided or overcome it or its consequences.
> (2) If the party's failure is due to the failure by a third person whom he has engaged to perform the whole or a part of the contract, that party is exempt from liability only if:
> (a) he is exempt under the preceding paragraph; and
> (b) the person whom he has so engaged would be so exempt if the provisions of that paragraph were applied to him.
> (3) The exemption provided by this article has effect for the period during which the impediment exists.
> (4) The party who fails to perform must give notice to the other party of the impediment and its effect on his ability to perform. If the notice is not received by the other party within a reasonable time after the party who fails to perform knew or ought to have known of the impediment, he is liable for damages resulting from such non-receipt.
> (5) Nothing in this article prevents either party from exercising any right other than to claim damages under this Convention.

Although the article does not expressly mention the term *force majeure*, in legal literature, it is submitted by authors that the above-mentioned article of the CISG reflects more civilian law traditions, which speak in terms of *force majeure*, rather than common law systems.[85]

---

[85] See NICHOLAS, B., "*Impractibility and Impossibility in the UN Convention on Contracts for the International Sale of Goods*" in Galston & Smit (eds.), *International*

Nevertheless, the provision also reflects influences of common law systems, as Rivkin points out, and adopts a compromise between civil law systems – which base impossibility on the lack of fault of the obligor and bar an award on damages – and the common law systems, which consider impossibility as an exemption from absolute liability and terminate the contract.[86]

As to the scope of the notion of the *force majeure*, it should be said that there is no uniform answer to questions, and the content and context may vary significantly especially for two main reasons.

The first one is related to the determination of the cases which would fall in the scope of the Article 79. Honnold enumerates some of the related settings – such as war, embargo and other governmental prohibitions, breakdown of transport facilities (such as the closing of the Suez Canal), strikes, shutdown or bankruptcy of a supplier – and underlines that these are "only points on a continuum of difficulties with varying degrees of scope, severity and unpredictability".[87]

The second reason is divergences existing in national legal systems and their potential influences on courts. In this direction, Tallon provides different interpretations and applications of the concept, diverging according to time and place, and notes that a number of theories emerged more recently, such as "*imprévision*" and "impracticability", which make the determination of the scope of the notion even more difficult.[88]

It can thus be said that a uniform and autonomous understanding and application of Article 79 can be considered a quite challenging task even after years of experience with the CISG.

In terms of Article 79, the party seeking exemption from liability in case of non-performance should prove four elements: 1) The failure is due to an impediment beyond his control; 2) He could not reasonably be expected to have taken the impediment into account at the time of the conclusion of the contract; 3) He could not reasonably be expected to

---

Sales: The United Nations Convention on Contracts for the International Sale of Goods, Matthew Bender, New York 1984, Juris Publishing, p. 5.1. See also ZIEGEL, J.S., "*Report to the Uniform Law Conference of Canada on Convention on Contracts for the International Sale of Goods*", July 1981, cisgw3.law.pace.edu.

86 See RIVKIN, D.R., "*Lex Mercatoria and Force Majeure*" in *Transnational Rules in International Commercial Arbitration*, E. Galliard (ed.), (ICC Publ No.480/4), Paris 1993, p. 200.

87 HONNOLD, J.O., *Uniform Law for International Sales under the 1980 United Nations Convention*, 3rd ed., Kluwer Law International, The Hague 1999, p. 472.

88 See TALLON D., in *Commentary on the International Sales Law*, C.M. Bianca, M.J. Bonell (eds.), Giuffrè, Milan 1987, p. 572.

have avoided the impediment or its consequences; and 4) He could not reasonably be expected to overcome the impediment or its consequences.[89] The last two elements apply subsequent to the time of contracting.[90]

The scope of the term "impediment beyond the control of the non-performing party" is a key issue in determining the scope of Article 79. As a result of the discussions during the conference, the word "circumstance" which was used in Article 74(1) of the Uniform Law on the International Sale of Goods (ULIS) has been replaced by the term "impediment". Rimke suggests that with this new terminology the CISG aims to avoid reference to existing concepts and develop its own autonomous system.[91] But what is the content of the term "impediment" in terms of the CISG?

It should first be said that there is no doubt that a case of physical impossibility is covered by the wording of Article 79 to the extent that requirements set forth by the article are fulfilled. Accordingly, the destruction of the seller's premises by fire can render performance impossible and fall within the field of application of Article 79, but if the seller failed to take necessary precautions to protect against fire, he cannot be exempt from liability in terms of this article.[92]

It is, however, not clear whether an economic "impossibility" can be considered within the scope of the article. On this matter, Hudson asks whether the term "control" means what is theoretically possible or what is commercially realistic, and points out that if the formulation of the Article 79 reflects the French rule of *force majeure* then the impediment must be understood as "unforeseeable, insurmountable, and irresistible", which requires that the performance should be impossible, not merely onerous.[93]

---

89 See the Secretariat's Commentary on Article 65 of the 1978 Draft, the Draft Counterpart of Article 79.

90 See HONNOLD, J.O., *Uniform Law for International Sales under the 1980 United Nations Convention*, 3rd ed., Kluwer Law International, The Hague 1999, p. 473.

91 See RIMKE, J., "*Force Majeure and Hardship: Application in international trade practice with specific regard to the CISG and the UNIDROIT Principles of International Commercial Contracts*" in *Pace Review of the Convention on Contracts for the International Sale of Goods*, Kluwer, 1999–2000, p. 242.

92 FLAMBOURAS, D.P., "*The Doctrines of Impossibility of Performance and clausula rebus sic stantibus in the 1980 Vienna Convention on Contracts for the International Sale of Goods and the Principles of European Contract Law: A Comparative Analysis*", 13 Pace Int'l L. Rev. 261–293 (Fall 2001), p. 266.

93 See HUDSON, A.H., "*Exemptions and Impossibility under Vienna Convention*" in *Force Majeure and Frustration of Contract*, McKendrick (ed.), Lloyds of London Press, London 1991, pp. 185–187.

It is generally admitted, however, that the impediment in terms of Article 79 should cover not only physical but also economic impossibility or "unaffordability", but under very narrow conditions.[94] It should be said that interpreting Article 79 from the perspective of French Law or any other national law would jeopardize the development of an autonomous content of the article, which is designed for a particular setting of contract. The formulations existing in the CISG inevitably reflect concepts existing in national laws but they should not be interpreted with reference to the concepts as understood in those national law systems. Instead, the point of reference should be the realities of and requirements of international trade.

Accordingly, economic "impossibility" should be considered a type of impossibility but the distinction between "economically impossible" and merely "more onerous" should be established carefully. We will come to this point later while examining hardship.

The impediment may have existed during the time of contracting. The party will still be exempt from liability if the case falls inside the scope of Article 79.[95]

Another controversial question is whether Article 79 applies also to cases of non-conformity. According to Honnold, the exemption provided by Article 79 does not apply to defective performance such as supply of non-conforming goods, as it must ordinarily be based on events that are widely known such as war, fire or embargo. He emphasizes that regarding "the care taken in a producer's manufacturing process" as covered by the wording of Article 79 would be anomalous and impractical.[96] Tallon, however, suggests that the expression "failure to perform" does not specify the nature of the non-performance and that it may be total or partial, delayed or defective.[97]

---

94 See SCHLECHTRIEM, P., *Uniform Sales Law-The UN Convention on Contracts for the International Sale of Goods*, Manz, Vienna 1986.

95 See the Secretariat's Commentary on Article 65 of the 1978 Draft, the Draft Counterpart of Article 79.

96 HONNOLD, J.O., *Uniform Law for International Sales under the 1980 United Nations Convention*, 3rd ed., Kluwer Law International, The Hague 1999, p. 472.

97 See TALLON, D., in *Commentary on the International Sales Law*, C.M. Bianca, M.J. Bonell (eds.), Giuffrè, Milan 1987, p. 575. In this direction see also FLECHTNER, H., "Article 79 of the United Nations Convention on Contracts for the International Sale of Goods (CISG) as Rorschach Test: The Homeward Trend and Exemption for Delivering Non-Conforming Goods", 19(1) Pace Int'l L. Rev. 29–51 (Spring 2007). See also LIU, C., "Perspectives from the CISG, UNIDROIT Principles, PECL and Case-Law", 2nd ed., at cisgw3.law.pace.edu.

It should be noted that the key element here is the fact that the impediment should be "beyond the control of the non-performing party" and this can only be evaluated by a case-by-case inquiry.[98] It should, however, not be forgotten that parties to an international commercial contract are "professionals", which necessitates a strict interpretation of both the terms "beyond the control" and "he could not possibly expected to have taken the impediment into account".

Indeed, as Kessedjian points out, a professional is

> expected to analyze the market, the situation in the countries where the manufacturing of the goods take place, where the delivery should occur, where the transport passes, and so on for each step in the performance of the contract.[99]

Having this point in mind, any type of failure to perform, including delivery of non-conforming goods, can be considered as treated by Article 79. As put forward in the literature, although it is hard to conceive of cases where a seller who delivers non-conforming goods might be exempt in terms of Article 79 (as impediments related to a seller's internal business operations cannot be considered beyond his control), such a possibility cannot be automatically excluded.[100]

This interpretation seems also to be in line with some benchmark court decisions from Germany. Indeed, in the *Vine Wax case*, the Federal Supreme Court of Germany, after referring to different points of view on the issue, ruled that the CISG "does not distinguish between an untimely delivery and a delivery of the goods not in conformity

98 See FLAMBOURAS, D.P., "*The Doctrines of Impossibility of Performance and clausula rebus sic stantibus in the 1980 Vienna Convention on Contracts for the International Sale of Goods and the Principles of European Contract Law: A Comparative Analysis*", 13 Pace Int'l L. Rev. 261–293 (Fall 2001), p. 266.

99 See KESSEDJIAN, C., "*Competing Approaches to Force Majeure and Hardship*", 5 International Review of Law and Economics (September 2005), p. 417. Basing on this fact, Professor Kessedjian suggests also that "A very good example of this could be the case of a manufacturer whose products contain a defect. He could never claim force majeure, for under no circumstance would a defect in the production process be considered beyond the control of the producer."

100 See LOOKOFSKY, J., "*Impediments and Hardship in International Sales: A Commentary on Catherine Kessedjian's 'Competing Approaches to Force Majeure and Hardship'*", 25 International Review of Law and Economics 436 (September 2005); see also SCHLECHTRIEM, P., "*Uniform Sales Law in the Decisions of Bundesgerichtshof*" at http://cisg.law.pace.edu/cisg/biblio/schlechtriem3.html.

with the contract. For both breaches of contract the same standard of liability applies".[101] In a more recent case, the same court stated that it may remain open whether Article 79 can generally be applied to goods that do not meet contractual requirements.[102]

It should also not be forgotten that whether a party would be exempt from liability in terms of Article 79 will depend on the terms of the contract in question. Accordingly, while guarantees will increase the scope of the liability, disclaimers and limitations will reduce it. In order to determine the scope of the liability provided by contractual terms Article 8 CISG will apply.[103]

Finally if we consider the last two elements (requirements) of Article 79, which apply subsequent to contracting, we should say that these also will be determined on a case-by-case basis. Accordingly, a party may be required to perform by providing a commercially reasonable substitute for the performance which was required under the contract, and the other party may reject the substitute performance if it is deficient compared to the original performance and constitutes a fundamental breach of contract.[104]

If the failure of performance by a party is due to the failure of a third person whom he engaged to perform the whole or a part of the contract, the party can be exempt from liability only if he and the third person would both be exempt in terms of Article 79(1). This paragraph will be examined below while comparing Article 79 with its counterparts existing in the PICC, PECL and DCFR.

Article 79 only deals with liability for damages and the impediment in question does not automatically terminate the contract. The other party may thus still avoid the contract if the failure to perform amounts to a fundamental breach of the contract.[105]

---

101 Germany, 24 March 1999, *Bundesgerichtshof* at http://cisgw3.law.pace.edu/cases/990324g1.html.

102 *Powdered milk case*, 9 January 2002, *Bundesgerichtshof*, Germany at http://cisgw3.law.pace.edu/cases/020109g1.html.

103 See SCHLECHTRIEM, P., *Uniform Sales Law-The UN Convention on Contracts for the International Sale of Goods*, Manz, Vienna 1986, p. 101.

104 See the Secretariat's Commentary on Article 65 of the 1978 Draft, the Draft Counterpart of Article 79.

105 ZIEGEL, J.S., "*Report to the Uniform Law Conference of Canada on Convention on Contracts for the International Sale of Goods*", July 1981, cisgw3.law.pace.edu.

UNIDROIT PRINCIPLES

The PICC deal with *Force Majeure* cases in Article 7.1.7. According to this article:

> (1) Non-performance by a party is excused if that party proves that the non-performance was due to an impediment beyond its control and that it could not reasonably be expected to have taken the impediment into account at the time of the conclusion of the contractor to have avoided or overcome it or its consequences.
> (2) When the impediment is only temporary, the excuse shall have effect for such period as is reasonable having regard to the effect of the impediment on the performance of the contract.
> (3) The party who fails to perform must give notice to the other party of the impediment and its effects on its ability to perform. If the notice is not received by the other party within a reasonable time after the party who fails to perform knew or ought to have known of the impediment, it is liable for damages resulting from such non-receipt.
> (4) Nothing in this article prevents a party from exercising a right to terminate the contract or to withhold performance or request interest on money due.

In the Comments on the article, it is stated that the PICC chose to use the term "*force majeure*" as the title of the article because it is widely known in international trade practice, which can be confirmed by the inclusion of "*force majeure* clauses" in international contracts. It is stressed, however, that the concept of *force majeure* as put forward by the Principles is not identical with any doctrine covering similar ground in domestic legal systems.[106]

Accordingly, explanations made for CISG Article 79 also apply for Article 7.1.7. PICC, and the term *force majeure* used in terms of this article does not refer to "an unforeseeable, insurmountable and irresistible contingency as understood in French law". Nicholas states in relation to Article 79 that the term "impediment" used in order to cover the ground is elastic and such elastic concepts are more undesirable in an international enactment than in a national one because of the lack of an already acquired patina of legal meaning, background and context.

---

106 UNIDROIT Principles of International Commercial Contracts 2016, Comments on Art. 7.1.7.

He acknowledges, however, that it is in the nature of definitions of this kind to be imprecise, and stresses that the important thing is that courts should see Article 79 in the context of the whole Convention and the practices of international trade.[107] These explanations apply also to Article 7.1.7 PICC.

If we compare the two articles, we see that the formulations are very similar. The most important difference between the two articles is that the counterpart of Article 79(2) is absent from the text of Article 7.1.7 PICC. This choice of the authors of the Principles to exclude Article 79(2) can be explained both by the difficulties in determination of the content of this paragraph and its limited scope of application.

First of all, it is difficult to define the term "third person". On this matter, it should be said that the "third person" in question cannot be the non-performing party's personnel because he is responsible for their poor performance as he organizes and controls their work.[108] Accordingly, the third person should be a sub-contractor or a similar legally "independent" party responsible for the performance of the whole or part of the contract.[109] The independence of this third party should nevertheless not be absolute. In other words, his non-performance should not be considered as an impediment beyond the control of the non-performing party in terms of the first paragraph.

Accordingly, the failure to perform by the supplier who has a monopoly or who was chosen by the buyer do not fall in the scope of the second paragraph and are dealt with by Article 79(1).[110] The aim of the second paragraph is thus to make exemption of a non-performing party more difficult by providing a double test of *force majeure* in cases

---

107 See NICHOLAS, B., "*Impractibility and Impossibility in the UN Convention on Contracts for the International Sale of Goods*" in *International Sales: The United Nations Convention on Contracts for the International Sale of Goods*, Galston & Smit (eds.), Matthew Bender, New York 1984, Juris Publishing, p. 5.1. See also ZIEGEL, J.S., "*Report to the Uniform Law Conference of Canada on Convention on Contracts for the International Sale of Goods*" (July 1981), cisgw3.law.pace.edu.

108 See SCLECHTRIEM, P., *Uniform Sales Law-The UN Convention on Contracts for the International Sale of Goods*, Manz, Vienna 1986, p. 104.

109 On the notion of "independent third party" see for instance TALLON, D., in Commentary on the International Sales Law, C.M. Bianca, M.J. Bonell (eds.), Giuffrè, Milan 1987, p. 584; LIU, C., *Remedies for Non-performance Perspectives from the CISG, UNIDROIT Principles, PECL and Case-Law*, 2nd ed. at cisgw3.law.pace.edu., fn 131 et seq.; GARRO, A.M., "*Comparison between provisions of the CISG regarding exemption of liability for damages (Art. 79) and the counterpart provisions of the UNIDROIT Principles (Art. 7.1.7.), Editorial Remarks*", 2005 at cisgw3.law.pace.edu.

110 See SCHLECHTRIEM, P., *Uniform Sales Law-The UN Convention on Contracts for the International Sale of Goods*, Manz, Vienna 1986, p. 104.

where the whole or a part of the contract is to be performed by an independent third party chosen by the party seeking an exemption. It has, however, a limited field of application as an exemption based on it would be very hard to establish, especially with the universal trend toward restrictive interpretation of the doctrine of *force majeure* in cases.[111]

Another difference between the two articles is the formulation of the last paragraph. Indeed, while the CISG states that nothing in the article prevents either party from exercising any right other than to claim damages, Article 7.1.7 gives a more restrictive list of possible remedies (the right to terminate the contract, withhold performance and request interest on the money due). Accordingly, two additional remedies which are reduction of the price (Article 50) and the right to compel specific performance (CISG Articles 46 and 62), available in the system of the CISG, are excluded by the UNIDROIT Principles.[112]

It should first be stated that Article 50 CISG (equivalent to PECL Article 9:401) on reduction of the price does not have a counterpart in the PICC. As to specific performance, it would be useless to compel specific performance when there is a failure to perform caused by impossibility.[113]

Apart from these points these is no significant difference between the two articles. The PICC, like the CISG, accept temporary impediment. It is noted in the Comments that in case of temporary impediment, the effect of the article would be to grant extra time for performance which may be greater or less than the length of the interruption. An illustration is given in the Comments: Climatic conditions make it impossible to lay a pipeline during winter in country *x*. Although the contract is timed to finish before winter, the start of work is delayed for a month by a civil war in a neighboring country, which makes it impossible to bring in all

---

111 See MELIS, W., "*Force Majeure and Hardship clauses in International Commercial Contracts in view of the practices of the ICC Court of Arbitration*", 1 Journal of International Arbitration 213 (1984), p. 215.

112 On this matter see for instance GARRO, A.M., "*Comparison between provisions of the CISG regarding exemption of liability for damages (Art. 79) and the counterpart provisions of the UNIDROIT Principles (Art. 7.1.7.), Editorial Remarks*", (2005) at cisgw3.law.pace.edu.

113 See HONNOLD, J.O., Uniform Law for International Sales under the 1980 United Nations Convention, 3rd ed., Kluwer Law International, The Hague 1999, pp. 494–495; See also FLAMBOURAS, D., "*Comparative Remarks on CISG article 79 & PECL Articles 6:111, 8:108*", May 2002, cisgw3.law.pace.edu.; also it should not be forgotten that hardship cases are treated separately by the PICC.

the piping on time. *A* may be entitled to an extension until the following spring even though the delay itself was one month only.[114]

PECL

According to Article 8:108 PECL entitled "excuse due to an impediment":

> (1) A party's non-performance is excused if it proves that it is due to an impediment beyond its control and that it could not reasonably have been expected to take the impediment into account at the time of the conclusion of the contract, or to have avoided or overcome the impediment or its consequences.
> (2) Where the impediment is only temporary the excuse provided by this Article has effect for the period during which the impediment exists. However, if the delay amounts to a fundamental non-performance, the creditor may treat it as such.
> (3) The non-performing party must ensure that notice of the impediment and of its effects on its ability to perform is received by the other party within a reasonable time after the non-performing party knew or ought to have known of these circumstances. The other party is entitled to damages for any loss resulting from the non-receipt of such notice.

This article should be read in conjunction with Article 8:107 ("Performance Entrusted to Another") which reads "A party which entrusts performance of the contract to another person remains responsible for performance".

The wording of Article 8:108 PECL has many similarities with equivalent articles of the CISG and PICC. The most important point here is that, unlike Article 79 CISG, the provisions in Article 8:108 PECL apply only to cases where the impediment prevents performance. Article 6:111 applies if performance became extremely onerous as a result of supervening unforeseen circumstances.[115] The preconditions of the article are those traditionally required for *force majeure*, namely to be unforeseeable, insurmountable or irresistible.[116]

---

[114] UNIDROIT Principles of International Commercial Contracts 2016, Comments on Article 7.1.7.

[115] See Comments on Article 8:108. See also FLAMBOURAS, D., "*Comparative Remarks on CISG Article 79 & PECL articles 6:101, 8:108*", Editorial Remarks at cisgw3.law.pace.edu.

[116] See Comments on Article 8:108. See also FLAMBOURAS, D., "*Comparative Remarks on CISG Article 79 & PECL Articles 6:101, 8:108*", Editorial Remarks at cisgw3.law.pace.edu.

Article 8:101(2) PECL states that where a party's non-performance is excused under Article 8:108 the aggrieved party may resort to any of the remedies provided in Chapter 4 PECL, except claiming performance and damages. The exclusion of claiming performance is reasonable and the explications made in relation to Article 7.1.7 PICC are also valid in terms of the PECL. Like the CISG, and differently than the PICC, price reduction is an available remedy under the PECL which provides for it in its Article 9:401. In case of a fundamental non-performance the creditor may terminate the contract by giving notice to the debtor under Article 9:303. If the contract is totally and permanently impossible to perform, however, it is "unnecessary to require a declaration" and "*force majeure* brings automatic termination of the contract".[117]

DCFR

According to Article III.–3:104 entitled "excuse due to an impediment":

(1) A debtor's non-performance of an obligation is excused if it is due to an impediment beyond the debtor's control and if the debtor could not reasonably be expected to have avoided or overcome the impediment or its consequences.
(2) Where the obligation arose out of a contract or other juridical act, non-performance is not excused if the debtor could reasonably be expected to have taken the impediment into account at the time when the obligation was incurred.
(3) Where the excusing impediment is only temporary the excuse has effect for the period during which the impediment exists. However, if the delay amounts to a fundamental nonperformance, the creditor may treat it as such.
(4) Where the excusing impediment is permanent the obligation is extinguished. Any reciprocal obligation is also extinguished. In the case of contractual obligations any restitutionary effects of extinction are regulated by the rules in Chapter 3, Section 5, Subsection4 (Restitution) with appropriate adaptations.
(5) The debtor has a duty to ensure that notice of the impediment and of its effect on the ability to perform reaches the creditor within a reasonable time after the debtor knew or could reasonably be expected to have known of these circumstances. The creditor is entitled to damages for any loss resulting from the non-receipt of such notice.

---

117 See Comments on PECL Article 8:108.

According to Article III.–2:106 which is entitled "performance entrusted to another", a debtor who entrusts performance of an obligation to another person remains responsible for performance.

In cases of impediment concerning an obligation arising from a contract, the first two paragraphs of the article should be read together and it is not difficult to note that the article has important similarities with above-mentioned corresponding articles of the CISG, PICC and that it is nearly identical to the provisions of the PECL.

In the Comments on Article III.–3:104, like in the Comments on PECL Article 8:108, it is underlined that the requirements laid down by the article are requirements which are traditionally sought for *force majeure* (*unforeseeable, insurmountable* and *irresistible*).[118] The external event should thus prevent performance, unlike in CISG Article 79.

It can be said that although the DCFR and PECL, like the CISG and the PICC, do not follow requirements which are identical to those set forth by a particular domestic legal system, the autonomous character of the articles seems to be less underlined in the Comments, which are more focused on a comparative law approach. In the Comments on the UNIDROIT Principles, by contrast, despite the fact that the PICC also clearly distinguish *force majeure* and hardship, any resemblance between Article 7.1.7 and any concept of *force majeure* is expressly excluded, with the fear that a uniform application would be jeopardized by the interference of domestic concepts.

The Comments on the DCFR describe the external character of the impediment as understood by Article III.–3:104.[119] In the light of these explanations it can be said that the article seems to have exactly the scope of Article 8:108 PECL.[120] Accordingly, the impediment should be outside the debtor's sphere of control. In this regard, the breakdown of a machine which is under the debtor's control or the failure of an employee cannot be considered covered by the article. It is the same for the failure of an independent subcontractor. Accordingly, the explanations made above in relation to Article 79 can generally apply for Article III.–3:104 DCFR (and Article 8:108 PECL).

It can however be noted that Article III.–3:104 DCFR (and Article 8:108 PECL) is more restrictive than Article 79 CISG with respect to some aspects of the determination of the external character of the

---

118 See DCFR Official Comments on Article III.–3:104.

119 See DCFR Official Comments on Article III.–3:104.

120 Compare with Comments on Article 8:108 PECL.

impediment. Indeed, according to illustrations given in the Comments, a strike in the debtor's company is excluded, as it is considered to be within the sphere of control of the debtor even if the strike was unforeseeable and if the company did not have the possibility to stop the strike by accepting the staff's demands. CISG Article 79 is more flexible than Article III.–3:104 DCFR (and Article 8:108 PECL) on deciding what is beyond the sphere of control of the parties in such cases.

Accordingly, the explanations made above in relation to the possible application of Article 79 to cases of delivery of non-conforming goods apply also to strikes which happen inside the company of the debtor. Thus, the employer's responsibility in case of a strike inside his company is decided on a case-by-case basis depending on the circumstances and the extent of the strike as well as the labor laws of the particular country.[121] Accordingly, despite the fact that Article 79(2) has a limited field of application because of the trend for a restrictive interpretation of exceptions to the *pacta sunt servanda* principle, there might be cases where the party would be exempt from liability in terms of Article 79(2) while it would not be the case in terms of Article III.–3:104 DCFR (or Article 8:108 PECL).

This difference should also be taken into account in cases of a failure of an independent subcontractor. According to DCFR Article III.–2:106 (counterpart of Article 8:107 PECL) a debtor who entrusts performance of an obligation to another person remains responsible for performance. Accordingly, the debtor cannot invoke the default of a subcontractor as an excuse for non-performance unless this was outside the debtor's control – for instance because there was no other subcontractor who could have been employed to do the work; and the impediment must also be outside the subcontractor's sphere of control.[122]

As we have already discussed above, in the system of the CISG, cases where the subcontractor has a monopoly (or is in any way completely beyond the control of the debtor) are dealt under paragraph (1) and not paragraph (2). Accordingly, the CISG is, here also, less strict as, unlike the DCFR (and the PECL), it is not necessary to check if the subcontractor is also exempt from liability under the system of Article 79. Beside such cases which would fall into the scope of application of

121 See SCLECHTRIEM, P., "*Uniform Sales Law-The UN Convention on Contracts for the International Sale of Goods*", Manz, Vienna 1986, p. 104, http://cisgw3.law.pace.edu/cisg/biblio/schlechtriem-79.html.

122 See DCFR Official Comments on Article III.–3:104.

the first paragraph, there might be cases where Article III.–3:104 (or Article 8:108) would be applied to situations covered by Article 79(2).

It should, thus, be kept in mind that here also there can be different interpretations between these instruments on deciding the sphere of control of the debtor, the CISG being more flexible.

Another difference between Article 79 and Article III.–3:104 concerns the requirement prescribed for the timing of the impediment. Indeed, as we explained above, in the system of the CISG, according to the Secretariat's Commentary, Article 79 applies even when the impediment in question has existed at the time of contracting without parties knowing it. Article III.–3:104 does not cover these cases and only applies to impediments subsequent to the time of contracting. The contract is, however, avoidable under the rules on mistake.

Finally, as to the effects of an impediment in terms of Article III.–3:104, it should be said that explanations made for Article 8:108 PECL are also available for Article III.–3:104.

Besides these points, the most important difference between the CISG and other instruments is the fact that, unlike the PICC, PECL and DCFR, the CISG does not contain express provisions on hardship, a point that we will examine under the next sub-section.

2.2.2.2. Hardship

Hardship and the CISG

One of the most challenging questions about the CISG is its position on hardship. In the absence of an express provision, a variety of answers are reached in the literature with reference to Articles 79 and 7 CISG and to the system of the Convention in general.

Before treating these answers, it should be noted that the preliminary issue here is to decide whether hardship is a matter governed by the Convention or not. As was submitted before, the CISG does not deal with issues related to validity. In some legal systems, however, hardship is considered as such.[123] Accordingly, if hardship is considered excluded by the Convention because of being a validity issue, then cases related to hardship would be dealt with by domestic laws.

---

123 E.g. Danish Contracts Act (*Aftaleloven*, paragraph 36), see KOFOD, R., "*Hardship in International Sales CISG and the UNIDROIT Principles*", Thesis, 2011, University of Copenhagen Faculty of Law, http://www.cisg.law.pace.edu/cisg/biblio/kofod.html.

According to Lookofsky in favor of such a solution, until we see some persuasive precedents which favor preemption within this context, "competition" between an Article 79 "exemption" and domestic rules of hardship remains a viable option. Thus, just as the PICC are sufficiently "roomy" to accommodate two distinctly separate conceptions and different remedial solutions for *force majeure* and *hardship*, the same may be said of the interface between CISG Article 79 and domestic laws. In support of this solution, Lookofsky writes that since the Convention drafters were not ready (in 1980) to legislate on sales contract validity, they can hardly have intended to put *hardship* into the Convention "through the back (Article 7(2)) door".[124]

The argument supporting that the CISG considered hardship to be a validity defense seems, however, to be without foundation and it cannot be extracted either from *travaux preparatoires* or from the wording of the Convention. A great number of national laws together with harmonized instruments such as the PICC, PECL and DCFR deal with the issue as a topic related to performance.[125] Promoting validity-based arguments against performance-based arguments without any concrete basis would be inconsistent with the main objective of interpretation, which is to promote uniformity in the CISG's application.

The fact that the UNIDROIT Principles (or other international or harmonized instruments) treat *force majeure* and hardship as two distinct concepts having different remedial solutions should not have an effect on this solution, as the UNIDROIT Principles (and other instruments) provide uniform solutions for hardship to be applied to cases which fall within its scope of application, while this is not the case for the CISG. If we accept that the CISG set forth uniform rules for *force majeure* and excluded hardship, then we will not have two separate concepts, as in the UNIDROIT Principles, but one separate concept of *force majeure* and an indefinite number of separate concepts of hardship as applied by national laws. The solution should, thus, be sought within the four corners of the CISG.

---

124 LOOKOFSKY, J., "*Walking the Article 7(2) Tightrope Between CISG and Domestic Law*", 25 Journal of Law and Commerce 87 (2005–06), p. 102.

125 On this matter, in relation with PICC see also CARLSEN, A., "*Can the Hardship Provisions in the UNIDROIT Principles Be Applied when the CISG is the Governing Law?*", http://www.cisg.law.pace.edu/cisg/biblio/carlsen.html; see also LIU, C., "*Remedies for Non-performance Perspectives from the CISG, UNIDROIT Principles, PECL and Case-Law*", 2nd ed., at cisgw3.law.pace.edu. See also KOFOD, R., "*Hardship in International Sales CISG and the UNIDROIT Principles*", Thesis, 2011, University of Copenhagen Faculty of Law, http://www.cisg.law.pace.edu/cisg/biblio/kofod.html.

As is submitted above, it is generally supported in the doctrine that cases of economic "unaffordability" can fall within the scope of application of Article 79 in extreme situations where "unaffordability" can be considered an "impediment" by virtue of this article. The choice of terminology of the article, which uses the autonomous term of "*impediment*" and does not refer to domestic concepts such as "*force majeure*", makes such an approach possible.

An economic "unaffordability", however, can never be considered a physical impossibility, as nothing is economically "impossible" in the strict sense of the word. Accordingly, "economic impossibility" can only be considered an extreme case of hardship. Thus, although Article 79 deals in general with impossibility and *force majeure*, its flexible approach makes possible that hardship cases might also fall within the scope of application of the article in some rare cases. A reasonableness test is again the criterion to decide whether a particular situation forms an "impediment" in terms of Article 79.

Accordingly, the article applies when performance has become so burdensome that the parties cannot reasonably be expected to overcome the "impediment" and perform.[126] The evaluation can only be made by an objective risk assessment made on a case-by-case basis,[127] and being exempt for "unaffordability" in terms of Article 79 can only be accepted in extreme cases.

On this matter Lookofsky writes that "I doubt that many arbiters would consider a 70% (or even 80%) price-increase to be sufficiently extreme to warrant a liability exemption … under Article 79."[128]

Then what will happen if there is a price increase of 80% in a given case where the CISG is applicable? Is there a gap to be filled in Article 79 or does the article close the door for such hardship cases and oblige the debtor to perform? In order to better understand the relationship between Article 79 and hardship, the history of the article should be taken into account. Three distinctive steps in the determination of the wording of the article are to be referred to on this matter.

---

126 See LINDSTROM, N., "Changed Circumstances and Hardship in the International Sale of Goods", 1 Nordic Journal of Commercial Law 2 (2006) fns. 45, 46 and 47: "it cannot be regarded as reasonable to require a party to save a plane that lays 100 meters below sea level."

127 See LINDSTROM, N., "Changed Circumstances and Hardship in the International Sale of Goods", 1 Nordic Journal of Commercial Law 2 (2006), fn. 50.

128 See LOOKOFSKY, J., "Not Running Wild with the CISG", 29(2) Journal of Law & Commerce 141 (2011), p. 165.

First, UNCITRAL proposed the following provision during the preparation of the 1977 Sales Draft, to be added within the text of the Convention:

> If, as a result of special events which occurred after the conclusion of the contract and which could not have been foreseen by the parties, the performance of its stipulations results in excessive difficulties for one of the parties, the performance of its stipulations results in excessive difficulties or threatens either party with considerable damage, any party so affected has a right to claim adequate amendment or its termination.

The Committee, however, did not follow this proposition.[129]

Second, Norwegian delegates put forward two alternative propositions for Article 79(3). The first proposition was to add the following provisions into the text:

> Where the impediment is temporary, the exemption provided by this article has effect for the period during which the impediment exists. Nevertheless, the party who fails to perform is permanently exempted to the extent that, after the impediment is removed, the circumstances are so radically changed that it would be manifestly unreasonable to hold him liable.

This proposal was supported by a significant number of the delegates but was rejected after the voting as some delegates were of the opinion that it would introduce the French doctrine of "*imprévision*" into the Convention.[130]

The alternative Norwegian proposition consisted of deleting the word "only" which was initially in the text of Article 79(3) which read "the exemption provided by this article has effect only for the period during which the impediment exists". This proposition, unlike the first two, was accepted.[131]

---

129 See RIMKE, J., "*Force Majeure* and Hardship: Application in International Trade Practice with Specific Regard to the CISG and the UNIDROIT Principles of International Commercial Contracts", *Pace Review of the Convention on Contracts for the International Sale of Goods*, Kluwer Law International, The Hague 1999–2000, pp. 197–243, p. 220.

130 See LINDSTROM, N., "Changed Circumstances and Hardship in the International Sale of Goods", 1 Nordic Journal of Commercial Law 2 (2006), fn. 56.

131 See for instance, LINDSTROM, N., "Changed Circumstances and Hardship in the International Sale of Goods", 1 Nordic Journal of Commercial Law 2 (2006), fn. 56.

Based on the history of the provision, different approaches are put forward in the doctrine. Accordingly, for the first group of scholars who base their argumentation on the express rejection of the first two propositions and on the drafting history of the article – which may seem to indicate that the autonomous term of "impediment" was also chosen in order to set aside any theory of changed circumstances[132] – hardship is excluded from the scope of Article 79. In favor of this solution, Flambouras points out that the CISG rejects the doctrine of *clausula rebus sic stantibus*, under which the validity of a contract depends upon the continuance of the surrounding circumstances at the time of contracting.[133]

Similarly, both Kritzer[134] and Jenkins[135] suggest that the CISG does not provide an exemption based on hardship. In the same direction, Sandvic and Lindström put forward that the CISG does not allow for any excuse based on hardship in cases where an impediment as provided by Article 79 ceases to exist, even if the circumstances are substantially altered during the time when the impediment was still effective.[136]

As a result, parties are fully liable under the contract even if the performance has become 70 or 80% more burdensome (or even more so) because of an unforeseeable and unavoidable event that occurred after the conclusion of the contract and non-performance is considered a breach of contract. In its most strict version, this approach may exclude economic impediments entirely from the scope of Article 79 to the extent that the article would only apply to cases of impossibility of performance.

According to a second approach, hardship cases can be considered within the scope of Article 79. In this direction, Honnold writes that the rejection of the first Norwegian proposal cannot be considered an

---

132 See Advisory Council Opinion No 7, Paragraphs 29 and 30.

133 See FLAMBOURAS, D.P., "*The Doctrines Impossibility of Performance and clausula rebus sic stantibus in the 1980 Vienna Convention on Contracts for the International Sale of Goods and the Principles of European Contract Law: A Comparative Analysis*", 13 Pace Int'l L. Rev. 261–293 (Fall 2001), p. 278.

134 See KRITZER, A.H., *Guide to Practical Applications of the United Nations Convention on Contracts for the International Sale of Goods*, Kluwer Law and Taxation Publishers, Boston MA 1989, p. 509.

135 JENKINS, S.H., "*Exemption for Non-performance: UCC, CISG, UNIDROIT Principles – A Comparative Assessment*", 72 Tulane Law Review 2015–2030, (1998), pp. 2020–2024, stating that the "Convention reflects more the traditional view of *pacta sunt servanda*" compared to the UCC.

136 See LINDSTROM, N., "*Changed Circumstances and Hardship in the International Sale of Goods*", 1 Nordic Journal of Commercial Law 2 (2006).

exclusion of hardship from the scope of Article 79, and the deletion of the word "only" from the original text shows that Article 79(3) does not lay down a rigid rule which does not take into account changed circumstances however important the changes.[137] Schlechtriem also shares the same position and states that such an approach is necessary in order to save the uniformity of application which is an important goal of the CISG.[138]

It should be noted that this approach may also be followed more or less strictly in practice, covering in its most strict version only some extreme cases of hardship which are described above as "economic *impossibility* cases" and leaving aside most other hardship cases even if the performance is 70 or 80% more onerous. On this matter, Slater stresses that it would not be easy to extend the word "impediment" in Article 79 to cover traditional cases of hardship as the article seems to be referring to greater obstacles.[139] It is indeed difficult to trace the line as the Convention created in Article 79 a novel and autonomous concept of "impediment" which is sometimes described as more flexible than "*force majeure*" and less flexible than "*impractibility*".[140]

The CISG Advisory Council Opinion No. 7, which states that

> A change of circumstances that could not reasonably be expected to have been taken into account, rendering performance excessively onerous ("hardship"), may qualify as an "impediment" under Article 79(1). The language of Article 79 does not expressly equate the term "impediment" with an event that makes performance absolutely impossible. Therefore, a party that finds itself in a situation of hardship may invoke hardship as an exemption from liability under Article 79,

however, seems to support that such an extension is possible.[141]

---

137 See HONNOLD, J., *Uniform Law for International Sales Under the 1980 United Nations Convention*, Kluwer Law and Taxation Publishers, Deventer/Netherlands 1989, pp. 442–443, and also the third edition, The Hague 1999, pp. 489–490.

138 See SCHLECHTRIEM, P., *Uniform sales Law, The UN-Convention on Contracts for the International Sale of Goods*, Manz, Vienna 1986, fns. 422a and 423.

139 See SLATER, S.D., "*Overcome by Hardship: The Inapplicability of the UNIDROIT Principles' Hardship Provisions to CISG*", Florida Journal of International Law, (Summer 1998), pp. 253–254.

140 Compare also with TALLON, D., in Commentary on the International Sales Law, C.M. Bianca, M.J. Bonell (eds.), Giuffrè, Milan 1987, p. 592.

141 CISG-AC Opinion No. 7, Exemption of Liability for Damages under article 79 of the CISG, Rapporteur: Professor Alejandro M. Garro, Columbia University School of Law, New York, NY, USA. Adopted by the CISG-AC at its 11th meeting of 12 October 2007.

Similarly, a German court decision is also in favor of such a broad interpretation of Article 79.[142] This of course does not mean that every change in contractual equilibrium would fall inside the scope of the article.

It should be said that, once the first approach – which excludes all remedies related to hardship when the CISG is the governing law – is rejected, another question presents itself. Is it possible for the court to adapt the contract in order to restore contractual equilibrium in terms of the CISG?

In the literature it is suggested that the Convention may be regarded as containing a gap to be filled with reference to Article 7 on matters of hardship. According to Schlechtriem, such a gap can be filled by applying the principle of good faith and fair dealing as an underlying principle of the Convention by virtue of Article 7(2). Furthermore, he submits that Article 50 CISG on price reduction in cases of non-conformity provides a basis to suggest that the Convention accepts adaptation of the contract if the contractual balance is altered.[143]

In the same direction, the above mentioned-opinion of the Advisory Council refers to Article 7(2) and the gap-filling process and states that "in a situation of hardship under Article 79, the court or arbitral tribunal may provide further relief consistent with the CISG and the general principles on which it is based".[144]

But can the detailed provisions on hardship of the UNIDROIT Principles be used in order to fill such a gap? An important decision of the Belgian Supreme Court created a lot of controversy concerning this issue. *Scafom International B.V. v. Lorraine Tubes S.A.S.* (Belgian Supreme Court Decision of 19 June 2009): The case concerned a number of contracts for the sale of steel tubes concluded between Scafom International (a Dutch Company – the buyer) and the seller (Exma – a French Company – predecessor of Lorraine Tubes). After the conclusion

142 See also *Electronic hearing aid case*, District Court Aachen, UNILEX, No. 43 0 136/92 (14 May 1993).

143 See SCHLECHTRIEM, P., *Uniform sales Law, The UN-Convention on Contracts for the International Sale of Goods*, Manz, Vienna 1986, p. 102 et seq. Compare also with Tallon who submits that "the adaptation of the contract by the judge is not expressly allowed in the Convention and must therefore be considered as impossible", TALLON, D., in *Commentary on the International Sales Law*, C.M. Bianca, M.J. Bonell (eds.), Giuffrè, Milan 1987, p. 592.

144 CISG-AC Opinion No. 7, Exemption of Liability for Damages under article 79 of the CISG, Rapporteur: Professor Alejandro M. Garro, Columbia University School of Law, New York, NY, USA. Adopted by the CISG-AC at its 11th meeting of 12 October 2007.

of the contracts, the seller gave notice to the buyer stating that the price agreed by the parties in the contract should be recalculated because of a 70% increase in steel prices. The contract did not contain any hardship clause. The buyer refused and sued the seller in the court of first instance (*Rechtbank van Koophandel Tongeren*). The Court, after acknowledging that the sudden and extraordinary price increase was duly proven by the seller. ruled that the CISG applicable to the contract in question deals only with *force majeure* and not with hardship. According to the Court, the seller should have agreed a price adjustment clause if it wanted the contract to be adapted to changed circumstances.[145] The seller appealed this decision in the Court of Appeal of Antwerp, which overturned the first instance decision and applied French law as the applicable domestic law, ruling that according to French law a duty to renegotiate the contract based on the good faith and fair dealing principle may be imposed in certain circumstances.[146] The case was brought to the Supreme Court, which rejected the application of French law, holding that there is a gap in the CISG to be filled by general principles of international trade, and ruled that these principles are to be found, among other sources, in the UNIDROIT Principles. The Court finally held that the seller was entitled to a renegotiation of the contract.[147]

It should first be said that the Supreme Court decision can be considered similar to the Advisory Opinion if not identical.[148] The approaches of both texts are highly criticized by some scholars based on different sets of arguments. The first category of arguments are based on the above-mentioned drafting history of the provision which is regarded by some scholars as expressly excluding any remedy for hardship. Accordingly, the suggestion that the Convention contains a gap on hardship is contested.[149]

---

145 Rechtbank van Koophandel Tongeren, 25 January 2005, http://cisgw3.law.pace.edu/cases050125bl.html.

146 Hof van Beroep, Antwerp, 29 June 2006.

147 *Scafom International BV v. Lorraine Tubes S.A.S.* Hof van Cassatie, 19 June 2009, http://cisgw3.law.pace.edu/cases/090619b1.html.

148 See KOFOD, R., "*Hardship in International Sales, CISG and the UNIDROIT Principles*" Thesis, 2011, University of Copenhagen Faculty of Law, http://www.cisg.law.pace.edu/cisg/biblio/kofod.html. See also Editorial Remarks on the *Scafom* Case, EISELEN, S., "*Editorial Remarks*", http://cisgw3.law.pace.edu/cases/090619b1.html.

149 For critics of the *Scafom* decision, see for instance, LOOKOFSKY, J., "*Remedies for 'Hardship' under the CISG International Sales Convention and the Decision by the Belgian Supreme Court in Scafom International v. Lorraine Tubes (2009)*", https://www.

We have already discussed this approach and the solution that it proposes for hardship cases governed by the CISG. There is not sufficient evidence in the drafting history of the CISG to ignore cases of contractual imbalance, especially when the Convention adopts price reduction as a remedy in case of non-conformity.

Second, there are authors who reject the use of the UNIDROIT Principles in order to supplement the Convention because of the chronology of the two texts; the Principles being subsequent to the Convention.[150] Veneziano suggests that the chronological argument, if taken seriously, would probably reach a result contrary to proponents of the CISG by undermining its use, as it fails to take into account the need to encourage the practical application and further development of the Convention.[151] The present author also shares this opinion. International trade is constantly evolving and the Convention should be further developed by courts in order to respond to actual needs. Article 7 should not be applied too narrowly in a way that would not leave room for development.

This does not mean, however, that the UNIDROIT Principles can be used automatically to supplement the Convention on any occasion. On this matter, the *Scafom* decision, which directly refers to the UNIDROIT Principles as a gap filler can be criticized. Fletchner rightly points out that the Supreme Court transforms "the general principles upon which the Convention is based" to "the general principles which govern the law of international trade" and searches for such general principles in

---

lexisnexis.com/legalnewsroom/international-law/b/commentry/posts/remedies-for-hardship-under-the-cisg-international-sales-convention-and-the-decision-by-the-belgian-supreme-court; KOFOD, R., "*Hardship in International Sales, CISG and the UNIDROIT Principles*", Thesis, University of Copenhagen Faculty of Law, http://www.cisg.law.pace.edu/cisg/biblio/kofod.html.

150 In favor of the chronological argument see DROBNIG, U., "*The UNIDROIT Principles and the Conflict of Law*", 3 Uniform L. Rev. 385 et seq. (1998); see also, SLATER, S.D., "*Overcome by Hardship: The Inapplicability of the UNIDROIT Principles' Hardship Provisions to CISG*", Florida Journal of International Law 231 (Summer 1998), p. 248; FERRARI, F., "*General Principles and International Uniform Law Conventions: A Study of the Vienna Sales Convention and the 1988 UNIDROIT Conventions on Factoring and Leasing*", 10 Pace Int'l L. Rev. 157 (1998), p. 168; SABOURIN, F., "*Quebec*" in M.J. Bonell (ed.), *A New Approach to International Commercial Contracts, The UNIDROIT Principles of International Commercial Contracts*, Kluwer Law International, The Hague 1999, p. 237 et seq.

151 VENEZIANO, A., "*UNIDROIT Principles and CISG: Change of Circumstances and Duty to Renegotiate according to the Belgian Supreme Court*", 15(1) Uniform L. Rev. 137 (2010), p. 141.

external sources.[152] Instead, it should have focused first on the underlying principles of the Convention.[153]

On this matter, Bonell's proposition on when to use the UNIDROIT Principles to supplement the CISG merits some attention. According to Bonell, the Principles may be used for this purpose only if they help for the clarification or support of an already existing general principle underlying the Convention.[154] Accordingly, if the good faith and fair dealing principle can be considered an underlying principle of the Convention, then hardship provisions provided by the UNIDROIT Principles may be used in order to supplement the CISG.

Lindström writes that this argumentation would build on far-fetched theories which are not possible in practice; namely Schlechtriem's theory of a general principle by virtue of Article 7(2) and Bonell's theory that provisions in the UNIDROIT Principles can be applied if they express a general principle of the CISG, even if the parties have not agreed on the application of the Principles.[155]

This author does not think that these theories are far-fetched. The status of the good faith principle as a principle on which the Convention is based is gaining more and more confirmation in literature and case law. In fact, there are a considerable number of authors who claim that a general duty of good faith imposed by the Convention can be extracted by referring to its different articles such as Articles 7(1), 7(2), 9(2) and 77,[156] and court decisions on this matter show that there is a tendency to give an important content to the good faith principle in terms of the Convention. These arguments can all serve as a basis to refer to the principle of

---

152 See FLETCHNER, H.M., "*The Exemption Provisions of the Sales Convention, Including Comments on 'Hardship' Doctrine and the 19 June 2009 Decision of the Belgian Cassation Court*", Legal Studies Research Paper Series Working Paper no. 2011-09, March 2011, p. 10.

153 For a similar position with the Court in relation to Article 25 CISG, see KOCH, R., "*Commentary on Whether the UNIDROIT Principles of International Commercial Contracts May Be Used to Interpret and Supplement Article 25 CISG*", http://www.cisg.law.pace.edu/cisg/biblio/koch1.html.

154 BONELL, J.M., *An International Restatement of Contract Law*, 3rd ed., Kluwer, 2015, p. 317 et seq.

155 See LINDSTROM, N., "*Changed Circumstances and Hardship in the International Sale of Goods*", 1 Nordic Journal of Commercial Law 2 (2006).

156 See explanations made in the section on good faith in the second chapter on §578 et s. Compare also with Felemegas who rejects a positive duty of good faith but accepts the status of the principle as an underlying principle in order to fill gaps in the Convention. FELEMEGAS, J., *The United Nations Convention on Contracts for the International sale of Goods:Article 7 and Uniform Interpretation*, Kluwer Law International, The Hague 2000–2001, Ch. 2, section 5.

good faith as a general principle to be applied in order to supplement the Convention on issues such as hardship by virtue of Article 7(2). This solution also provides the basis for further development of the Convention and of the autonomous content of the concepts that it governs. This does not mean, however, that we should automatically refer to the PICC when there is a gap in the CISG. The reference should be made via application of Article 7(2), as suggested by Bonell. For that purpose, the *Scafom* decision can be criticized.[157]

Finally, it is put forward in doctrine that the *Scafom* decision could pave the way for conflicting decisions in common law jurisdictions, where the doctrine of economic hardship is underdeveloped.[158] In this author's opinion, however, reference by the courts to the Unidroit Principles can only be helpful for a uniform application of the Convention.[159]

Hardship and the UNIDROIT Principles

Unlike the CISG, the PICC dedicates an entire chapter to hardship. After underlining the exceptional character of hardship in Article 6.2.1, the Principles define the concept in Article 6.2.2 and finally enumerate its effect on Article 6.2.3.

According to Article 6.2.2 ("definition of hardship")

> There is hardship where the occurrence of events fundamentally alters the equilibrium of the contract either because the cost of a party's performance has increased or because the value of the performance a party receives has diminished, and

---

157 In favor of Bonell's approach see also VENEZIANO, A., "*UNIDROIT Principles and CISG: Change of Circumstances and Duty to Renegotiate according to the Belgian Supreme Court*", Unif. Law. Rev. 137 (2010), p. 141. In favor of the reference of the Court to Unidroit Principles see also, PHILIPPE, D., "*Renégociation du Contrat En Cas de Changement de Circonstances Dans La Vente Internationale*", philippelaw.eu/UploadDirectory/UserFiles/files/rdcavril2011.pdf.

158 See, EISELEN, S., "*Editorial Remarks*" in *Scafom International BV v. Lorraine Tubes S.A.S.*, http://cisgw3.law.pace.edu/cases/090619b1.html. For a comparative analysis of American and Italian Laws on this matter see PERILLO, J.M., "*Hardship and Its Impact on Contractual Obligations: A Comparative Analysis*", http://www. cisg.law.pace.edu/cisg/biblio/perillo4.html.

159 According to Hansebout, reference by the Court to the Unidroit Principles shows that judges are up to date with recent economic and legal developments in international trade. HANSEBOUT, A., "*Landmark Supreme Court Decision on Hardship under CISG*", http://www.internationallawoffice.com/Newsletters/Company-Commercial/Belgium/ALTIUS/Landmark-Supreme-Court-decision-on-hardship-under-CISG.

(a) the events occur or become known to the disadvantaged party after the conclusion of the contract;
(b) the events could not reasonably have been taken into account by the disadvantaged party at the time of the conclusion of the contract;
(c) the events are beyond the control of the disadvantaged party; and
(d) the risk of the events was not assumed by the disadvantaged party.

Article 6.2.3 deals with the effects of hardship. Accordingly,

(1) In case of hardship the disadvantaged party is entitled to request renegotiations. The request shall be made without undue delay and shall indicate the grounds on which it is based.
(2) The request for renegotiation does not in itself entitle the disadvantaged party to withhold performance.
(3) Upon failure to reach agreement within a reasonable time either party may resort to the court.
(4) If the court finds hardship it may, if reasonable,
    (a) terminate the contract at a date and on terms to be fixed; or
    (b) adapt the contract with a view to restoring its equilibrium.

Both Articles 6.2.1 and 6.2.2 stress that a remedy for hardship can only be possible if the equilibrium of the contract is "fundamentally altered". The numeric criterion to be used to describe a fundamental alteration is, however, very controversial.

In the 1994 Commentary on the PICC it was provided that whether an alteration is "fundamental" in a given case will depend upon the circumstances. It is also submitted that if, however, the performances are capable of precise measurement in monetary terms, an alteration amounting to an increase of 50% or more of the cost of the performance is likely to amount to a "fundamental alteration".[160] The numeric threshold provided in the Comments on the PICC was, however, found to be too low by a number of authors in the literature.[161] As a consequence it has been deleted since the 2004 edition.[162]

---

160 See 1994 PICC Official Comments p. 147.

161 See VAN HOUTTE, H., "*The UNIDROIT Principles of International Commercial Contracts and International Commercial Arbitration: Their Reciprocal Relevance*" in *The UNIDROIT Principles for International Commercial Contracts: A New Lex Mercatoria?*, (ICC Publication No. 490/1), International Chamber of Commerce, Paris 1995, p. 190; DOUDKO, A.G., "*Hardship in Contract: The Approach of the UNIDROIT Principles and Legal Developments in Russia*", 5(3), Uniform L. Rev. 483 (2000), p. 496.

162 It is submitted in *travaux preparatoires* that the threshold was criticized in the legal literature as being "too low and in any event rather arbitrary", see UNIDROIT 2003,

Accordingly, it can be supported that, although there might be exceptions, a threshold below 50% would generally not be considered as a fundamental alteration. The question whether a percentage increase above this threshold can be considered such an alteration can only be evaluated on a case-by-case basis, taking into account all relevant circumstances such as the duration and the purpose of the contract, the level of risk assumption, experience, economic status and financial capabilities of the parties, whether the counter-performance was also burdened, etc.[163] Girsberger and Zapolskis rightly stress that such an approach would prevent a conflict with the concepts of equitable justice, reasonableness and good faith because of a strict application of *pacta sunt servanda*.[164]

Such criteria are also applicable in the determination of the scope of application of Article 79. Accordingly, giving numbers such as 70% or 80% may be misleading. An alteration of 70% can be considered within the scope of the article in some cases, as it was in the *Scafom* case, based on surrounding circumstances, and can be excluded in others.

The disadvantaged party is entitled to request renegotiation of the contract in terms of the PICC. If an agreement cannot be reached after renegotiation conducted in good faith by either party,[165] either party may resort to the court. The court may terminate or adapt the contract in order to restore the equilibrium if reasonable. If not, the court may direct parties to resume negotiations or confirm the terms of the contract as they stand.[166]

Study L-Doc. 85 at http://www.unidroit.org/english/documents/2003/study50/s-50-085-e.pdf.

163 See GIRSBERGER D., ZAPOLSKIS P., "*Fundamental Alteration of the Contractual Equilibrium under Hardship Exemption*", 16 March 2012, p. 128, at https://www.mruni.eu/upload/iblock/434/7_Girsberger.pdf.

164 See GIRSBERGER D., ZAPOLSKIS P., "*Fundamental Alteration of the Contractual Equilibrium under Hardship Exemption*", 16 March 2012, p. 128, at https://www.mruni.eu/upload/iblock/434/7_Girsberger.pdf.

165 Although it is not expressly mentioned in the article, the conduct of both parties during the renegotiation process is subject to the good faith principle, see PICC Official Comments 2016 on Article 6.2.3.

166 See PICC Official Comments 2016 on Article 6.2.3.

Hardship and the PECL

According to the PECL Article 6:111, entitled "change of circumstances",

> (1) A party is bound to fulfil its obligations even if performance has become more onerous, whether because the cost of performance has increased or because the value of the performance it receives has diminished.
> (2) If, however, performance of the contract becomes excessively onerous because of a change of circumstances, the parties are bound to enter into negotiations with a view to adapting the contract or terminating it, provided that:
>   (a) the change of circumstances occurred after the time of conclusion of the contract,
>   (b) the possibility of a change of circumstances was not one which could reasonably have been taken into account at the time of conclusion of the contract, and
>   (c) the risk of the change of circumstances is not one which, according to the contract, the party affected should be required to bear.
> (3) If the parties fail to reach agreement within a reasonable period, the court may:
>   (a) terminate the contract at a date and on terms to be determined by the court; or
>   (b) adapt the contract in order to distribute between the parties in a just and equitable manner the losses and gains resulting from the change of circumstances.
>
> In either case, the court may award damages for the loss suffered through a party refusing to negotiate or breaking off negotiations contrary to good faith and fair dealing.

It can first be said that beside the fact that PECL Article 6:111, which covers all three Articles 6.2.1, 6.2.2 and 6.2.3, seems to be better presented than related articles of the PICC, there is not a substantial difference between the system of the PECL and the system of the PICC.

The PECL chooses to use the term "excessively onerous" instead of the term "fundamental alteration" in order to describe the situations of changed circumstances. According to Kessedjian, choices of terminology of the PECL are better than that of the PICC, first because the PECL prefers the neutral term of "change of circumstances" to the term "hardship", and second because the term "contract becomes excessively onerous" more clearly defines the events that would trigger the provision.[167] According to McKendrick, however, the requirement of "excessively onerous" is implicit within the requirement of "fundamental alteration".[168]

An important difference between the two articles is the time factor to be taken into account. In the system of the PECL, if, unknown to either party, circumstances which make the contract excessively onerous for one of them already existed at the time of contracting, the rules of mistake apply.[169] According to Article 6.2.2 PICC, however, hardship provisions apply even if the events occurred before the time of contracting. The criterion to be taken into account is the time when they become known to the disadvantaged party. Again, Article 6:111 seems to be more coherent than its PICC counterpart.

The requirement set forth by Article 6.2.2, according to which the events should be beyond the control of the disadvantaged party, does not exist in Article 6:111. This may be because such a requirement could be seen as unnecessary when the essence of the concept of hardship is taken into account. Finally, the last requirement of Article 6.2.2, which states that "the risk of events was not assumed by the disadvantaged party", does not exist as such in the PECL. On this requirement Kessedjian points out that, it is quite impossible that the disadvantaged party assumes a risk which became known to him after the conclusion of the contract according to the first requirement.[170]

Moreover, according to the second requirement it is also necessary that the same party could not reasonably have taken into account the risk at the time of conclusion. The PECL, thus, did not follow the same formulation and provided for a more objective requirement according to which the risk of the change of circumstances is not one which, according to the contract, the party affected "*should be*" required to bear.

The article does not deal with the request for negotiation in a detailed way such as its PICC counterpart does. It states instead that parties are bound to enter into renegotiations in case of changed circumstances.

---

167 KESSEDJIAN, C., "*Competing Approaches to Force Majeure and Hardship*", 25 International Review of Law and Economics 415 (September 2005), pp. 421–423.

168 McKENDRICK, E., in *Commentary on the UNIDROIT Principles of International Commercial Contracts*, Vogenauer S., Kleinheisterkamp J. (eds.), Oxford University Press, Oxford 2009, pp. 719–720.

169 See Comments of PECL on Article 6:111.

170 KESSEDJIAN, C., "*Competing Approaches to Force Majeure and Hardship*", 25 International Review of Law and Economics 415 (September 2005), p. 421.

Again, the court may either terminate the contract or modify its terms under the PECL. It may require the parties to make a last effort at renegotiation or use the means that are available to it under its national law. It may not, however, rewrite the contract for the parties.[171]

Hardship and the DCFR

According to Article III.–1:110 DCFR, the title of which is "Variation or termination by court on a change of circumstances",

> (1) An obligation must be performed even if performance has become onerous, whether because the cost of performance has increased or because the value of what is to be received in return has diminished.
> (2) If, however, performance of a contractual obligation or of an obligation arising from a unilateral juridical act becomes so onerous because of an exceptional change of circumstances that it would be manifestly unjust to hold the debtor to the obligation a court may:
>   (a) vary the obligation in order to make it reasonable and equitable in the new circumstances;
>   or
>   (b) terminate the obligation at a date and on terms to be determined by the court.
> (3) Paragraph (2) applies only if:
>   (a) the change of circumstances occurred after the time when the obligation was incurred;
>   (b) the debtor did not at that time take into account, and could not reasonably be expected to have taken into account, the possibility or scale of that change of circumstances;
>   (c) the debtor did not assume, and cannot reasonably be regarded as having assumed, the risk of that change of circumstances; and
>   (d) the debtor has attempted, reasonably and in good faith, to achieve by negotiation a reasonable and equitable adjustment of the terms regulating the obligation.

Although the formulation of the DCFR article is not identical to that of Article 6:111 PECL and seems to be more complicated than the latter, it should be said that the articles are again quite similar. The most important difference between the two articles is the fact that Article III.–1:110 also applies to unilateral acts, unlike Article 6:111.

---

171 See PECL Comments on Article 6:111.

Another point is that the requirement of "excessively onerous" set forth by the PECL is revisited by the DCFR, which provides that the court may vary or terminate the performance when the performance "becomes so onerous because of an exceptional change of circumstances that it would be manifestly unjust to hold the debtor to the obligation". The double tests of "exceptional change" and "manifestly unjust performance" are added.[172]

Although this choice can be explained by the intention to stress that hardship is an exceptional concept to have recourse to, this author believes that this formulation complicates unnecessarily the criterion to be applied. It is in any cases the circumstances of a given case which will be decisive.

3. CONCLUSION

Sometimes an event which was not foreseen at the time of contracting can render the contract impossible to perform (*force majeure*) or without purpose (*frustration of purpose*). It may also completely change the contractual equilibrium (*hardship*). We have focused on these issues in the chapter on gap filling because these concepts share the same underlying reason with gaps, which is the lack of foresight at the time of contracting.

For this purpose, we have examined related provisions contained in the CISG, PECL, PICC and DCFR and once again, we observed that the CISG (having a gap on hardship) contains less detailed provisions than the other instruments. Thus, the possibility to have recourse to the PICC in order to fill the gap on hardship and possible foundations for such a solution became relevant. This author believes that the principle of good faith and fair dealing as a principle on which the Convention is based provides the basis for such a solution.

---

172 See GIRSBERGER D., ZAPOLSKIS P., "*Fundamental Alteration of the Contractual Equilibrium under Hardship Exemption*", 16 March 2012, p. 124, https://www.mruni.eu/upload/iblock/434/7_Girsberger.pdf.

CONCLUSION

In conclusion, contract interpretation can be briefly described as the understanding of the "meaning" of a contract and of rights and obligations that are created by it. Accordingly, the first aim in this book was to understand the notion of "contractual meaning". Instead of examining this notion as a linguistic or philosophical concept, this book has focused on it in the sense of the "meaning attached to contractual clauses by contracting parties".

From this perspective, there are three definitions of "contractual meaning" traditionally put forward in the literature. When we enumerate them from the most "objective" to the most "subjective" one, we can say that the textualist approach gives us the most objective definition, which is: "That to which either party ought to be referring according to the common and ordinary usage of the words". It should be noted that we do not discuss here the meaning that each party ought to refer to by the application of overriding legal rules such as any application of the principle of good faith and fair dealing. As a result, from this point of view, the notion of "party intent", whether "actual" or "presumed", is not taken into consideration in ascertaining contractual meaning and the contract is understood as the written document.

It must be noted here that language is not as objective as it is generally presumed to be, as all understanding of language is necessarily construed against contextual background knowledge. When, for instance, the author of an utterance uses the sentence "blue bicycle", he/she necessarily refers to background information on the color called "blue" and the object called "bicycle." Accordingly, in order to "understand" this sentence, the listener would need to have the knowledge of that background information. When we communicate or understand language, we often think that the other party shares the same background knowledge while it might not always be the case. A "common or ordinary meaning" of language is thus a very debatable concept.

However, while from an intentionalist point of view there is no meaning and no language apart from "intention", it is hard to conclude that language in general has meaning only when the author's (whether subjective or objective) intention is at stake. Indeed, one's actual or presumed intention does not play an important role when one communicates a scientific fact.

In considering the prescriptive language of the contract, however, if we are concerned with preserving the essence of "party autonomy", meaning should inevitably be considered with reference to the intention of the contracting parties, whether actual (subjective) or presumed (objective). This is, in this author's opinion, to treat the contract as an agreement and not merely as a written document.

Accordingly, when we eliminate a textualist approach, we have two competing definitions of contractual meaning, each corresponding to a competing "interpretative" approach; namely, objective and subjective theories of contract interpretation. Indeed, from a more objective point of view, contractual meaning is "that to which either party has reason to believe the other is referring" and from a more subjective one it is "that to which either party refers".

In a subjective approach, interpretation is the establishment of the meaning that the parties actually attributed to the expressions contained in the contract and thus, the determination of the existence of the parties' common intention at the time of contracting. This approach is in line with a will theory of contract, according to which commitments are enforceable because the promisor has willed or chosen to be bound by his commitment. This constitutes an affirmation of the principle of freedom of contract, as the idea lying behind such an approach is the self-imposed character of the contractual obligation. Whenever the parties' subjective intention can be shown, it prevails over objective manifestations.

In an objective approach, contracts should not be interpreted by looking into the parties' actual intent but rather by looking into what they have expressed and written down. This approach is in accordance with the reliance theory of contract, which suggests that we ought to be liable in contract law for our assertive behavior when it creates foreseeable and justifiable reliance by others. The priority given to the understanding of the listener leads to the construction of some sort of a "presumed intent" where the foreseeable character and reasonableness of the listener's understanding are questioned. Accordingly, the theory refers to an objective point of view which is called the "reasonable person" criterion.

It is very important to emphasize that the degree of objectivity of an interpretation system can only be understood by the extent of the contextual information that it takes into account. While the subjective approaches by definition are always contextual, objective approaches can significantly vary on that point, on a scale which goes from strict textualism to a high level of contextualism where it might sometimes be difficult to distinguish between relevant circumstances and subjective declarations of intent.

It can, thus, be said that in an objective test, the "degree of objectivity" of the reasonable person and the extent of that person's "third party" character depend on its construction and the degree of context to be taken into account.[1] Accordingly, any construction of the reasonable person may be situated on a scale between "a neutral, third-party listener" and "a highly approached objectified substitute of the actual parties". When the reasonable person is placed in the shoes of the contracting parties and construed as an objective substitute of the actual parties, the test becomes more "subjective". Conversely, it is also possible for the reasonable person to be construed merely as a properly informed ordinary speaker of the language. All depends on the weight given to the text and the degree of context taken into account in its construction.

As reliance and will theories are one-sided, they are generally combined in practice. Thus, interpretation rules in most systems combine the objective and subjective theories and adopt tempered solutions. In any case, the "objectivity" or "subjectivity" of an interpretation method can only be determined with reference to the "context" taken into account in the ascertainment of the contractual meaning, which puts the notion of "context" in the center of all discussions on the interpretation rules adopted in a given system.

When we examine the interpretation rules contained in the CISG, PICC, PECL and DCFR on the basis of this necessary theoretical background, we see that these instruments bring together different approaches and create an autonomous interpretation system which is sometimes known in the literature as the "inter-subjective" method of interpretation.

The first test to be applied is a subjective test where the common intention of the parties prevails over the written document. In the same direction, if the intent of a party differs from the wording and the other party knew or could not have been unaware about this actual intent, this latter party cannot rely on the reasonable meaning of the words. In the

1 Although we are mainly focused here on the notion of context, it should not be forgotten that the reasonable person may also be objectively construed with the application of the principle of good faith and fair dealing, and become objective in this sense.

international commercial setting where parties are generally located in different places, however, the applications of this subjective test can rather be limited. Thus, the subjective test is completed with an objective test of the "reasonable person" to be applied in cases where the first test does not yield a solution.

In both tests, "all relevant circumstances" (such as preliminary negotiations, subsequent conduct, usages, practices established between the parties, interpretation which has already been given to similar clauses by the parties, the meaning commonly given to terms and expressions in the trade concerned, and the nature and the purpose of the contract) are taken into account, which makes the reasonable person a highly party-based construction in terms of these instruments. This – on a case-by-case basis – construction of the reasonable person is sometimes classified in literature by concepts such as "*business common sense*" or "*generally accepted view*" in the quest for uniformity of application.

In this author's opinion, although these general notions may be of help in the quest for uniformity of application, their importance should not be over-estimated and the circumstances of the given case should not be forgotten. After all, in the highly contextualist system of these instruments, the statement of a tractor salesman from a developed country to a Nusquamian peasant is to be interpreted as it would be understood by the reasonable Nusquamian peasant.[2]

In the light of this highly contextual approach, it should be noted that the CISG, PICC, PECL and DCFR reject formalistic interpretation rules from common law countries such as the plain meaning rule, four corners rule and parol evidence rule in contract interpretation. From a law and economics perspective, however, these formalistic rules are generally considered more adapted to commercial settings where the actors are generally well informed parties. In other words, the context of the commercial contracts may necessitate the rejection of a contextual interpretation technique.

Accordingly, opting for a fully contextualist interpretation approach may be considered controversial especially for the CISG and PICC, which only apply to commercial contracts. While, from a comparative law perspective, interpretation of contracts is a less controversial topic than before as globalization has showed its effects and brought different systems closer to one another, the controversy, thus, remains

---

2 For this example, see FELTHAM, J., "*The United Nations Convention on Contracts for the International Sale of Goods*", J. Bus. L. 349 (1981).

in the context of international commercial contracts. In order to better understand this important point, this book has classified different types of context which form the unique context of an international commercial contract.

For this purpose, first a distinction between two competing "*specific contexts*" in which an international commercial contract is placed, namely, "commercial" and "international" context is made. Then, three different types of "*general context*" that may affect not only the interpretation of international commercial contracts but also interpretation of every contract are examined.

When we focus on the "commercial context", we observe that in a world where contextualist approaches continue to gain ground over formalism, neoformalistic arguments, claiming that commercial context itself may necessitate a rejection of the context in terms of commercial contracts, are indeed becoming more and more present. From that point of view, formalistic rules increase predictability and certainty in contractual relationships and reduce transaction costs. They are also more adapted to commercial contracts because they promote efficiency in contracting, given the ability of firms to maximize welfare by negotiating efficient contracts. Finally, they mitigate the risks of judicial discretion and reduce litigation costs.

So why did the instruments that we are examining here, and especially the CISG and PICC, not opt for interpretative rules that are considered more cost effective and, thus, efficient and adopt a highly contextual interpretation technique? In order to understand this choice, the second competing context, namely, international context should be examined.

Indeed, as an international commercial contract cannot solely be defined by its commercial character, it is not sufficient to take only economic criteria into consideration in deciding on the most suitable rules of interpretation to be applied. The "*international character*" of the contract which brings a particular factual reality into the equation needs also to be taken into account. Accordingly, in an international setting, where the same language and the same legal and cultural background information to process that language are often not shared by the parties (or the court), linguistic errors are more likely to be observed.

While the "objectivity of the language" is already the subject of a big debate in homogeneous domestic contexts, the debate gains another dimension in a heterogeneous international setting. Can (or should) a contract between a Chinese company and a Russian company, written in English, be interpreted by a French arbitrator according to the ordinary meaning of the contractual clauses as understood by a competent user of the English language? Can we obtain "predictability" in commercial transactions with such an approach?

If parties are very well-informed big corporations, immune to linguistic and cultural errors, who regularly enter into the same kind of transactions in the same foreign language, and if the interpreter focuses exclusively on the linguistic information in solving the litigation and puts aside his or her legal, linguistic and cultural background, this goal can be reached. But does this ideal picture reflect the realities of international commercial contracts?

It should first be emphasized that not all the actors in international trade are such well-informed parties. Indeed, the increasing globalization of commerce and improvement of transportation and communication technologies have enabled new, smaller economic players to take part in international commerce. Moreover, a dichotomy between consumer and merchant is also challenged as small businesses show resemblances with consumers in their sophistication.

Uniform and harmonized instruments, conceived in order to respond to the growing needs of international business, could not and did not overlook cultural and linguistic "diversity" in the world whose relevance grew and continues to grow with the evolution of new technologies in transportation and communication. Moreover, one important goal of these instruments is to help promote and facilitate international trade.

Adopting interpretative approaches, advantageous to most experienced parties, which may "exclude" or "scare" newcomers and less experienced actors would certainly be at odds with such a goal. The CISG is ratified by 89 countries so far. One can hardly imagine the linguistic and cultural diversity, as well as varying levels of ability, of the actors involved.

Apart from commercial and international contexts, there are three different types of "*general context*" that may affect the interpretation process of not only international commercial contracts but also every contract.

From this perspective, first, there are elements inherent to contractual parties such as their abilities (including linguistic) and the "context" in which each of them is situated at the time of contracting. All four instruments that we are examining in terms of this book consider this first type of context relevant by adopting first a subjective test and then by construing the reasonable person as someone in the shoes of the actual parties.

Second, there are elements inherent to the contract itself and the "context" in which the contract itself is concluded. Again, all four instruments consider all relevant circumstances related to the contract during the interpretation process in both subjective and objective tests.

And finally, third, there is the context in which the "interpreter" or the "reader" is situated which is mainly constituted of his/her linguistic, cultural and legal background. Accordingly, as a user of the language he/she has a view concerning the meanings of words used by contracting parties (that he/she can "extract" with more or less reference to the contextual matrix of the contract) as well as the purpose and the function of contract interpretation. He/she has a view on fairness and on to what extent it should be taken into account when interpreting a particular contract and so forth.

While factual information on the first and the second contexts may generally be considered relevant (in varying degrees) in contextualist approaches, the third set of context is indeed a matter of concern. Both textualists and contextualists agree on this point: the court should respect the principle of freedom of contract and not make the contract for the parties according to its own beliefs.

While there is "subjectivity" in all "interpretation" and subjective elements inherent to the interpreter's context are not desirable in the interpretation process, solutions that are traditionally put forward in order to minimize the risk of interference do simply not fit within the setting of international contracts.

First, to make a distinction between the notions of "interpretation" and "understanding of a text" based on the common and ordinary speaker of the language and to consider the problem a matter of grammar and dictionary in order to reach objectivity and efficiency is of little help where the language of the contract is generally foreign to at least one of the parties and/or the court.

Second, a classical, neutral conception of the reasonable person is insufficient to cover the diversity among "the real-life reasonable parties" who enter into international commercial contracts and to bring predictability and certainty in commercial transactions. In the absence of data related to the actual parties, the interpreter will turn to his or her own "context" to resolve the dispute, which definitely is the complete opposite of the result that is aimed for. From that point of view, the more the reasonable person is placed in the shoes of the contracting parties, the more this hypothetical personality stays outside the shoes of the interpreter.

Minimizing the interference of the interpreter's context has indeed a very important aspect in the setting of international commercial contracts. In a domestic setting, the interpreter may have a *false consensus bias* as to the "meaning" of the words and falsely think that his or her categorization of the linguistic data is naturally shared by others as the predominant view. This potential "linguistic" bias is also valid for international settings and may even become more problematic because of linguistic divergences and "*faux amis*" (the same term (legal or other) having different meanings in different places). In addition, in an international setting, *cultural biases* also become more likely to occur because of the cultural heterogeneity. In any case, it is not easy to separate language from culture as the former is necessarily contextual.

Accordingly, an interpretation method which focuses only on the written language of the contract could create more uncertainty than certainty and increase transaction costs as costs related to linguistic information. Such an approach would moreover be more disadvantageous for parties which will have to contract in the language of their partner, which could create a fear of entering into contractual relationships and thus prevent the promotion of international trade. Although these effects would be less important for experienced firms which constantly enter into the same type of international contracts in a given language and a given country, they could be more present for newcomers and less experienced actors.

What are the practical impacts of the fully contextual interpretation method adopted by the CISG, PICC, PECL and DCFR on the litigation process? Will the court gather all information about the whole factual matrix related to the characteristics of the parties and the contract, preliminary negotiations, subsequent conduct, practices established between the parties, usages, etc. in construing the reasonable person each time when there is a dispute over the meaning of a contractual clause? The list of relevant circumstances provided by the CISG, PICC, PECL and DCFR is a non-exhaustive one. Accordingly, it is possible to ask where this inquiry is going to start and where it is going to end. At the end, the litigation process needs to have some efficiency and should not waste time and money in vain.

The answer to this question can also be found in the notion of "context" itself. Adopting a fully contextualist approach means that the interpretation rules in a given system make all contractual data available for the court to resolve issues related to the interpretation of contracts. This does not mean, however, that there must not be any selection between all available circumstances in a given case. The context itself provides the best criteria for the selection of the relevant context. From this point of view, it can be said that arguments put forward by new formalism on the commercial context have some relevancy even when we opt for a fully contextualist approach.

Characteristics related to the parties and the contract provide the best guidance for the court in order to decide on the relevant context to be taken into account. How informed are the contracting parties? What is the nature of the contract? How detailed is the contract? It is important for the court to have access to contextual information in order to be able to decide which circumstances are indeed relevant in a given case. Accordingly, the reasonable person in the shoes of a well-informed big multi-national corporation who enters repeatedly into the same kind of detailed, well-negotiated contracts in a given country, in a given language may not be construed in the same manner as the reasonable peasant from a developing country.

Consequently, the court may find that it would be unreasonable for the first kind of reasonable person to rely on preliminary negotiations in the circumstances of the case and not consider preliminary negotiations as relevant context in a given case, but do the exact opposite and give them significant weight in construing the second kind of reasonable person in another case. In both cases, the result should also be in accordance with the principle of good faith and fair dealing, which in this author's opinion, has a very important function in the fully contextual interpretation method adopted by uniform and harmonized instruments, as it provides the "flexibility" that "international commercial context" requires. It is, thus, crucial that the principle acquires a uniform and autonomous content determined by the "international commercial context" and not by the interpreter's own context.

It should also not be forgotten that parties are invited to provide interpretation clauses in their contract in order to provide guidance to the court about their intention. An individually negotiated merger clause, for instance, will prevent recourse to preliminary negotiations in order to contradict or supplement the writing. It will not, however, prevent the court from having recourse to prior negotiations in order to interpret the contract. If parties, however, do not want prior negotiations to be used in order to interpret the contract either, they can agree on an individually negotiated clause expressly stating this intention.

Another important pillar of this research is the principle of good faith and fair dealing and its scope of application in interpretation and gap-filling processes in terms of the CISG, PICC, PECL and DCFR. While the PICC, PECL and DCFR recognize a duty to act in good faith addressed to contractual parties and give a very important content to the principle in both interpretation and gap-filling processes, the position of the CISG on the issue is a matter of debate, especially because of the drafting history of the Convention. This point has important effects on our research subject. The principle can shape both the reasonable person criterion itself and the interpretation of the wording in general as an overriding principle, not to forget its effects on the implication process in general. But the answer given to the question on the content of the good faith principle in terms of the CISG has also another important aspect. Indeed, if we do not accept a positive duty of good faith in terms of the CISG, reference to the related articles of the PICC, PECL and DCFR in interpreting and supplementing CISG Article 8 would lose both its foundation and practicability, as the principle has a very important content in terms of these three instruments.

From a first point of view, the Convention and the content of Article 7 exclude a possibility to extract such a duty from the terms of the Convention. This view, based upon the literal reading of the Convention, sees good faith as a criterion to be applied by judges and arbitrators only in the interpretation of the CISG itself.

According to a second view, Article 7(1) CISG imposes a positive duty of good faith because "the need to promote ... the observance of good faith in international trade" stated in this article is also necessarily directed to the parties to each individual contract of sale.

Third, it is suggested to consider good faith as a general principle on which the Convention is based, and apply Article 7(2) in order to impose a duty of good faith on the parties. From that point of view, although the term good faith is not directly referred to in different articles of the Convention, the term reasonableness is. This author believes, however, that this solution is rather confusing because good faith and reasonableness are two different concepts which may or may not have the same content.

If the first approach is accepted, the answer would be sought in the rules of private international law, and domestic laws would apply to problems of fairness. Considering the broadness of application of the principle, such a solution would undermine certainty and predictability in international transactions even more than any difficulties that we might have in order to determine a uniform content of the principle in terms of the CISG.

In favor of the second view, recognizing a general duty of good faith in terms of the CISG is in accordance with the interpretation of the Convention according to the goals set forth in Article 7(1), namely, promoting uniformity of application and observance of good faith in "international trade". First, the good faith principle has a very broad field of application and national laws attribute divergent contents to this principle, application of the national laws to questions of fairness in relation to international contracts governed by the CISG would jeopardize the uniformity of application of the Convention. Secondly, the Convention aims for the observance of good faith in "international trade". Such a goal can only be reached by the establishment of an autonomous concept of good faith applied to international transactions. Accordingly, like the rest of the Convention, Article 7 should itself be interpreted by taking these points into account.

It should also be noted that the recognition of a general duty of good faith in terms of CISG would pave the way for the use of other harmonized instruments which recognize such a duty (especially of the PICC which has the closest scope of application to the CISG) in order to interpret and supplement CISG Article 8, and could help in the development of an autonomous international content to be applied to international commercial contracts.

If such a duty is rejected, in my opinion, recourse to non-binding instruments such as the PICC or PECL in order to interpret or supplement CISG rules on interpretation and gap filling would lose both its foundation (in cases where the parties did not expressly refer to these instruments) and its practicality, as the general duty to act in good faith is an omnipresent principle in all aspects of interpretation and gap filling in the system of these instruments.

These points gain even greater importance if one considers the fact that when it comes to the determination of the content of the contract, rules provided by Articles 8 and 9 CISG fall quite short of covering all the aspects of the issue as they are not as detailed as the provisions contained in other harmonized instruments including the PICC. The acceptance of a general duty of good faith could at least lead to a "relative uniformity".

It should, however, not be understood that recourse to the PICC should be systematic in all cases involving interpretation of contracts. In this respect, a solution should first be sought within the CISG and if necessary, the directions of Article 7(2) should be followed and reference to underlying principles of the Convention should be made in order to supplement the Convention.

It should be noted that an examination of the case-law shows that the principle of good faith and fair dealing finds its way more and more as a general principle of the Convention. It does not mean, however, that this makes the uniform application of the Convention an easy goal. Although courts all use the term "principle of good faith and fair dealing", the content of this principle may be different according to the legal background of the judge. It is indeed not surprising to see for instance that German courts refer more extensively to the principle than others. This does not mean of course that an autonomous international content is not forming over time. For this purpose, this author is of the opinion that with each decision a new step forward is taken.

Finally, after examining the scope of application of the good faith and fair dealing principle in interpreting international commercial contracts governed by the CISG, PICC, PECL and DCFR, it can be said that the subject of interpretation and gap filling in international commercial contracts cannot be fully grasped without referring to the notion of "fairness in contractual relationships" according to the needs of international trade. Again, on this matter, international commercial contracts have their own context to be taken into account, and the highly contextualist approach of interpretation will certainly help for this purpose.

From these same perspectives the book also examined the mechanisms of gap filling in terms of the CISG, PICC, PECL and DCFR together with *force majeure* and hardship issues, as these latter, like gaps, are consequences of a lack of foresight at the time of contracting. An important controversy here was to decide if hardship was an issue covered by the CISG (which only contained Article 79, dealing primarily with *force majeure* cases although without expressly using the term) or if it was excluded from the scope of the Convention as a validity issue to be dealt with by domestic laws.

This author is of the opinion that such exclusion can be deduced neither from the history nor from the text of the Convention. As a great number of national laws, together with the PICC, PECL and DCFR, deal with the issue as a topic related to performance, there is no need to exclude hardship from the scope of the Convention on the basis of validity arguments. This answer, on the other hand, does not solve all the problems of scope in terms of the CISG, as the drafting history of Article 79 may be interpreted as suggesting that hardship is excluded from the scope of the article.

Being against a strict literalist interpretation technique for both statutory and contractual interpretation, this author believes that in extreme circumstances there might be cases of changed circumstances which might fall within the scope of Article 79 and that such a possibility should not be categorically rejected with arguments based on the drafting history of the provision before treating the circumstances of the case in the light of the system of the Convention as a whole. This point of view is also in line with the CISG Advisory Council Opinion No. 7, which further states that in such cases relief consistent with the CISG and the general principles on which it is based can be provided by the court. But can the PICC be used in order to fill the existing gap in the CISG to provide further relief?

The controversial *Scafom* decision of the Belgian Supreme Court of 19 June 2009 not only took the same path as the above-mentioned Advisory Council Opinion, but also applied the PICC in order to fill the gap as underlying principles of the Convention. As I have submitted above, this author is in favor of a broad interpretation of Article 79. Chronological arguments which suggest that the PICC, being subsequent to the Convention, cannot be used to supplement this former should not be retained, as it would be an important obstacle to the further development of the Convention and to the formation of an autonomous international content. Besides, this chronological argument seems to be quite incoherent given the fact that law is constantly evolving and so are the rules contained in the "applicable law by virtue of the rules of private international law" that apply in cases where gaps cannot be filled via the application of the principles on which the Convention is based. Indeed, these rules will apply regardless of whether they are subsequent or not to the Convention.

This does not mean that the PICC should be used automatically to supplement the Convention. On this matter, the *Scafom* decision, which directly refers to PICC as a gap filler can be criticized. As it is rightly pointed out in the literature, the Supreme Court transforms "the general principles on which the Convention is based" to "the general principles which govern the law of international trade" and searches for such general principles in external sources. Instead, it should have focused first on the underlying principles of the Convention.

BIBLIOGRAPHY

ALFORD, D., "*A Guide on the Harmonization of International Commercial Law*" (2005), http://www.nyulawglobal.org/globalex/Unification_Harmonization.htm.

ANDERSEN BAASCH, C., "*Good Faith? Good Grief!*", 17 Int'l Trade and Bus. L. Rev. (2014), pp. 310–321.

ARNOLD, L.D., "*I Didn't Say That! No Oral Modification Clauses in Energy Transactions*" (2011), http://www.nortonrosefulbright.com/files/us/e_templates/CRD/publications/IDidntSayThat0311.pdf.

ATIYAH, P.S., *The Rise and Fall of Freedom of Contract*, Oxford University Press, Oxford 1979.

——, *Promises, Morals and Law*, Clarendon Press, Oxford 1981.

AUER, M., "*Good Faith: A Semiotic Approach*", 10(2) European Review of Private Law (2002), pp. 279–301.

AYRES, I., "*Default Rules for Incomplete Contracts*" in *The New Palgrave Dictionary of Economics and the Law*, P. Newman (ed.), Palgrave MacMillan 2002, pp. 585–590.

AYRES, I., GERTNER, R., "*Majoritarian vs. Minoritarian Defaults*", 51 Stan. L. Rev. (1999), pp. 1591–1614.

Bacon's Maxims III, *The Works of Francis Bacon, Baron of Verulam, Viscount St. Alban, and High Chancellor of England: Law Tracts. Maxims of the Law*, Printed for C. and J. Rivington, London 1826.

BARNES, N.J., "*Good Faith under the UNIDROIT Principles of International Commercial Contracts: A Struggle for Meaning*", http://www.dundee.ac.uk/cepmlp/car/html/CAR9_ARTICLE14.pdf.

BARNETT, R.E., "*A Consent Theory of Contract*", 86 Columbia Law Review (1986), pp. 269–321.

BARNHIZER, D.D., "*Context as Power: Defining the field of Battle for Advantage in Contractual Interactions*", 45 Wake Forest L. Rev. (2010), pp. 607–640.

BARON, J.B., "*Law, Literature and the Problems of Interdisciplinarity*", 108 Yale L.J. (1999), pp. 1059–1086.

BEALE, H., FAUVARQUE-COSSON, B., RUTGERS, J., VOGENAUER, S., *Cases, Materials and Text on Contract Law*, Ius Commune Casebooks for the Common Law of Europe, Hart Publishing, Oxford/Portland OR, 2010.

BEALE, H., "*General Clauses and Specific Rules in the Principles of European Contract Law: The 'Good Faith' Clause*" in *General Clauses and Standards in*

European Contract Law, Comparative Law, EC Law and Contract Law Codification, S. Grundmann, D. Mazeaud (eds.), Kluwer law International, The Hague 2006, pp. 205–218.

BEALE, H.G., BISHOP, W.D., FURMSTON, M.P., *Contract Cases and Materials*, 5th ed., Oxford University Press, Oxford 2008.

BERG, A., "*Thrashing through the Undergrowth*", 122 L.Q.R. (2006), pp. 354–362.

BERNSTEIN, L., "*Private Commercial Law in the Cotton Industry: Creating Cooperation Through Rules, Norms and Institutions*", 99 Mich. L. Rev. (2001), pp. 1724–1790.

BLUM, B.A., *Contract Examples & Explanations*, Aspen Publishers, New York 2007.

BOLGAR, V., "*The Contract of Adhesion, A Comparison of Theory and Practice*", 20 Am. J. Comp. L. (1972), pp. 53–78.

BONELL, M.J., "*Interpretation of Convention*" in *Commentary on the International Sales Law*, C.M. Bianca, M.J. Bonell (eds.), Giuffrè, Milan 1987.

——, *An International Restatement of Contract Law, The Unidroit Principles of International Commercial Contracts*, 3rd ed. Transnational Publishers Inc., New York 2005.

BOUT, P.X., "*Trade Usages: Article 9 of the Convention on Contracts for the International Sale of Goods*", http://www.cisg.law.pace.edu/cisg/biblio/bout.html.

BRUNNER, C., *Force Majeure and Hardship under General Contract Principles, Exemption for Non-Performance in International Arbitration*, Kluwer Law International, The Hague 2009.

BURROWS, A., *A Casebook on Contract*, 5th ed., Hart Publishing, Oxford 2016.

BUSCH, D., *The Principles of European Contract Law and Dutch Law: A Commentary*, Kluwer Law International, The Hague 2002.

CANARIS, C.W., GRIGOLEIT, H.C., "*Interpretation of Contracts*" in *Towards a European Civil Code*, 4th ed., Kluwer Law International, The Hague 2011, pp. 587–618.

CARLSEN, A., "*Can the Hardship Provisions in the UNIDROIT Principles Be Applied when the CISG is the Governing Law?*", http://www.cisg.law.pace.edu/cisg/biblio/carlsen.html.

CHARNY, D., "*Hypothetical Bargains: Normative Structure of Contract Interpretation*", 89 Mich. L. Rev. (June 1991), pp. 1815–1879.

CHERRY, C., *On Human Communication – A Review, a Survey and a Criticism*, 3rd ed., MIT Press, Cambridge MA August 1980.

CHOMSKY, N., *Aspects of the Theory of Syntax*, MIT Press, Cambridge MA 1965.

CHRISTIE, G.C., "*Vagueness and Legal Language*", 48 Minn. L. Rev. (1963–1964), pp. 885–912.

COHEN, G.M., "*Implied Terms and Interpretation in Contract Law*" in *Encyclopedia of Law and Economics*, Bouckaert, B., De Geest, G. (eds.), Edward Elgar, Cheltenham 2000, pp. 78–99.

COOTER, R.D., ULEN, T., *Law and Economics*, Pearson Series in Economics, 6th ed., Berkeley Law Books, 2016.

CORBIN, A.L., "*The Interpretation of Words and The Parol Evidence Rule*", 50 Cornell L.Q. (1964–1965), pp. 161–190.

CRASWELL, R., "*Efficiency and Rational Bargaining in Contractual Settings*", 15 Harv. J.L. & Pub. Policy (1992), pp. 805–838.

CREMADES, B.M., "*Good Faith in International Arbitration*", 27 Am. U. Int'l L. Rev. (2012), pp. 761–788.

CSERNE, P., "*Policy Considerations in Contract Interpretation: The contra proferentem rule from a comparative law and economics perspective*", http://works.bepress.com/peter_cserne/28.

——, "*Reasons for Limiting Freedom of Contract: Questions of Philosophy and Policy*", http://jesz.ajk.elte.hu/cserne13.html.

CUNNINGHAM, L.A., "*Hermeneutics and Contract Default Rules: An Essay on Lieber and Corbin*", 16 Cardozo L. Rev. (1994–1995), pp. 2225–2248.

CURTIS, C.P., "*A better theory of legal interpretation*", 3 Vand. L. Rev. (1949–1950), pp. 407–437.

DE LY, F., "*Interpretation Clauses in International Contracts, (Characterization, Definition, Entire Agreement, Headings, Language, NOM-Clauses, Non-Waiver Clauses and Severability)*", 6 I.B.L.J. (2000), pp. 719–812.

——, "*Sources of International Sales Law: An Eclectic Model*", 25 Journal of Law and Commerce (2005–2006), pp. 1–12.

DEMOGUE, R., *Traité des Obligations en Général*, Librairie Arthur Rousseau, Paris 1931.

DENNING, L.J., *The Discipline of Law*, London 1979.

DEWEY, J., *Logic - The Theory of Inquiry*, Henry Holt and Company, New York 1938.

DiMATTEO, L.A., "*The Counterpoise of Contracts: The Reasonable Person Standard and the Subjectivity of Judgement*", 48 South Carolina L. Rev. (Winter 1997), pp. 293–356.

——, "*The CISG and the Presumption of Enforceability: Unintended Contractual Liability in International Business Dealings*", 22 Yale Journal of International Law (1997), pp. 111–170.

——, "*Reason and Context: A Dual-Track Theory of Interpretation*", 109 Penn. State L. Rev. (2004), pp. 397–486.

——, *The Law of International Contracting*, 2nd ed., Wolters Kluwer Law & Business, Alphen aan den Rijn 2009.

——, "*False Dichotomies in Commercial Contract Interpretation*", 11(1) J.I.T.L & P. (2012), pp. 27–43.

DiMATTEO, L.A., OSTAS, D.L., "*Comparative Efficiency in International Sales Law*", 26 Am. U. Int'l L. Rev. (2011), pp. 371–440.

DiMATTEO, L.A, MORANT, B.D., "*Contract in Context and Contract as Context*", 45 Wake Forest L. Rev. (2010), pp. 549–578.

DiMATTEO, L.A., DHOOGE L.J., GREEN, S., MAURER, V.G., PAGNATTARO, M.A., *International Sales Law A Critical Analysis of CISG Jurisprudence*, Cambridge University Press, Cambridge 2005.

——, "*The Interpretive Turn in International Sales Law: An Analysis of Fifteen Years of CISG Jurisprudence*", 34 Nw. J. Int'l L. & Bus. (Winter 2004), pp. 299–440.

DOUDKO, A.G., "*Hardship in Contract: The Approach of the UNIDROIT Principles and Legal Developments in Russia*", 5(3) Uniform L. Rev. (2000), pp. 483–509.

DROBNIG, U., "*The UNIDROIT Principles and the Conflict of Law*", 3 Uniform L. Rev. (1998), pp. 385–396.

DUPICHOT, J., "*Pour un retour aux textes : Défense et illustration du petit guide-âne des articles 1156 à 1164 du Code Civil*" in *Etudes offertes à Jacques Flour*, Répertoire du notariat Defrénois, Paris 1979.

DURKHEIM, E., "*Durkheim and the Law*", S. Lukes, A. Scull (eds.), Martin Robertson, Oxford 1983.

EISELEN, S., "*Remarks on the manner in which the Principles of European Contract Law may be used to interpret or supplement Article 29 of the CISG*", http://www.cisg.law.pace.edu/cisg/text/peclcomp29.html#8.

——, "*Editorial Remarks*", (on Belgium, 19 June 2009, Court of Cassation Decision), http://cisgw3.law.pace.edu/cases/090619b1.html.

EISENBERG, M.A., "*The Emergence of Dynamic Contract Law*", 88(6) Cal. L. Rev. (2000), pp. 1743–1814.

EMMERT, F., "*The Draft Common Frame of Reference (DCFR): The Most Interesting Development in Contract Law since the Code Civil and the BGB*", http://ssrn.com/abstract=2025265.

ENDERLEIN, F., MASKOW, D., *International Sales Law*, Oceana Publications, New York 1992.

EORSI, G., "*General Provisions*" in *International Sales: The UN Convention on Contracts for the International Sale of Goods*, N.M. Galston, H. Smit (eds.), Matthew Bender, New York 1984, §2-1–2-36.

ESSER, M., "*Commercial Letters of Confirmation in International Trade: Austrian, French, German and Swiss Law under the 1980 Sales Convention*", 18 Georgia Journal of International and Comparative Law (1988), pp. 427–460.

FARIA, J.A.E., "*Future Directions of Legal Harmonization and Law Reform: Stormy Seas or Prosperous Voyage?*", 14 Uniform Law Rev. (2009), pp. 5–34.

FARNSWORTH, E.A., "*'Meaning' in the Law of Contract*", 76 Yale L.J. (1967), pp. 939–965.

——, *Contracts*, Little, Brown Co., Boston MA 1982.

——, "*Duties of Good Faith and Fair Dealing under the Unidroit Principles, Relevant International Conventions, and National Laws*", 3 Tulane Journal of International and Comparative Law (1995), pp. 47–64.

FARNSWORTH, A., "*Formation of Contract*" in *International Sales: The United Nations Convention on Contracts for the International Sale of Goods*, N.M. Galston, H. Smit (eds.), Matthew Bender, New York 1984, §3-1–3-18.

——, "*Article 8*" in *Commentary on the International Sales Law*, C.M. Bianca, M.J. Bonell (eds.), Giuffrè, Milan 1987, pp. 95–102.

FARNSWORTH, E.A., "*The Interpretation of International Contracts and the Use of Preambles*", 3/4 I.B.L.J. (2002), pp. 271–280.

——, *Farnsworth on Contracts*, 3rd ed., Aspen Publishers, New York 2004.

FELEMEGAS, J., "*The United Nations Convention on Contracts for the International sale of Goods: Article 7 and Uniform Interpretation*" in *Review of the Convention on Contracts for the International Sale of Goods (CISG)*, Kluwer Law International, The Hague 2000–2001, pp. 115–265.

FELTHAM, J., "*The United Nations Convention on Contracts for the International Sale of Goods*", J. Bus. L. (1981), p. 346.

FERRARI, F., "*Trade Usage and Practices Established Between the Parties under the CISG*", 5 I.B.L.J. (2003), pp. 571–580.

——, "*General Principles and International Uniform Law Conventions: A Study of the Vienna Sales Convention and the 1988 UNIDROIT Conventions on Factoring and Leasing*", 10 Pace Int'l Law Revi. (1998), pp. 157–186.

FISH, S., "*Is there a Text in this Class?*", Harvard University Press, Cambridge MA 1982.

——, "*There is no Textualist Position*", 42 San Diego L.R. (2005), pp. 629–650.

FISS, O.M., "*Objectivity and Interpretation*", 34 Stanford L.R. (April 1982), pp. 739–764.

FLAMBOURAS, D.P., "*The Doctrines of Impossibility of Performance and clausula rebus sic stantibus in the 1980 Vienna Convention on Contracts for the International Sale of Goods and the Principles of European Contract Law: A Comparative Analysis*", 13 Pace Int'l Law Review (Fall 2001), pp. 261–294.

FLAMBOURAS, D., "*Comparative Remarks on CISG article 79 & PECL Articles 6:111, 8:108*", May 2002, http://www.cisg.law.pace.edu/cisg/text/peclcomp79.html.

FLECHTNER, H., "*Article 79 of the United Nations Convention on Contracts for the International Sale of Goods (CISG) as Rorschach Test: The Homeward Trend and Exemption for Delivering Non-Conforming Goods*", 19(1) Pace Int'l Law Review (Spring 2007), pp. 29–52.

FLETCHNER, H.M., "*The Exemption Provisions of the Sales Convention, Including Comments on 'Hardship' Doctrine and the 19 June 2009 Decision of the Belgian Cassation Court*", 2011 Annals of the Faculty of Law in Belgrade, International Edition, 2011, pp. 84–101. Legal Studies Research Paper Series Working Paper no. 2011-09, March 2011, p. 10.

FLORESTAL, M., "*Is a Burrito a Sandwich? Exploring Race, Class, and Culture in Contracts*", 14(1) Michigan Journal of Race and Law (2008), pp. 1–60.

FONTAINE, M., DE LY, F., *Drafting International Contracts, An Analysis of Contract Clauses*, Transnational Publishers Inc., New York 2006.

GARRO, A.M., "*Comparison between provisions of the CISG regarding exemption of liability for damages (Art.79) and the counterpart provisions of the UNIDROIT Principles (Art.7.1.7.), Editorial Remarks*", 2005, http://www.cisg.law.pace.edu/cisg/text/anno-art-79.html#uni.

GARVIN, L.T., "*Small Business and the False Dichotomies of Contract Law*", 40 Wake Forest L. Rev. (2005), pp. 295–388.

GIRSBERGER D., ZAPOLSKIS P., "*Fundamental Alteration of the Contractual Equilibrium under Hardship Exemption*", 16 March 2012, https://www.mruni.eu/upload/iblock/434/7_Girsberger.pdf.

GOETZ, C.J., SCOTT, R.E., "*The Limits of Expanded Choice: The Analysis of the Interactions between Express and Implied Contract Terms*", 73 Cal. L. Rev. (1985), pp. 261–322.

GOLDSTEIN, B.H., "*The Plain Language Law: Some Reflections on its Basic Assumptions*", 1 Comm. & L. (1979), pp. 69–80.

GOODE, R., KRONKE, H., MCKENDRICK, E., *Transnational Commercial Law, Text, Cases and Materials*, Oxford University Press, Oxford 2007.

GREENAWALT, K., "*A Pluralist Approach to Interpretation: Wills and Contracts*", 42 San Diego L. Rev. (2005), pp. 533–606.

HANSEBOUT, A., "*Landmark Supreme Court Decision on Hardship under CISG*", http://www.internationallawoffice.com/Newsletters/Company-Commercial/Belgium/ALTIUS/Landmark-Supreme-Court-decision-on-hardship-under-CISG.

HARDY, R., "*The DCFR Rules on Contract Interpretation: Efficient Defaults?*" in *The Draft Common Frame of Reference: national and comparative perspectives*, V. Sagaert, M. Storme, E. Terryn (eds.), Intersentia Publishing Ltd., Cambridge/Antwerp/Portland OR 2012, pp. 201–218.

HARTKAMP, A., "*Formation of Contracts According to the Principles of European Contract Law*", Festskrift til Ole Lando, Gadjura, Copenhagen 1997, p. 180.

HERBOTS, J.H., "*What Precisely is Interpretation*" in *Elgar Encyclopedia of Comparative Law*, 2nd ed., J.M. Smits (ed.), Edward Elgar, Cheltenham 2012, pp. 421–448.

HESEN G., HARDY, R., "*Contract Interpretation, Interpretative Criteria*" in *Economic Analysis of the DCFR, The Work of the Economic Impact Group within the CoPECL Network of Excellence*, P. Larouche, F. Cihirico (eds.), Sellier, Munich 2010, pp. 83–95.

HESSELINK, M.W., "*The Concept of Good Faith*" in *Towards a European Civil Code*, 4th ed., Kluwer Law International, The Hague 2011, pp. 619–649.

HILLMAN R., "*Article 29(2) of the United Nations Convention on Contracts for the International Sale of Goods: A New Effort at Clarifying the Legal Effect of 'No Oral Modification Clauses'*", 21 Cornell International Law Journal (1988), pp. 449–466.

HONNOLD, J.O., *Uniform Law for International Sales under the 1980 United Nations Convention*, 3rd ed., Kluwer Law International, The Hague 1999.

HUBER, P., "*Some Introductory Remarks on the CISG*", http://www.cisg.law.pace.edu/cisg/biblio/huber-09.html.

HUDSON, A.H., "*Exemptions and Impossibility under Vienna Convention*" in *Force Majeure and Frustration of Contract*, E. McKendrick (ed.), Lloyds of London Press, London 2013, pp. 267–286.

ILIFF, A., HALLS, P., TEDJESKE, J., "*The Shifting Sands of Contract Drafting, Interpretation and Application*", 32 Constr. Lawyer (2012), pp. 1–11.

JENKINS, S.H., "*Exemption for Non-performance: UCC, CISG, UNIDROIT Principles – A Comparative Assessment*", 72 Tulane Law Review (1998), pp. 2015–2030.

JOSSERAND, L., *Cours de droit civil positif français*, Imprenta Paris, Receuil Sirey, Paris 1938.

JUNGE, W., "*General Provisions*" in *Commentary on the UN Convention on the International Sale of Goods (CISG)*, P. Schlechtriem (ed.), Oxford University Press, Oxford 1998.

KACZOROWSKA, A., "*Règles uniformes d'interprétation d'un contrat international*", 43 Revue de droit International et de droit compare (1991), pp. 294–313.

KASSIS, A., *Théorie générale des usages du commerce, Droit Comparé, Contracts et Arbitrage Internationaux, Lex Mercatoria*, L.G.D.J., Paris 1984.

KASTELY, A.H., "*Unification and Community: A Rhetorical Analysis of the United Nations Sales Convention*", Symposium: Reflections on the International Unification of Sales Law, 8 Nw. J. Int'l L. & Bus. (1988), p. 574 et seq.

KATZ, A.W., "*The Economics of Form and Substance in Contract Interpretation*", 104 Colum. L.Rev. (2004), pp. 496–538.

——, "*Contractual Incompleteness: A Transactional Perspective*", 56 Case W. Res. L. Rev. (2005), pp. 169–186.

KEILY, T., "*Good Faith and the Vienna Convention on Contracts for the International Sale of Goods (CISG)*", 3(1) Vinodoba Journal of International Commercial Law and Arbitration (1999), pp. 15–40.

KESSEDJIAN, C., "*Competing Approaches to Force Majeure and Hardship*", 25 International Review of Law and Economics (September 2005), pp. 415–433.

KIM, N.S., "*Evolving Business and Social Norms and Interpretation Rules: The Need for a Dynamic Approach to Contract Disputes*", 84 Neb. L. Rev. (2005), pp. 506–570.

——, "*Reasonable Expectations in Sociocultural Context*", 45 Wake Forest L. Rev. (2010), pp. 641–668.

KLEIN, J., "*Good Faith in International Transactions*", 15 Liverpool Law Rev. (1993), pp. 115–141.

KOCH, R., "*Commentary on Whether the UNIDROIT Principles of International Commercial Contracts May Be Used to Interpret and Supplement Article 25 CISG*", http://www.cisg.law.pace.edu/cisg/biblio/koch1.html.

KOFOD, R., "*Hardship in International Sales CISG and the UNIDROIT Principles*", Thesis, 2011, University of Copenhagen Faculty of Law, http://www.cisg.law.pace.edu/cisg/biblio/kofod.html.

KONERU, P., "*The International Interpretation of the UN Convention on Contracts for the International Sale of Goods: An Approach Based on General Principles*", 6 Minnesota Journal of Global Trade (1997), pp. 105–152.

KORNET, N., *Contract Interpretation and Gap Filling: Comparative and Theoretical Perspectives*, Intersentia, Antwerpen/Cambridge 2006.

KOSTRISTSKY, J.P., "*Incomplete Contracts: Judicial Responses, Transactional Planning, and Litigation Strategies*", 56 Case W. Res. L. Rev. (2005), pp. 135–149.

KÖTZ, H, "*Interpretation of Contracts*" in *European Contract Law*, H. Kotz (ed.), G. Mertens and T. Weir (trans.), 2nd ed., Oxford University Press, Oxford 2017, pp. 91–108.

KRAMER, A. "*Implication in fact as an instance of Contract Interpretation*", 63(2) Cambridge Law Journal (2004), pp. 384–411.

KRITZER, A.H., *Guide to Practical Applications of the United Nations Convention on Contracts for the International Sale of Goods*, Kluwer, Dewenter 1989.

——, Editorial Remarks, ICC Arbitration Case No. 7331 of 1994 (*Cowhides case*), http://cisgw3.law.pace.edu/cases/947331i1.html.

—— (ed.), "*Reasonableness, Overview Comments*", http://www.cisg.law.pace.edu/cisg/text/reason.html.

KUOPPALA, S., "*The Application and Interpretation of the CISG in Finnish Case Law 1997–2005*", 2009, http://cisgw3.law.pace.edu/cisg/biblio/kuoppala2.html.

LAUTENSCHLAGER, F., "*Current Problems Regarding the Interpretation of the Statements and Party Conduct under the CISG – The Reasonable Third Person, Language Problems and Standard Terms and Conditions*", 11(2) Vindobona Journal of International Commercial Law & Arbitration, (2007), pp. 259–290.

LEONHARD, C., "*Beyond the Four Corners of a Written Contract: a Global Challenge to U.S. Contract Law*", 21 Pace Int'l L. Rev. (2009), pp. 1–36.

LEWISON, K., *The Interpretation of Contracts*, Sweet & Maxwell, London 2004.

LEYHANE, J., "*The Two Faces of Contract Ambiguity Claims*", 100 Illinois Bar Journal (2012), p. 264.

LIAO, J., "*The Role of Subsequent Conduct in Contract Interpretation*", 11 N.Z. Bus. L. Rev. (2005), pp. 66–81.

LIEBER, F., "*Art. III – On Political Hermeneutics or on Political Interpretation and Construction, and also Precedents*", 18 Am. Jurist. & L. Mag. (1837–1838), pp. 281–294.

LINDSTROM, N., "*Changed Circumstances and Hardship in the International Sale of Goods*", 1 Nordic Journal of Commercial Law (2006), p. 2, http://www.cisg.law.pace.edu/cisg/biblio/lindstrom.html.

LIU, C., "*Changed Contract Circumstances*", April 2005, http://www.cisg.law.pace.edu/cisg/biblio/liu5.html.

——, "*Remedies for Non-performance Perspectives from the CISG, UNIDROIT Principles & PECL*", 2003, http://www.cisg.law.pace.edu/cisg/biblio/chengwei.html.

LOOKOFSKY, J.M., "*Article 9 Commercial Custom and Usages*" in *The 1980 United Nations Convention on Contracts for the International sale of Goods*, 2000, http://www.cisg.law.pace.edu/cisg/biblio/loo9.html.

——, "*Understanding the CISG in the USA: a compact guide to the 1980 UN Convention on contracts for the international sale of goods*", Kluwer Law International, The Hague 2004.

——, "*CISG Foreign Case Law: How Much Regard Should We Have?*" in Ferrari/Flechtner/Brand (eds.), *The Draft UNCITRAL Digest and Beyond*, Sellier European Law Publ., Munich 2004, pp. 216–234.

——, in *The 1980 United Nations Convention on Contracts for the International Sale of Goods*, J. Herbots (ed.)/R. Blanpain (general ed.), *International Encyclopaedia of Laws – Contracts*, Suppl. 29, Kluwer Law International, December 2000, pp. 1–192.

LOOKOFSKY, J., "*Impediments and Hardship in International Sales: A Commentary on Catherine Kessedjian's 'Competing Approaches to Force Majeure and Hardship'*", 25 International Review of Law and Economics (September 2005), pp. 434–445.

——, "*Walking the Article 7(2) Tightrope Between CISG and Domestic Law*", 25 Journal of Law and Commerce (2005–2006), pp. 87–106.

——, "*Not Running Wild with the CISG*", 29(2) Journal of Law and Commerce (2011), pp. 141–170.

——, "*Remedies for 'Hardship' under the CISG International Sales Convention and the Decision by the Belgian Supreme Court in Scafom International v. Lorraine Tubes (2009)*", https://www.lexisnexis.com/legalnewsroom/international-law/b/commentry/archive/2012/02/02/remedies-for-hardship-under-the-cisg-international-sales-convention-and-the-decision-by-the-belgian-supreme-court.aspx?Redirected=true.

Lord HOFFMANN, "*The Intolerable Wrestle with Words and Meanings*", 114 S. African L.J. (1997), p. 656 et seq.

Lord STEYN, "*Written Contracts: To What Extent May Evidence Control Language?*", Current Legal Problems (1988), p. 23 et seq.

LU, S., "*Gap Filling and Freedom of Contract*", http://www.digitalcommons.law.uga.edu/cgi/viewcontent.cgi?article=1029&context=stu_llm.

MAGNUS, U., "*Guide to Article 7, Comparison with UNIDROIT Principles of International Commercial Contracts*", Editorial Remarks, http://www.cisg.law.pace.edu/cisg/principles/uni7.html.

——, "*General principles of UN-Sales Law*", L. Haberfellner (trans.), Max Planck Institute for Foreign and International Private Law, Rabels Zeitschrift for Foreign and International Private Law, Hein Kotz in Honor of his 60th Birthday, Part I, Volume 59 (1995), Issue 3-4, (October), https://www.cisg.law.pace.edu/cisg/biblio/magnus.html.

——, "*Die allegemeinen Grundsatze im UN-Kaufrecht*" (General principles of UN Sales Law) (English Translation), 3 International Trade and Business Law Annual, Australia 1997, pp. 33–56.

MALEVILLE, M.H., "*Pratique de l'Interprétation des Contrats, Etude Jurisprudentielle*", Publications de l'Université de Rouen, Vol. 164, Rouen 1991.

MANTYSAARI, P., *The Law of Corporate Finance: General Principles and EU Law, Volume II: Contracts in General*, Springer, 2010.

MASKOW, D., "*Hardship and Force Majeure*", 40 American Journal of Comparative Law (1992), pp. 657–670.

McBAINE, J.P., "*The Rule Against Disturbing Plain Meaning Of Writings*", 31 Cal. L. Rev. (1942–1943), pp. 145–166.

McGOWAN, M.O., "*Against Interpretation*", 42 San Diego L.R. (2005), pp. 711–734.

McKENDRICK, E., "*The Interpretation of Contracts: Lord Hoffmann's Restatement*" in *Commercial Law and Commercial Practice*, S. Worthington (ed.), Hart Publishing, Oxford/Portland OR 2003.

——, "*Introduction to Section 6.2 of the PICC*" in *Commentary on the UNIDROIT Principles of International Commercial Contracts*, S. Vogenauer, J. Kleinheisterkamp (eds.), Oxford University Press, Oxford 2009, p. 711 et seq.

McLAUCHLAN, D.W., "*In Defence of a Role for Subsequent Conduct in Contract Interpretation*", 12 N.Z. Bus. L. Q. (2006), pp. 30–49.

McMEEL, G., "*Language and the Law Revisited: An Intellectual History of Contractual Interpretation*", 34 Comm. L. World Rev. (2005), pp. 256–286.

——, *The Construction of Contracts*, 3rd ed., Oxford University Press, Oxford 2017.

——, "*Prior Negotiations and Subsequent Conduct: The Next Step Forward for Contractual Interpretation?*", 119 L.Q.R. (2003), pp. 272–297.

MELIS, W., "*Force Majeure and Hardship clauses in International Commercial Contracts in view of the practices of the ICC Court of Arbitration*", 1 Journal of International Arbitration (1984), pp. 213–222.

Merriam-Webster's Dictionary of Law, Merriam Webster Inc., Springfield MA 1996.

MILLER, M.R., "*Contract Law, Party Sophistication and New Formalism*", 75 Missouri L. Rev. (2010), pp. 493–536.

MILLS, S., JACOBSEN, L., "*Entire agreement and non-reliance clauses*", 22 Company Law Rev. (2001), pp. 189–191.

MITCHELL, C., *Interpretation of Contracts, Current Controversies in Law*, Routledge-Cavendish, Abingdon 2007.

MUGASHA A., "*Good faith obligations in commercial contracts*", 27 Int'l Bus. Law (1999), pp. 355–365.

MURRAY, J.E., in *Corbin on Contracts*, Desk Edition, Matthew Bender, New York 2009.

——, "*An Essay on the Formation of Contracts and Related Matters under the United Nations Convention on Contracts for the International Sale of Goods*", 8 Journal of Law and Commerce (1988), pp. 11–51.

MUTHORST, O, "*Contract Interpretation under the German BGB and under the DCFR*" in *Interpretation in Polish, German and European Private Law*, B. Heiderhoff, G. Zmij (eds.), Sellier European Law Publishers, Munich 2011, pp. 47–60.

NEUMAYER, K.H., MING, C., *Convention de Vienne sur les contrats de vente internationale de marchandises*, F. Dessemontet (ed.), CEDIDAC, Paris 1993.

NICHOLAS, B., "*Impractibility and Impossibility in the UN Convention on Contracts for the International Sale of Goods*" in Galston & Smit (eds.), *International Sales: The United Nations Convention on Contracts for the International Sale of Goods*, Matthew Bender, New York 1984, Juris Publishing, Ch. 5, §§5.1–5.24.

OGDEN, C.K., RICHARDS, I.A., *The Meaning of Meaning*, Routledge & Kegan Paul Ltd., London 1969.

PAMBOUKIS, Ch., "*The Concept and Function of Usages in the United Nations Convention on the International Sale of Goods*", 25 Journal of Law and Commerce (2005–2006), pp. 107–132.

PATERSON, J., ROBERTSON, A., HEFFEY, P., *Principles of Contract Law*, LawBook Co., Sydney 2005.

PATTERSON, D., "*Interpretation in Law*", 42 San Diego L.R. (2005), pp. 685–710.

PATTERSON, E.W., "*The Interpretation and Construction of Contracts*", 64 Columbia L. Rev. (1964), pp. 833–865.

PEDEN, E., "'*Cooperation' in English Contract Law: To Construe or Imply?*", 16 Journal of Contract Law (2000), pp. 56–67.

——, "*Policy Concerns Behind Implication of Terms in Law*", 117 L.Q.R. (2001), pp. 459–476.

PERCONTI, P., "*An Epistemic Commitment in the Very Idea of 'Speaker's Intention'*", in *Pragmemes and Theories of Language Use*, K. Allan, A. Capone, I. Kecskes (eds.), Springer, 2016, pp. 791–798.

PERELL, P.M., "*Plain Meaning for Judges, Scholars and Practitioners*", 20 Advoc. Q. (1998), pp. 24–84.

PERELMAN, C., *Le Raisonnable et le Déraisonnable en Droit. Au-delà du Positivisme Juridique*, L.G.D.J., Paris 1984.

PERILLO, J.M., *Calamari and Perillo on Contracts*, Thompson Reuters, St Paul MN 2009.

——, "*Editorial Remarks on the Manner in which the UNIDROIT Principles may be used to Interpret or Supplement CISG Article 8*", http://www.cisg.law.pace.edu/cisg/principles/uni8.html.

——, "*Hardship and Its Impact on Contractual Obligations: A Comparative Analysis*", http://www.cisg.law.pace.edu/cisg/biblio/perillo4.html.

——, "*Force Majeure and Hardship under the UNIDROIT Principles of International Commercial Contracts*" in *Contratación internacional, Comentarios a los Princios sobre los Contratos Comerciales Internacionales del Unidroit*, Universidad Nacional Autónoma de México - Universidad Panamericana, 1998, pp. 111–132.

PHANG, A., "*Implied terms, Business Efficacity and Officious Bystander, A modern History*", J. Bus. L. (January 1998), 1–34, http://resourcelists.kent.ac.uk/items/E8392D21-733A-1992-93A6-C137175CCE46.html.

PHILIPPE, D., "*La Clausula rebus sic stantibus et la Renégociation du Contrat dans la Jurisprudence Arbitrale Internationale*", http://www.philippelaw.eu/UploadDirectory/UserFiles/files/La%20clausula.pdf.

——, "*Unidroit Principles and Belgian Case Law*", Diritto del Commercio Internazionale, Anno XXVI, Fasc. 4-2012, (2012), pp. 940–942.

——, "*Renégociation du Contrat En Cas de Changement de Circonstances dans la Vente Internationale*", http://www.philippelaw.eu/UploadDirectory/UserFiles/files/rdcavril2011.pdf.

PIROZZI, R., "*Developments in the Change of Economic Circumstances Debate*", 16 Vindobona Journal of International Commercial Arbitration (2012), pp. 95–108.

POSNER, R.A., *Economic Analysis of Law*, 5th ed., Aspen Law and Business, New York 1998.

——, "*The Law and Economics on Contract Interpretation*", 83 Tex. L. Rev. (May 2005), pp. 1581–1614.

Principles of the European Contract Law, Parts I and II, Prepared by The Commission on European Contract Law, O. Lando, H. Beale (eds.), Kluwer Law International, The Hague 2000.

PUELINCKX, A.C., "*Frustration, Hardship, Force Majeure, Imprévision, Wegfall der Geschäftsgrundlage, Unmöglichkeit, Changed Circumstances*", 3(2) Journal of International Arbitration (1986), pp. 47–66.

RAMBERG, J., "*Autonomy of Contract and Non-Mandatory Law*", 37 Scandinavian Stud. L. (1993), pp. 141–156.

RILEY, C.A, "*Designing Default Rules in Contract Law, Consent, Conventionalism and Efficiency*", 20(3) Oxford Journal of Legal Studies (2000), pp. 367–390.

RIMKE, J., "*Force Majeure and Hardship: Application in international trade practice with specific regard to the CISG and the UNIDROIT Principles of International Commercial Contracts*" in *Pace Review of the Convention on Contracts for the International Sale of Goods*, Kluwer, 1999–2000, pp. 197–243.

RIVKIN, D.R., "*Lex Mercatoria and Force Majeure*" in *Transnational Rules in International Commercial Arbitration*, E. Galliard (ed.), ICC Publ No. 480/4; Paris 1993, p. 161 et seq.

ROBERTSON, A., "*The Limits of Interpretation in the Law of Contract*", 47 Victoria U. Wellington L. Rev. (2016), pp. 191–207.

ROTHELMEL, F., "*Role of Course of Performance and Confirmatory Memoranda in Determining the Scope, Operation and Effect of 'No Oral Modification' Clauses*", 48 Univ. Pittsburgh L. Rev. (1987), pp. 1239 et seq..

QUINE, W., *Word and Object*, The M.I.T Press, Cambridge MA 1964.

SABOURIN, F., "*Quebec*" in *A New Approach to International Commercial Contracts, The UNIDROIT Principles of International Commercial Contracts*, M.J. Bonell (ed.), Kluwer, The Hague 1999, p. 237 et seq.

SAIDOV, D., "*Cases on CISG Decided in the Russian Federation*", 7(1) Vindobona Journal of International Commercial Law and Arbitration (2003), pp. 1–62.

SCALIA, A., "*Common Law Courts in a Civil Law System: The Role of the United States Federal Courts in Interpreting the Constitution*" in *A Matter of Interpretation: Federal Courts and the Law*, A. Gutmann (ed.), Princeton University Press, Princeton, NJ 1997, pp. 3–48.

SCHLECHTRIEM, P., *Uniform Sales Law: The UN Convention on Contracts for the International Sale of Goods*, Manz, Vienna 1986.

——, *Commentary on the UN Convention on The International Sale of Goods (CISG)*, Oxford University Press, Oxford 1998.

——, "*Good Faith in German Law and in International Uniform Laws*", Centro di studi e ricerche di diritto comparato e straniero diretto da M.J. Bonell, Saggi, Conferenze e Seminari 24, Rome 1997, https://www.cisg.law.pace.edu/cisg/biblio/schlechtriem16.html.

——, "*The Seller's Obligations Under the United Nations Convention on Contracts on the International Sale of Goods*" in *The United Nations Convention on Contracts for the International Sale of Goods*, Matthew Bender, New York 1984, Juris Publishing, Ch. 6, §§6-1-6-35.

——, "*Uniform Sales Law in the Decisions of Bundesgerichtshof*" at http://www.cisg.law.pace.edu/cisg/biblio/schlechtriem3.html.

SCHMITTHOFF, C.M., "*The Unification or Harmonisation of Law by Means of Standard Contracts and General Conditions*", 17 Int'l & Comp. L.Q. (1968), pp. 551–570.

SCHROETER, U.G., "*Freedom of Contract: Comparison between Provisions of the CISG (Art. 6) and Counterpart Provisions of the Principles of European Contract Law*", July 2002, http://www.cisg.law.pace.edu/cisg/text/peclcomp6.html.

SCHWARTZ, A., SCOTT, R.E., "*Contract Theory and the Limits of Contract Law*", 113 Yale L.J. (2003), pp. 541–620.

——, "*Contract Interpretation Redux*", 119 Yale L. J. (2010), pp. 926–964.

SHAVELL, S., "*On the Writing and Interpretation of Contracts*", 22(2) Journal of Law, Economics, and Organization (2006), pp. 289–314.

SHEEHY, B., "*Good Faith in the CISG: The Interpretation Problems of Article 7*", https://papers.ssrn.com/sol3/papers.cfm?abstract_id=777105, pp. 1–48.

SIM, D., "*The Scope and Application of Good Faith in the Vienna Convention on Contracts for the International Sale of Goods*" (2001), http://www.cisg.law.pace.edu/cisg/biblio/sim1.html.

SIMMONDS, N.E., "*Imperial Visions and Mundane Practices*", 46(3) Cambridge L.J. (1987), pp. 465–472.

SLATER, S.D., "*Overcome by Hardship: The Inapplicability of the UNIDROIT Principles' Hardship Provisions to CISG*", 12 Florida Journal of Int'l Law (Summer 1998), pp. 231–262.

SMITH, S.A., *Contract Theory*, Oxford University Press, Oxford 2004.

SOLAN, L.M., "*Pernicious Ambiguity in Contracts and Statutes*", 79 Chicago-Kent L. Rev., 2004, pp. 859–888.

SOLAN, L., ROSENBLATT, T., OSHERSON, D., "*False Consensus Bias in Contract Interpretation*", 108 Columbia L. Rev. (June 2008), pp. 1268–1300.

SPAGNOLO, L., "*The Last Outpost: Automatic CISG Opt Outs, Misapplications and the Costs of Ignoring the Vienna Sales Convention for Australian Lawyers*", 10 Melb. J. Int'l L. (2009), pp. 141–216.

STANIVUKOVIC, M., "*Editorial Remarks on the Manner in which the PECL may be used to Interpret or Supplement CISG Article 8*", http://www.cisg.law.pace.edu/cisg/text/peclcomp8.html.

STEYN, J., "*Contract Law: Fulfilling the Reasonable Expectations of Honest Men*", 113 L.Q.R. (1997), pp. 433–442.

STORME, M.E., "*The Binding Character of Contracts - Causa and Consideration*" in *Towards a European Civil Code*, A.S. Hartkamp, M.W. Hesselink, E.H. Hondius (eds.), 2nd revised and expanded ed., Kluwer/Ars aequi, 1998, pp. 239–254.

——, "*Freedom of Contract: Mandatory and Non-Mandatory Rules in European Contract Law*", https://papers.ssrn.com/sol3/papers.cfm?abstract_id=2672648.

——, "*Good Faith and the Contents of Contracts in European Private Law*", http://www.ejcl.org/71/art71-1.pdf.

STOUT, J., "*What is the Meaning of a Text?*", 14(1) New Literary History (Autumn 1982), pp. 1–12.

SUN, C.L., "*Interpreting an International Sale Contract*", http://www.cisg.law.pace.edu/cisg/biblio/sun1.html.

SUND-NORRGARD, P., KOLEHMAINEN, A., SUHONEN, O.A., "*The Principle of Loyalty and Flexibility of Contracts*", https://www.ulapland.fi/loader.aspx?id=ec90abd9-ff6d-49cd-bf4c-c5a80d363ba4, pp. 190–208.

TALLON D., "*International Sales: The United Nations Convention on Contracts for the International Sale of Goods*", Matthew Bender, New York 1984, Ch. 7, §§7-1–7-20.

——, "*Article 79*" in *Commentary on the International Sales Law*, C.M. Bianca, M.J. Bonell (eds.), Giuffrè, Milan 1987, pp. 572–595.

TRAYNOR, R.J., Opinion, Pacific *Gas & Electric Co. v. G.W. Thomas Drayage etc., Co.* 69 Cal. 2d 33 (1968).

TOULLIER, C.B.M., *Le droit civil français suivant l'ordre du Code*, 5th ed., Paris 1842.

UNBERATH, H., "*Long-term Contracts and the DCFR, Interpretation and Adjustment*" in *The Common Frame of Reference; A View from Law & Economics*, G. Wagner (ed.), Sellier European Law Publishers, Munich 2009, pp. 87 et seq.

UNIDROIT Principles of International Commercial Contracts 2010.

VAN HOUTTE, H., "*The UNIDROIT Principles of International Commercial Contracts*", 2 Int'l Trade & Bus. L. Ann. (1996), pp. 1–20.

——, "*Changed Circumstances and Pacta Sunt Servanda*" in E. Gaillard (ed.), *Transnational Rules in International Commercial Arbitration* (ICC Publ. Nr. 480/4), Paris 1993, pp. 105–123.

——, "*The UNIDROIT Principles of International Commercial Contracts and International Commercial Arbitration: Their Reciprocal Relevance*" in *The UNIDROIT Principles for International Commercial Contracts: A New Lex Mercatoria?* (ICC Publ. No. 490/1), International Chamber of Commerce, Paris 1995, pp. 181–197.

VANTO, J., "*Remarks on the Manner in which the Principles of European Contract law may be Used to Interpret or Supplement Article 46 of the CISG*", http://www.cisg.law.pace.edu/cisg/text/peclcomp46.html.

VENEZIANO, A., "*UNIDROIT Principles and CISG: Change of Circumstances and Duty to Renegotiate according to the Belgian Supreme Court*", 15(1) Uniform L. Rev. (2010), pp. 137–151.

VOGENAUER, S., "*Interpretation of Contracts: Concluding Comparative Observations*" in *Contract Terms*, A. Burrows, E. Peel (eds.), Oxford University Press, Oxford July 2007, pp. 123–150.

——, "*Interpretation of Contracts*" in *The Max Planck Encyclopedia of European Private Law*, Vol.1, Basedow, J., Hopt, K.J., Zimmermann, R., Stier, A. (eds.), Oxford University Press, Oxford 2012, pp. 973–977.

VOGENAUER, S., KLEINHEISTERKAMP, J. (eds.), *Commentary on the Unidroit Principles of International Commercial Contracts (PICC)*, Oxford University Press, Oxford 2015.

WARNER, R.H., "*All Mixed Up about Contract: When is Contract Interpretation a Legal Question and when is it a Fact Question?*", 5 Va. L. & Bus. Rev. (Fall 2010), pp. 81–130.

WAGNER-VON PAPP, F., "*European Contract Law: Are No Oral Modification Clauses Not Worth the Paper They Are Written On?*", 63(1) Current Legal Problems (January 2010), pp. 511–596.

WEISZBERG, G., "*Le raisonnable en Droit du Commerce International*", http://www.cisg.law.pace.edu/cisg/biblio/Reasonableness.html.

WHITE, J.B., "*Law as Language: Reading Law and Reading Literature*", 60 Tex. L. Rev. (1981–1982), pp. 415–446.

WHITTAKER, S., ZIMMERMANN, R., "*Good faith in European Contract Law: surveying the legal landscape*" in *Good Faith in European Contract Law*, R. Zimmermann, S. Whittaker (eds.), Cambridge University Press, Cambridge 2000, pp. 7–62.

WILLISTON, S., "*Freedom of Contract*", 6 Cornell L.Q. (May 1921), pp. 365–380.

WILSON, N.S., "*Freedom of Contract and Adhesion Contracts*", 14 Int'l Comp. L.Q. (1965), pp. 172–193,

WINSHIP, P., "*International Sales Contracts under the 1980 Vienna Convention*", 17 UCC L.J. (1984), pp. 55–71.

ZAMIR, E., "*The Inverted Hierarchy of Contract Interpretation and Supplementation*", 97 Columbia L. Rev. (1997), pp. 1710–1803.

ZELLER, B., "*Four-Corners – The Methodology for Interpretation and Application of the UN Convention on Contracts for the International Sale of Goods*", May 2003, PhD Thesis at the University of Melbourne, http://www.cisg.law.pace.edu/cisg/biblio/4corners.html.

——, "*Determining the Contractual Intent of Parties under the CISG and Common Law-A Comparative Analysis*", 4(4) European Journal of Law Reform (2002), pp. 629–643.

——, "*Good Faith – The Scarlet Pimpernel of the CISG*", Int'l Trade & Bus. L. Rev. (2000), pp. 227–246.

ZIEGEL, J.S., SAMSON, C., "*Report to the Uniform Law Conference of Canada on Convention on Contracts for the International Sale of Goods*" (July 1981), http://www.cisg.law.pace.edu/cisg/wais/db/articles/english2.html.

ZWEIGERT, K., KOTZ, H., *An Introduction to Comparative Law*, 3rd ed., T. Weir (trans.), Oxford University Press, Oxford 1998.

ABOUT THE AUTHOR

Ayşe Nihan Karadayı Yalım is a postdoctoral researcher in the Business and Law Research Group at the University of Antwerp. She obtained her LLB from Galatasaray University, Istanbul, LLM from Free University of Brussels, and PhD in law from University of Antwerp. The Board of the Faculty of Law at the University of Antwerp nominated her PhD thesis for the prestigious "St. Petersburg International Legal Forum Private Law Prize 2018". She is also a member of the Working Group on International Contracts chaired by Prof. Dr. Filip De Ly. Her main research interests are "international commercial contracts" with a special focus on "context" and "efficiency", and "comparative analysis of uniform and harmonized instruments".

www.ingramcontent.com/pod-product-compliance
Ingram Content Group UK Ltd.
Pitfield, Milton Keynes, MK11 3LW, UK
UKHW021012120926
8556IPUK00039B/1044